10/14/...

Aloysius James Mullally

To

My Daemon

Barbara & Paul,

How my life was affected
by Alcohol

Dear friends, great in Lusino, especially apt. houses and leaders in their field, beyond all of us. I've enjoyed knowing you for all these years!

A. J. Mullally, author of My Daemon.

My Daemon

How my life was affected
by Alcohol

For Geraldine

*Whose great patience and
enduring love forever
changed this author's life*

PREFACE

My youngest son presented me with a handsome leather-bound book filled with empty pages, saying to me, "I would like you to write an autobiography of your life". Far too old to write anymore, I thought it might be an easy task simply to dictate the highlights of my life. Then I realized my life had followed diverse paths, that it would be difficult to describe all my life's changing exploits. As Newman has said, "to grow is to change and to grow much, to change often".

At the early age of fifteen, I did not like what I saw; how my life was taking shape without moral constraints. So, I spent four years attempting to change what I had become, resulting in a major psychosis: bone crushing pressure in the head, mind rushing out of control, wild dreams; the terrifying realization that I was losing consciousness. I went through all of this at the time and far, far more, which would be difficult, if not impossible, to relate.

In a long life, raising a large family and living a life of action, I began to drink to excess. I almost lost my marriage, my health and my fortune as I become addicted to alcohol. This period of addiction was the low point of my life. My wife decided to leave me. How, I wondered, could I tell any of this?

In thinking about it, I suddenly realized thirty years ago I had written a story about my experience as an alcoholic in a treatment center I named Maplewood. "Mark" tells what happens in that short period of six weeks. This book sat on my shelf for thirty years unread.

At one time, spanning at least ten years, I was extremely active in Alcoholics Anonymous. During that period, with the help of my sponsor, I attended many meetings. I spoke before groups charged with DUI's, at the Federal Building, to inmates at the low intensity prison near Fircrest, students at many high schools, occasionally church parishioners, veterans and business groups such as Rotary: before any group that wanted to hear of the dangers of alcohol.

After living eighty-eight years, I have seen so many lives destroyed through addiction to alcohol. I have also seen many lives rescued through the efforts of Alcoholics Anonymous, by seriously following the programs teachings, by seeing the truth (that one has become powerless over the drug), by calling upon a Higher Power to rescue us from addiction, and by following the other steps, which literally call for a radical change from what we had become as alcoholics. In other words to become a new man.

Mark is an extreme case. He realizes the change that is necessary to find a different life. The purpose of the story is to tell how Mark struggled to find that new life.

All alcoholics are liars; the blindest of all men. Alcohol deceives them, inflates their ego and allows them to think that they are masters of the universe. Often, while drinking they feel there are no moral constraints. Friends, a job, not even a loving wife can stand in the way of their drinking. A doctor's caution that their health is failing, their liver baldly damaged, often has no effect upon them. And, records show (you often read about it in the newspaper) that alcohol often plays a role in accidents and crime.

Years ago, I stood with a leading official of the Washington State Patrol, tracing rust marks of a car driven by a drunk driver that had straddled the berm at the side of the road at high speed. It was evident where the car had leaped back on to the highway, out of control, crossing the center line and hitting a 1978 van, estimated speed: 68 mph. My oldest daughter, mother of two children, was sitting in the back seat in the center. On one side was her husband, on the other, our friend. She was propelled into the dashboard and killed almost immediately. The driver, too, died. The drunk driver, a young woman, and her boyfriend were also killed. Three of the five passengers in the van were severely injured. My son-in-law, crippled for life.

I mentioned to the State Patrol Officer that I was an active speaker in AA and our national records showed that almost 50% of all fatal accidents involved alcohol. He responded back saying, in the eighteen years he has investigated accidents on state highways, in almost 90% of all fatal accidents, (heavy drinking was involved).

Mark tells my story in the novel, My Daemon. The descriptions and opening chapter are accurate. I wondered what had happened to the picture Mark describes until I saw it, once again, on the wall in the living room of my son's home. The picture has not changed. The young man appeared young and prosperous, as Mark described him, where as I have grown old, very old, indeed.

This manuscript sat on a shelf amongst my books. I had not burned it as I intended. Reading it again, I thought I had described alcoholism in a forceful manner. I considered this story well told. Most of all, the characters in the book are very real, exactly as I knew them: how they acted, what they did, and who was able to change from this dread disease. All of us were deeply wounded members of our society, fighting to overcome one of the worst diseases known to man. Bernice, Mary, Dean, Bill, The Colonel, Lucy, Audrey, and Peg the Hippie; Eva, Ralph, Pamela, Roy, and Stella all played their roles and spoke and acted much as Mark describes them. Ralph really was a good guy, harshly treated in the book.

I, along with other members of our group, did not agree with all our instructions at Maplewood. Like a few others, I could not accept rejecting old relationships because their drinking might affect ones efforts towards sobriety. This was loudly debated. And, Mark did get into a lot of trouble with Lucy, as the story shows. He was almost kicked out of Maplewood. All this is true. A few of us were quick to see Pamela's story did not ring true. She was a delightful dish; very pretty indeed, when she lost weight. Ralph finally married her. And, as I far as I know they lived happily ever after. Ralph's little spelling bee was true. Some members were quick to see how limited his education was.

All the staff members, with the exception of Dr. Neilson, had limited sobriety and education. They were almost fanatic in their dedication to helping those under their charge. Mark tells my story; I believe he is forceful, sometimes poetic. The battle against spirits may be overdone. As Saint Paul once said, "our battle is against principalities and powers of the world of darkness". Dr. Bogleman played a real part as my Daemon, but of course he is exaggerated. Lucy also plays a real part, true for the most part, as I describe her. Mark was sick, perhaps not far from breaking into a thousand pieces, losing all identity to this life, like Mary and Bernice.

Newman again speaks of coming out of the shadows into reality. When we see Truth, we will see our loved ones and friends once more. This is my attempt to tell a story, mostly a true story, seen through the eyes of a recovering alcoholic who has not touched alcohol for over 37 years. For that Grace, I give thanks to our Almighty and Merciful God.

CHAPTER 1

The clock had hardly moved. Time always moves slowly in a doctor's office. How long had I been sitting there, waiting? Waiting for what? To see a doctor–but not an ordinary doctor. I looked around the room: so drab, so small, so brightly lighted. Color, nondescript. Furniture, sparse. The floor was cold and uncarpeted. Through a small opening into the nurse's office I could see several grey filing cabinets, a typewriter, and a glass coffee pot. The whole aura of the office was grimly utilitarian.

What was I doing here? Several nights ago, before supper, my wife told me I needed help. A friend had recommended a Doctor Bogleman, reputed to be competent, someone who would be helpful. An appointment had been made.

Stunned with the idea of seeing a psychiatrist, I had drunk almost a fifth of Scotch. I began to weep.

As I recalled that drinking scene, the thought of what I had done now caused me to twist in my chair. To break down, to weep, like a child. Such weakness! How could I possibly lose my control? In the past my emotions had always been so consciously guarded. After all, repression of anger or guilt or any disturbing emotion–was a stoic quality much to be admired. Wasn't it?

Wait–delay–time lost. Doctors were all alike, guarding their time as if it were a precious commodity, treating others as if they were waiting to seek a favor. I felt the fire begin to smolder within me. Patience not being my long suit, I looked up at the clock again. Five minutes–that is all I'd give him–then I'd leave. I'd solve my problem unaided, as I had done so many times in the past. My mind did not seem to move. Each thought came slowly, and with effort. Looking at something in the room, several moments seemed to elapse before I recognized the object. I first noticed this when reading–even trade journals whose subject matters were familiar. The words were clear enough but I had difficulty grasping their meaning. Was it boredom that made my mind move like a snail?–as slow as the hands on the wall clock.

The time was up. I'd just slip out.

"Mark?"

My name, someone was calling my name.

I felt myself rise, almost automatically, and limbs of lead somehow propelled me toward the doctor's inner office. It was larger than the waiting room, but done in the same aggressive tastelessness which had earlier offended me. Tiled floor; cold pale colors. The sparse furnishings consisted of a desk, three chairs, and a scarred stand which held an ash tray. A shaded window admitted just enough light to emphasize the drabness of the room.

As I absorbed my surroundings, the other presence in the room–the doctor I had come to see–moved to his desk, sat down, and took out a cigarette.

Rather an odd looking man, clothes too large, shabby; unkempt. It was obvious that he had been trying to lose weight. A big head, heavy features, dark coarse skin: he appeared flushed. Was it blood pressure? A drinking problem? No matter, I was here to determine what was wrong with me–to see if a prominent psychiatrist could offer some insight into a life going nowhere.

"Mr. Mark Malone," he said, "my name is Dr. Raymond Bogleman. You may call me Dr. Bogleman, Mark, or whatever you are comfortable with. There is a great deal to be said for informality, so I plan to call you 'Mark.'

Bogleman's voice was soft, almost indifferent. As I glanced at him, he didn't seem to be looking directly at me.

"We must begin somewhere," he said, "so tell me about yourself. What hobbies do you enjoy? What are your interests? What kind of people do you like? How do people affect you? Say whatever comes to mind, ramble."

Curious how this would interest him, but I began talking. What was my life like? A family, a business, never enough money, and problems—a never ending stream of problems. When one problem was solved, another followed. There were some diversions—the occasional fishing trip, the weekends at Harrison Hot Springs or Vancouver, the cocktail parties which seemed such a bore with the constant chit chat, the repetition of events and stories. At these affairs, all ideas traveled across the surface of things revealing no depth or insight. No one listened—everyone was talking or laughing or drinking without any evidence of sincere expressions of warmth or affection. Cocktail party chatter was little more than a catharsis, an emptying, a pouring out. It left me drained, exhausted. What could I tell this hulk of a man before whom I sat? That I was depressed? Lost? That life had lost its meaning? That I was fearful—and at the same time bored?

I didn't say any of these things. I answered as simply as I was able.

"My wife and I travel some. We have a family and a business that take up considerable time. Our business, until a recent recession, did well. Our holdings are large. We go out to dinner once or more a week. And, oh yes, we socialize—cocktail parties—but people bore me." I laughed. "Perhaps, I bore them even more."

His voice did not change its soft tone. "Do you listen to others at these parties?"

"Sometimes."

"Why do you feel people at these parties are not interesting?"

So, the first judgment had been made. How did he know what they were like? Did he know them? Could he see their faces, hear their voices?—loud, excited, self important, laughing at the most trivial matters—uttering words, just words, without thought or substance or meaning. Such trivial utterances, such a waste. Their world was not my world. They did not reach me, nor I them. The "cocktail hour" communicants might as well have been in foreign lands for all the feelings or thoughts we were able to exchange.

I attempted to answer with caution. "Perhaps, it is a lack of interest in the ordinary things of life."

Then another thought struck me.

I said, "I lack wit: I am rather slow. I do not have the quickness that startles and draws interest." In my mind I felt I was mouthing only childish prattle. Perhaps, though, this self deprecating approach would impress Bogleman.

"You have good health?"

"Fat, but good health."

"Much energy?"

"Not much."

At that I lit a cigarette and looked into his face. He seemed to be appraising me.

What category was I fitting into? What sort of problem did he see in me? What combination of weaknesses? Some pride, of course–a big ego–a lack of control. The marks of excess, certainly, going to extremes. Surely he saw no evidence of moderation. Only those who smile and accept and move along quietly in the herd are truly normal. Since I obviously was not <u>one</u> of them, into which slot, in which file did I belong?

"Your wife tells me that you recently took a trip to Los Angeles. Care to tell me about it?" he asked.

His tone was casual, mild. If there was any direction or ultimate purpose in the question it was not apparent.

"We flew to L.A.," I said, "spent the day at the airport waiting for my car."

"A new car?" he asked.

"Yes," I said. "Foreign. Something new on the market. Road & Track gave it the highest rating. Great car for cornering, very fast, holds the road."

"Your wife says you stopped in a motel in San Francisco." He looked at me with those dark, cloudy eyes. There was no change in the tone of his voice: no sign of unusual interest.

"Yes, we spent the night."

"Your wife says you threatened to kill her." He was watching me intently now.

"That's putting it bluntly," I smiled, "and seeing too much in a family quarrel. She was in the bathroom getting ready to go out for dinner while I was watching TV and having a few drinks. Through one window I could see the lights of the city. The night was unusually warm for San Francisco, and I opened the door to the balcony. Through the openings in the railing, I could see the park, the brightly lighted fountain and shrubbery below. I don't remember how the discussion began."

"Hardly a discussion," he smiled, without malice, "if you threatened her."

How to answer this? All I remember was my wife saying over and over again: "You are cruel, cruel! You are the cruelest person I've ever met!" But what had I said that caused such an outburst? For the life of me I could not remember.

Rather lamely I replied, "I recall only saying to her that if she left me, we would go together. Our lives would end now!"

"Go together? By that you were saying?" He paused, slowly shifted about in the chair (all his movements were slow and ponderous)–then seemed to alter his approach. "What brought on such a threat of violence?"

"I don't know."

"Were you drinking much?"

"Not any more than usual. Some Scotch."

"Do you feel you drink too much?"

"Of course I drink a lot. All my friends do. The last few years I've drunk more than usual." Quickly, I added, "But I have been active in many undertakings. My business does well. My family certainly doesn't suffer. My resistance is lower no doubt, and I am simply tired much of the time. Probably middle age. Or the result of too much pressure. Or boredom, possibly. I need a vacation."

He appeared to think about this flurry of justifications and excuses for a moment. Then, raising his head to look at me, he asked, "Would you like a cup of coffee before we continue?"

I nodded and watched him as he lifted his ponderous hulk from the chair and walked through the door behind him. He returned with two large cups of black coffee. Accepting a cup I watched him slowly resume his seat at the desk. Sipping the black hot coffee gave me time to study his face: placid, yet indicating in its dark lines an inscrutable depth, etched with the pain and frustration of years of struggle–the often unrewarding efforts of helping those who did not respond to treatment. I felt that to Bogleman, I must appear like some familiar and well examined book, the contents of which was known, and with only a change in title and binding to differentiate it from all the others. The narrative was certainly commonplace, evoking feelings, thoughts and ambitions which, to the doctor, could only be, by this time in his career, trite beyond measure. The same old weaknesses and failings were again hauled out for examination, revealing nothing new, startling, or original. With me, he would plumb no depths that hadn't been explored previously.

Having finished his coffee, he looked straight at me, yet his appraisal seemed to take in the entire room. His impersonal look seemed to say, "It does not matter what you say–I already know the answer."

"Doesn't it strike you as odd and highly irregular for you to threaten your wife in a motel, while you two are ostensibly enjoying a pleasure trip? What was the provocation? Had she insulted you? Belittled you? In some way attacked your pride? Were you ill? Something was said that set you off. Such anger! Why? You must have some idea. Can you dismiss such a threat to your wife simply by telling me that you are a good provider? What was it you said . . .? You at least indicated that you thought of yourself as a 'doer'–you indicated a certain success in your business. Well and good–but a man who loves his wife certainly does not threaten to kill her."

He stopped talking. His look was as impersonal as if he had just finished commenting upon the latest market report. No use telling him that I had been filled with fear for several days after that outburst of uncontrolled anger–particularly when I realized that I could not remember what had caused it.

"For some time," I began, "there has been considerable strain in our business because of a recent recession. Our expenses have been high, what with supporting several children in college and maintaining a staff the expenses have continued while our income has fallen to the point where I have been going behind each month. The bank is uneasy, and another downtrend in the market could increase the pressure causing undue haste in liquidating properties at a fraction of their real worth." Pausing for a moment I looked up at the doctor to see how he was taking all this. As before, I learned nothing from his expression. His dark face, his eyes darker still, showed no expression. I tried again, deciding to end the explanation.

"What can I say further? A combination of pressures, together with a few drinks caused this eruption. It won't happen again. Nothing really happened anyway."

He appeared almost to smile. "You are in control then. You have no serious problems that might lead to another violent outburst. I hope so," he said as if speaking to himself. Pausing he glanced at his watch. Looking up, he said, "Our time is up. Is next week, same time, agreeable?"

I nodded, relieved that our interview was over, and that I was to be allowed to regain the freedom of the bright out of doors. That drab, dim office and Bogleman's probing had been more of an ordeal than I would have cared to admit.

But as time went on, and the weekly interviews became a part of my accustomed routine, the sessions were less onerous. The visits to the psychiatrist became a matter of course, and what anxieties had existed originally had been quelled. Now, I listened attentively to his questions, and then answered pleasantly, without showing any sign of emotion. Why I assumed this phlegmatic pose, I do not know–self protection, perhaps. But assume it I did, showing little visible interest in either his questions or in the more or less automatic responses I gave to them.

We continued on this low key course for some time. Then, one day, he jolted me out of my complacency.

Speaking with an intensity which was unfamiliar to me, he said, "You've come to the end of the line. You've used up all the enzymes in your system, and your body just will not take any more beating. Drinking alcohol has nearly done you in. You <u>must</u> stop!"

"But why? What makes you say that?"

"You resist. My God!" He sounded resigned. "Your mind is clouded. You're always depressed. Your marriage is affected–even your health is endangered. Yet you resist. You will not stop drinking. What further signs of trouble do you need?"

All this was said without a smile–without inflection–without raising his voice. There were just those words coming out of that dark mouth. I dismissed his words. He did not know me or my problems or my innermost feelings. Many men drank excessively during periods of stress. That did not make them drunkards.

I nodded my head slowly saying nothing. For several moments he stared at me, then indicated that the week's session was at an end. I walked out of the room feeling his eyes following me.

I knew how to rid myself of the feeling of depression that was closing in on me.

CHAPTER 2

By evening I had forgotten the doctor's remarks; all my desires were set upon having a few drinks. As I drove into the wide parking area below the east wing of the house I noticed the carport was empty. Walking up the stairs between the rows of shrubbery and turning left, facing the glass entrance, I saw no one. Opening the locked door I stepped inside and listened: there was the hum of a circulating pump, a car making the curve near the house, the muffled sound of city traffic, the slight movement of rafters overhead caused by the cooling change in temperature–then, almost total silence.

I walked down the long hallway to the kitchen, plucked a bottle from the liquor cabinet and poured myself a stiff drink of scotch. At that moment I saw the note lying on the counter.

It was brief and to the point. "Dear Mark," she wrote, "You have made a decision, and drink is now more important to you than our life together. You are no longer the man I married. Your personality has changed; your outlook and thinking are different. You're not sweet and thoughtful anymore but harsh and bitter. You are either unwilling or unable to accept my help, or for that matter, the help of anyone who is close to you. Your mental and physical health are both deteriorating, and since you reject my love and my help, I cannot bear to stay near you and watch you destroy yourself. For all of these reasons, and for some too confused in my own mind to even express, I see no reason to remain a part of this household. I will, of course, be in touch with the children, and I'll get word to you when my plans have become more settled."

"Gone at last!" I sighed. The sound of my own voice in that big, empty house momentarily startled me.

I raised my glass and muttered, "I'll drink to that." Then I repeated the phrase, over and over, until I realized that I was shouting. "What a relief!" I yelled. My words rang through the family room, and echoed down the hallway.

The sense of the new found freedom lifted my spirits. Now, tonight, all alone (there would never be a tomorrow) I could wander about the house doing as I pleased, recalling and reliving scenes of the past—the great parties, the big crowds, the countless faces. Let them all come back now, one by one, late into the night! Let the night go on and on forever!

On this high counter that served as a table and a bar, friends had crowded around: they leaned against it or sat on bar stools. Here I had served untold hundreds of drinks. On more formal occasions, or with larger crowds, two bartenders worked; sometimes in the outer cabana near the pool in the summer, or in the larger bar below in the winter. With the liquor flowing, the voices had risen higher and higher. The house had been designed for parties. The architect had called for high, arched ceilings, and the soffits above the doors and windows extended into the family room, concealing the lights that illuminated the ceiling. On the lower side of these soffits, along the outer walls, were lights controlled by rheostats. The formal dining room separated the two main rooms of the house, the living room and the family area. These two rooms were graced by massive doors of wood and glass (often open in the summertime) which led to the lanai around the swimming pool.

The Scotch whisky was beginning to have its usual magical effect on me, and from where I now stood, I could see the pool, and flowers, and the carefully tended green shrubbery. In the middle distance, poplar trees moved lightly in a freshening breeze.

Feeling a need to watch the trees more closely, I walked through the dining room and opened two of the large doors in the living room. I stepped outside and sat in a camp chair with my back to the children's wing of our home. To the left of me was a high fence, now all but concealed by flowers and shrubs; on my right was the deep interior of the living room whose details I could make out only dimly through the open doors. With a half filled glass in my hand and a bottle of Scotch beside me, I sat facing the pool, the sun and the trees.

The wind was now blowing in stronger gusts. The leaves danced and twisted, catching the reflections of the fading sun, rustling as they touched and turned: the branches bowed with the weight of the leaves–ever moving in a graceful, rhythmic dance. Deep shadows began forming around the pool. The last rays of the sun appeared through openings in the trees, and overhead, the clouds–only a short time before white, radiant and still in a blue sky–had changed. They were now black, ominous, set in a darkening sky.

Once, as a boy, long ago, I sat in the back seat of a Model A Ford. All day from early morning my dad had driven the car from Aberdeen across the prairie, many miles separating the small towns, until we had reached Mobridge, South Dakota. The Missouri River flowing rapidly below the bridge was a spectacular sight. Toward evening, we left the main road and began crossing over the barren countryside of North Dakota, where the land was wild and untamed. There were hills and sagebrush and prairie grass. The grey unbroken soil was covered with rocks. In the distance were high buttes, steep on all sides, strangely different with the flat surface on top. I sat in the back seat straining my eyes to look beyond, to penetrate the purple haze that hovered over all the hills to see what exciting world was there. To me all life was exciting: the opening of doors every day to new sights and sounds–my world of dreams for life was an unending adventure.

Past dreams faded as present needs intruded. Suddenly, I craved more Scotch. I drank deeply and felt in complete and utter harmony with all of nature. The peace which was now infusing my soul was what I had always been seeking. It seemed strange to me that I could ever have felt at odds with anyone. My wife–all my problems– seemed far away. I wondered if they ever existed. Feeling the cooling air I looked up to see the first star–then another–then across a patch of dark blue, the outline of the moon.

With my refilled glass–the bottle only half empty–I drank deeply before walking back in the living room. The house was silent, save when a rafter or some joint in the sturdy roof groaned under the contraction of changing temperature. I sat in the dark at one end of the living room. Even without lamps I could see quite clearly from the light given off by the stars and the gas lights just beyond the pool. Above me was the balcony that enclosed our master bedroom, and higher still, the cedar lined vaulted ceiling. The outer wall, of heavy doors of wood and glass, supported beams and columns with large sections of glass above the doors. On fine days, the sun shone brightly through the glass, restricted only by draperies which could be opened or closed at our whim. Now, it was the moon and the stars which were etched on the glass, and upon which I found my attention strangely directed. Then my glance was diverted to the open staircase near the main entrance, by which one reached the upper levels of the house. My eyes shifted again, to sweep over the inner brick wall of the living room, and its dramatic pit fireplace occupying one whole corner of the room. The black hole at the far end of the room was nothing more threatening than the door to the dining room beyond. And to the right of the dining room door began the brick inner wall which extended to the fireplace. A reflective fireplace screen was brought to life by the shadow dance of the limbs and leaves of the trees outside. The wildly dancing shadows were first apparent only upon the screen; then I noticed their gyrations also on the brick wall, and even across the face of an eighteenth century portrait in its niche in the wall. The wind was rising.

I smiled as I watched the leaves dance in the dark. How utterly contented I felt as I recalled certain strange nights when I was a boy. Many nights in fall or winter, after concluding some game with my friends, I would sit on the curb in the street outside my home. The wind moaned above me in the trees; the single bulb from the overhead street lamp cast some light upon a dirt road and the bare cottonwoods, but I feared going into the house and to my bedroom.

Often in that upper room I had awakened, so it seemed, to see the leaves and branches of the trees outside my upper window reflected on the wall across from my bed. In the still room whose silence was broken only by the lonely sound of a train whistle, I watched this eerie dance. Somehow it always happened: my eyes were drawn to a closet near the entrance to the room; my skin grew tense as I detected the slightest movement of the door. As the door slowly opened I was unable to bear the paralyzing fear: unable to cry out. I leaped from the bed, plunged into the closet, reaching out wildly to grapple with whatever demon I was able to grasp. Then, in a state of great agitation, I wakened. Such wild dreams that occurred so long ago amused me at this moment.

My eyes were drawn away from the wall with the dancing trees to the large picture in an ornate frame–the eighteenth century painting of an aristocratic young man. His face was round and full, eyes soft and alert, the nose large, his lips relaxed almost in a smile. Rich,– undoubtedly rich and gifted–in an age of pioneering, of great struggle and poverty, when few were successful and almost everyone poor. He had reached the top; he could afford a talented painter; he could show a relaxed face; he was young and possessed so much. No doubt his wife was beautiful. He looked innocent, just over indulgent. There was nothing about his looks that suggested the hard, sensuous face of a Don Juan. In my fantasy I conjectured that his money had been gained from a family business–lumber or shipping perhaps–as a merchant selling in a growing town. So many ways to make money–and lose it too. But what happened to that wife, that successful business, the children, their heirs? Does anything remain? Do I have it all in this picture? Does this masterpiece in oil tell a tale of success and the folly of it all? I have you, all that is left of you! Now you can just hang there–hang, hang and embellish my room. My laughter at this thought startled me.

High above in the arched ceiling the rafters groaned again, and the leaves continued their dance upon the wall. The pale features of the young merchant with the soft eyes continued to meet my gaze never blinking, never changing–always the same, always watching me. The night was so dark, so still: almost imperceptibly, at first, I began to feel a closeness in the room. My mood changed. I thought of my achievements. By any standards, I had done well. But success was bitter without charm or appeal. There was no pleasure, nor joy, nor satisfaction in my success for me–only a constant weariness. Goals which had been attained were never high enough: there were always much greater heights to scan. Only those who benefited from my success cared: they cared for themselves; they cared to know me if it reflected to their advantage, and, it seemed, for that reason alone. Otherwise, toward me, there was, I felt, contempt or jealousy or the malice of envy. So easy to be hated if one was successful. What a price to pay! Fear–constant fear–a fear never ending; nightmares, the threat of bankruptcy if the market turned at the wrong time. I had attained an upper ledge, and was secure for the moment. But would it last? How long could I retain my grasp, and even if I held on, did it all have a meaning? What has been achieved anyway? Success be damned, business be damned! Save for the sycophants and the leeches, who cared for anyone who has made a lot of money? I had become an unwilling "Money Machine." With this thought I drained the bottle.

I looked up again into those soft painted eyes, not feeling as relaxed and content as I had an hour before. By what right do I own your elaborate portrait? What was I thinking about you a moment ago? Oh yes–your wife and children. Where are they now, ancient nobleman? Were your heirs prosperous like you, or did your family fortune disappear in one of those financial crashes to which your times must have also been prey? The soft eyes and the full, round face, so smooth and guileless, began to bother me. In a fit of pique, I shouted at my two dimensional companion. "You wouldn't look like that if your face had been painted when you were my age!" I waved the bottle, half intending to throw it. "Your eyes wouldn't be soft, they would be hard–would gleam sometimes with hatred, sometimes with avarice, sometimes with cruelty–but always calculating and watchful."

I paced the room on unsteady legs. Raising my voice again I began to shake with anger, "Would your face be bloated like mine, your hair white, dark holes for eyes, a twisted mouth with thin lips if you had lived as long as I and lived the same life–my life?" I sat down. The sofa was soft. "Well, I'm smarter than you," I growled to myself, "smart enough not to be painted so some art collector can buy me at an auction and use me to embellish a room. Looking up, someone would say, 'What technique, must have cost a fortune'; another would say how they captured that face–those eyes; other descriptions, the lost look of despair. The old fool: dissipated, appears to have gone through life indulging himself and from one fraud to another. What cold features. Probably cruel too." The judgment of others: the thought caused me to shrug. I felt nothing about such things.

The eyes in the painting were watching me closely. I mocked them. What an elaborate, baroque frame inlaid with gold leaf! An artist of merit has preserved all that is left of you for me to gaze upon–to gaze at you forever, if I like, with pleasure or contempt. Whatever my mood, you will not change. You cannot complain; your features are forever set, captive for me. That innocent look of contentment is frozen upon your face while I look at you and judge you as I like. You are held, fixed within that gold frame as surely as if you were sealed in a tomb. You neither protest, resist, nor escape. You are my possession; my work of art. With a feeling of malice I smiled as I thought again how good it would be to have the other painting of him in his old age.

Was it the creak of the overhead beams, a cold breeze through the open doors that drew my eyes to the other wall where the limbs of the trees and the leaves were moving up and down wildly in a mad, frenetic dance? Electric shocks darted up and down my legs, my clothes hung tight to my skin, my body was quivering. Was it from a chill? My grip tightened on the empty bottle. I listened and scanned the room, not missing any part of the dark. There was someone?–some creature?–something deadly–near me. I could feel it.

The picture was alive. The eyes were no longer soft: they were mocking me. This intensified my fear that almost overwhelmed me. With fear came hate rising like a volcano within. A movement came at last, something huge in the dark entrance to the dining room; then it disappeared behind the bricks. Was it coming down the hall from the other side? I could not hear a sound, only the hum of the pump, the moving of the wind. I was now the quarry, the victim; I cursed determined to lash out. I think it was the mocking eyes that caused me to make a move: carefully across the carpet I moved toward the smiling face, nearer, step by step toward the dark entrance to the other room. I could not see, only sensed a presence. With a scream I leaped into the opening swinging the bottle with all my strength at the creature behind the wall.

CHAPTER 3

Silently the door opened. As I was wheeled into the white room the overhead lights forced me to close my eyes. Lying on my back I turned my head to one side to avoid the glaring lights and then opened my eyes slowly. Standing near me were men dressed in white. On their faces they wore masks. No one spoke.

All eyes were upon me. My face and hands were wet. My heart was pounding. Fear possessed me. Someone gave a signal. Everyone moved at once. My legs and arms were pinned to the table. A large mask was placed over my face covering my nose, mouth and eyes.

"Breathe deeply," said a harsh voice.

The odor was vile, choking me. I fought in terror.

"Hold him," someone cried.

"Stop fighting. Lie still," said an ugly voice.

"He's going," said another in relief.

The voices faded away. My world was gone. I felt suspended in a narrow tunnel where I could not move or see but a few feet in a strange brown darkness. The narrow cylinder in which I was lying was made; it seemed, of countless strands of wire that appeared to revolve emitting a loud buzzing noise. I felt no pain. Physical pain would have been a delight compared to the terror I felt.

The loneliness was the worst. The sense of loss was my pain and horror, confined here, isolated, cut off forever from all my friends. Never to see anyone again. This was my fate. A living, breathing death–forever.

I shuddered, as I waited to see Bogleman, each time I recalled the nightmares of the previous night. Why after all these years, I wondered, were vivid scenes of my childhood surgery and the accompanying nightmares coming back to haunt me?

My head was throbbing. My hand, stitched across the palm and up my arm, hurt whenever I moved. I needed pain pills. The gash from the broken bottle had been deep, and the doctor who had attended me had said that the artery had been partially severed. But, he had added, I must have tucked my arm beneath my body as I fell, in such a way as to close the wound, allowing the blood to clot. Otherwise, he suggested, I would have bled to death while unconscious. No need then to sew me up.

There had been the waiting–forever waiting–waiting for the doctor to come. I recalled the earlier hours of the day.

There had been so much blood on the carpet. When I had heard the phone ringing, I felt a terror of forever being confined in that nightmare, helpless, unable to move, abandoned, unable to see clearly. There was a world of darkness into which I had been condemned.

I had felt pain as consciousness returned. The phone kept ringing, louder and louder, the shrill sound reverberating in the empty house. The effort in moving increased the pounding in my head. My arm throbbed.

When I struggled to the phone and answered, it was Bogleman. His voice was slow and deliberate.

"Can you come in today? I have an opening at two this afternoon."

For the longest moment I paused, examining my arm and hand. The blood had begun to drip on the floor. The gash was very deep, needing surgical attention to draw it together. The carpet was drenched with blood. I swore as the room began to turn.

"What did you say?" Bogleman inquired.

"I'll be there," I said. Then I hung up. What was the time? Ten o'clock. It was then that I had telephoned the other doctor.

I should have worn dark glasses. This dismal room: everything white and cold and sterile. The furnishings were sparse: Formica table of imitation walnut with chrome legs; chrome chairs with padded seats. Brown tile on the floor–these bright lights and white walls.

My eyes. Always felt that people who wore dark glasses were affected. My arm hurt. Raising my bandaged arm, I saw stains of blood lightly spotting the bandages.

"Won't you come in?"

I hadn't heard the door open. He was looking at me expressionless. There was no indication that he was aware of what had happened. How could he know? Did he sense a change? His seeming indifference, his slow, ponderous movements gave the appearance of strength and self assurance as he stepped aside to let me enter his office.

With a sigh of weariness I sat down in a familiar chair while the doctor assumed his seat in back of his desk.

He looked up only after lighting a cigarette. His eyes studied me like a lab assistant looking over one of his choice white rats in a laboratory. I waited for him to initiate the conversation as he sipped coffee. For the first time he did not offer me a cup. Was his attitude calculated, I wondered, to irritate me?

"You look sick. You don't appear to be making any progress," he said bluntly.

My head was throbbing. The pain in my hand and arm had increased. I could not ask him for a pain pill. He looked at me, then at his cigarette, back to his coffee, then glanced at me wondering, I suppose, why I didn't say something.

I felt a fire within me begin to burn with increasing intensity. With each moment it was becoming harder to control. This room, the brightness, the floral drapes, and the cold asphalt tiled floors–the whole dreary place was so depressing–as cold and tasteless as the doctor himself.

"You don't see yourself as you are. You don't know the difference," he said, slowly shaking his head.

"The difference of what?"

"Between a social drinker and an alcoholic–which you certainly are."

"Prove it. Set me straight. What is so different about me? How do I differ from any other social drinker?"

The pain I felt seemed to increase my hatred of this man. I was watching him closely: he would glance at me and then lower his eyes. Was he afraid of me? How could he set himself up as my judge?

He began, "Often it takes time to tell."

Looking up, his eyes searched my face. Dropping his eyes and reaching for his cigarettes he continued, "No, you don't see. You resist. You are blind. That is the frightful part of the disease–blindness–the victim cannot or will not see. There in the dark he steps off the cliff never seeing where his steps have been leading him. There is a profound significance in taking it or leaving it alone. Social drinkers can go on for ages either taking a drink or leaving it alone.

"Alcohol is such a part of your life that you cannot function without it. It seems to give your life the meaning it has at the moment. You have no resistance. Whatever enzymes which resist addiction have long since been burned out of you. You are not happy. Where is the joy that wine brings to the heart? The peace, the lightness. You are a hardened and embittered man. There is a frightening violence in you, seething within. You could explode and do things–evil things –beyond your control. What you are, what you are becoming, is the result of alcoholism."

"I ask you for an answer, and you examine my soul," I said, mocking him. "Surely you can do better."

Bogleman listened without betraying any emotion.

Leaning forward in my chair, I continued. "You judge me. But look at yourself! Fat–at least thirty pounds overweight. There is a heaviness, a dark side to your appearance. There isn't a trace of lightness in you, yet you would reform me. Doesn't scripture say something about failing to see the plank in your eye while you search for a speck of sawdust in another's eye? Remove the plank before you presume to teach me."

I sat back in my chair. "This is my last visit to you. I should have known better than to try to learn something from a psychiatrist who specializes in drunks. For all I know, you could be one yourself."

Quite forgetting myself, I turned up my right arm, revealing the heavy bandages and their telltale stains.

He was neither intimidated nor angry. His dark eyes were clouded as he rose slowly from his chair and moved around the desk. He examined my bandaged palm and the blood soaked bandages on my arm.

"Stitches?" he asked.

"Many."

"Care to tell me about it?"

"Why not?" I said.

This would be the last time I'd be seeing him. I felt reckless. Give it all to him. Let him judge me mad if he liked. Let him pass on some wild tale to those who had sent me here.

I began my narrative with accounts of my strange nightmares as a boy, and concluded with a description of my last twenty four hours. Only briefly did I refer to the note from my wife and my vigilance before the portrait. I dwelt more on my sitting in the dark alone, watching the stars and the trees. For Bogleman, I fixed the precise location of the portrait on the living room wall (to the left of the archway into the dining room) through which arch I had seen movement and the face of some malignant creature.

Absorbed in what I was saying, the doctor asked, "Did you see evidence of an intruder in the morning? Was anything missing?"

I nodded, feeling more anxious than foolish.

"You dreamed it," he said. Leaning back in his chair with his hands behind his head, he seemed to reconsider. "No," he continued, "you saw it. You want a sign of alcoholism. You want proof. Unfortunately you cannot see yourself. Alcoholics lie–you lie. You are not telling me the truth. Perhaps you cannot.

"Let me reconstruct that night. You were alone because your wife had left you. You decided to celebrate, you were free–free to do as you pleased–to drink without being censored, to survey your castle, to relive the past, to dream of the future, to enjoy nature without anyone to trouble you. You could even revel in your greatness and your many successes without contradiction. You recalled scenes of your childhood, perhaps imagined yourself a great artist. Certainly the painting of the young man fascinated you–a prized possession like your books and antique furniture–someone you could totally possess. You were elated at first.

"Life smiled upon you, perhaps even the man in the painting smiled, too. The air was warm, the trees danced for you, casting their reflections on the interior walls of the room. All of nature and all of life seemed so richly rewarding at that hour. But as the night wore on, your mood changed; in the dark the picture no longer smiled–perhaps it even mocked you. Your hearing became acute. Every object in the room seemed alive, watching you. Somewhere near was danger. An intruder? You saw something move–something dark and sinister, like in your dreams–just beyond the portrait in the darkness of the dining room. Your very nature rebelled against you, yet you ask for proof of your sickness."

"Sickness?" I asked. "Nervous, perhaps, unstrung. Is life easy? You could be considered strange with your ponderous movements, your heavy handed ways. I thought you said alcoholism–not sickness– and isn't that a matter of will power?"

"Will power has little to do with it, strong or weak. You have simply burned up all the enzymes in your system. You are defenseless. You are on the edge of a precipice, alone. You hear the roar of the sea and you tremble, fearful to move. You do not know where to step. You are at the end of the line. Another drink and you will fall into the abyss."

"How dramatic."

"Sad to say it is true. You will fail rapidly now–suicide is even a possibility."

"My," I taunted him, "you have been seeing too many movies. There must be a dramatic climax, something to build interest. Perhaps I could jump out of your window, but then that would not be good for your practice."

"If you change you will see. Otherwise," his voice trailed off, "you have no future."

"I'm not interested in old wives' tales. You will never move me by fear."

He appeared to ignore what I said as if he didn't hear me. Although he had surprised me by his unusual perception in piecing together the events of the previous night, I could only believe that this was accidental. A series of shrewd guesses.

"You received a note from your wife. What did she say?" he asked.

"Not much. She told me that she was leaving for good if I did not stop drinking."

"You won't?"

"I will not!"

"Will you then take a test? You presume to be honest. Will you face this challenge?" He raised his hand. "Do you have the courage to prove me wrong by going into a treatment center for a recommended period? There you will be without liquor; you will hear lectures, have regular hours, and eat good basic foods. For a short time you will be cut off from the world, from society, from all your friends and business associates. Who knows, you might enjoy yourself? Anyway, this is all I can offer you."

If I say no?"

He dealt his trump card. "Surely, your wife will do as she threatened. She will not come back again."

He had waited for this moment, built up to it carefully. I was the pawn who had been carefully manipulated. During all these interviews, appearing to show little interest in me or my remarks, he had been studying, analyzing, waiting, trying to determine what was the weakest chink in my armor. He seemed to be saying to me, "If you have love enough for your wife to accept my counsel, and do as I suggest, there may be hope for you, and for your marriage. Otherwise, I wash my hands of you. I cannot help those who are determined not to accept help."

I had grown to respect his intuition. It was plain that if I did not care enough for my wife to accept the doctor's challenge–for her–his further services were useless for me.

(This pain–the weariness, the frustrations. All my dreams had faded long ago. Now I was no longer young. It had not always been that way . . . . It seemed only yesterday promise. Where had all the years gone? And what had I done with them?)

I was very young and working in a strange city, living in a boarding house managed by two elderly sisters. Their young half-sister, Evelyn, had been transferred to Seattle and came to live with them. She was wearing some outrageous hat when I first met her, but I liked her smile, the feeling of strength and calmness that radiated from her. Being with Evelyn seemed to pull together all the conflicting forces within me. She was reserved. Our acquaintanceship grew and my loneliness disappeared. We went to dances, drank little, and began dreaming of the future.

In those days I had imagined that I was going to become something of a scholar. Accordingly, one night I determined to tell her that I was going to leave Seattle, go back to the Midwest to a small college and pursue my studies. I would not see her again. Her grief at hearing this was so intense, so obviously genuine, that she melted my heart completely. No one had ever shown such affection for me.

I walked out into the summer night and wept bitterly. For what seemed like hours I walked, weeping, considering my future and feeling the intense pain of hurting someone who cared for me. By morning I had resolved that if there was one person in this life who cared that much for me, I would build my life around her and <u>her</u> future, and attempt to make her happy.

Together, facing life, we would enjoy all seasons, share in whatever success we achieved, raise a family and overcome all obstacles. No one would overcome us and our life together would be an exciting adventure. My wife, forever my wife! The life I would offer Evelyn was all that was within me.

The intensity of her love was overwhelming. Two weeks after saying that I was leaving, I asked her to marry me! She was ecstatic, almost in a trance. I thrilled to see Evelyn so happy. Three months later, in a small church ceremony, we were married. Her half-sister gave us a fine breakfast with a few friends after the wedding. In the afternoon a DC 3 flew us to British Columbia where our honeymoon began in a Vancouver hotel. The following day we took a boat to Victoria where we stayed for a week in the Craigflower Auto Courts.

How simple and innocent we were! How little we knew about life, how filled with hope. With budding ambition, we dreamed our dreams, not of any great success but of just a small place in the world to be happy.

Neither one of us cared if we were never recognized by anyone. We had each other. What dreams those had been, and how slowly our world had changed. Children came, and with them was the constant need for money in ever increasing sums. A growing business and success brought attendant problems–a never ending stream of problems–as we reached higher and higher upon each rung of that mythical ladder of success. Somehow it had all gone wrong. The joy and thrill of success had faded, and only disillusionment remained.

Dreams had become tarnished. Only the dust and ashes of our vision remained. Weary, now, from cares and endless problems–jarred and jolted from unforeseen downturns in the market–our ambitions had been tempered. Even success had proved a mockery: the bright, gleaming star of promise, so desirable so many years ago, promising such great fulfillment, had left in its wake so much bitterness, had conceived so much pain, so much envy, that the price was not worth the victory.

The dreams that had faded ushered in the cold reality of a new life, propped up by the increasing need of drugs for stimulant, for social lubricant, to assuage the pain of failure, to celebrate success; in all situations it was needed for the wheels of commerce so I needed alcohol. Existence without it had become intolerable. I could bear any pain, any loss, the greatest suffering or disappointment as long as I had a drink. But I had not lost control. Dependent on alcohol? Of course. Addicted, no.

But now, my wife, Evelyn, presented a stumbling block for me. If she never returned there would be nothing remaining of my vision; not even a memory, not even the ashes. Better if I did not exist if all our efforts together had led to this final parting. What price had I paid to be the victim of my success!

On the other hand, was there even a remote possibility that in all this, the relentless onslaught of Dr. Bogleman's analogies, held some grain of truth–perhaps a ray of hope. Perhaps I could go into a treatment center somewhere, as Dr. Bogleman had suggested, stay in seclusion for a limited period, resting, going along with the program and shedding weight while emptying my mind of business. After all, I had many books; I could read, hike in the woods, and forget society. Freedom–for the first time in years!

I could be free.

And when I returned home from the treatment center, I would drink only with great caution. I would never again be out of control, because I would have learned all of the dangers and pitfalls.

"You're smiling. Has something amusing about all this occurred to you?" Bogleman's question interrupted my reverie.

I looked up at him, wondering if he was being sarcastic. He appeared only curious.

"You're asking a great deal of me, suggesting I go into such a place. What will people say?"

"What will they say? Do you care?" He was kind enough not to repeat my words regarding the opinions of others.

"What about my wife? What if I go through all this torture and she still insists on leaving me? What then?"

"Do you know so little of her after all these years?" the doctor asked. "She is made of that steel you once referred to; she wants you back, as you were, before alcohol possessed you."

"When will I go?"

"Now," he said. "Right now."

"This hour? You're very sure of yourself. How am I expected to get there?"

"Your driver is waiting," he replied. "This is, as I see it, your last chance. I was not sure you would–or could–make the right decision. You have. Perhaps you will make it. Perhaps you will not."

Dr. Bogleman paused and looked at me for what seemed like an eternity. His face grew darker and ominous; his eyes began to slowly ignite as if there was a hidden fire within him. Slowly–even more slowly than before–he began to speak measuring each word. His voice carried the sound of doom.

"You are going to be faced, I fear, with your greatest challenge. You are a chosen one. You are soon going to be aware of the forces that will rage within you and threaten your sanity. Without alcohol, with your peculiar nature, your sensitivity–your unusual gift–you will see yourself as you have never seen yourself before. You might even come face to face with a force that now controls your life. That will be frightening. A terrifying struggle will follow. Then you will–if there is hope for you–become aware of your daemon.

"I have been selected to look after you, to see that you do not fail. No matter what happens never despair! None of this, of course, makes sense to you now. Even my vision is clouded when I attempt to look beyond your coming struggle to see the outcome."

With that he arose, nodded, and shuffled out the door. I sat there for several minutes, frightened, thinking over what he had said. Finally I arose and left the room, wondering if I would ever see that strange doctor again.

CHAPTER 4

With a sense of relief I walked out of Bogleman's office. Pushing the elevator button, I turned and looked back down the long hallway into the small waiting room. The overhead lights reflected upon the white walls, and a cold, searing light outlined the chrome chairs and Formica tables. The brown asphalt floors contrasted sharply in the light. I felt the searing light, the pain of isolation, and the harsh reality of my life, filled now with disillusionment, so utterly different from what I had dreamed it would be As the door of the elevator opened and closed, cutting out this dismal scene, I wondered if I would ever see Bogleman again—and who would be waiting for me when I stepped out of the building.

"Boss! Over here!"

Art—faithful Art—a man who drove himself almost beyond endurance. No construction worker produced more: in the sun or in the cold rain of winter, under the harshest conditions, taking pride in his performance that outshone most men. He played hard, too—drank more than most men, womanized, drove a Cadillac, and lived life to the lees.

"I haven't seen you around lately," he said by way of greeting.

"What are you doing with all this?" I asked, pointing an accusing finger at the big car. I climbed docilely into the rear seat. "Obviously the company is doing well, or am I paying too much? Sets a bad example to the other men, don't you think?"

Art laughed. "You know me, boss. I need lots of room to maneuver. These modern girls want the best. I give it to them—all they want."

Settling back in the seat I asked, "What's the program? Where are you taking me?"

"Some place called Maplewood. Heard it was a sanitarium. Hope it's not serious, boss." He hesitated a moment, then said, "I brought you a little gift to make the ride more comfortable."

Turning in his seat he handed me a fifth of Vodka, a large paper cup and a can of orange concentrate. Without hesitation I accepted. From long experience I quickly spooned a scoop of concentrate into the cup and mixed it with Vodka. As the car threaded its way through traffic, I drank; filled and drank again. I waited several minutes before mixing the third drink, to give the alcohol time to take effect. I felt much better. The pounding in my head subsided: I no longer felt the pain in my arm. A feeling of adventure came over me.

"How is the job going, Art?" I asked. The car gained speed as Art accelerated onto the freeway heading north

"Everything's going great. The appliances are coming in, the painters have two floors finished, the plasterboard people are done–I didn't think they'd ever finish."

"That figures–always some holdup."

I settled down with the bottle and gazed out at the passing countryside. Great white clouds hung listlessly in the blue sky. The bright sun made the clouds seem white and the sky stretched on beyond the hills and the mountains–an endless expanse of pale blue, contrasting with the whiteness of the clouds. Puffy cumulus were drifting lazily, forming new shapes, at times radiating the brilliance of the sun or again molding out an inert shape, still and lifeless. My eyes were attracted to the trees standing so erect and still on this windless day. They were silent, never changing spectators as we sped by. Ancient firs, sturdy, rugged, having withstood all seasons and many storms, bowed only to the wind and listened to its mournful tales. They rustled or churned in what may have been anguish, but no one knew what response they gave: they kept their own counsel and were not disturbed by the petty troubles of men. What strength and grandeur! If only I could be made like one of those great trees–to bear up well in all seasons; never troubled by rain or sleet or snow, or the howling winds of winter–or the loss of ideals. Rooted solidly in the forest, I would not have to understand the futility in wealth, feel the pain of loss, watch youth slip away, see hopes unfulfilled, or find dreams an illusion. And I would not have to harbor a broken heart left hardened and embittered. As hope ends, joy ceases; pleasure sought turns to pain; there is a nagging sense of loss, pervading depression, haunting loneliness. Beyond that is fear: the emptiness of despair.

Oh! To leave it all behind, all memories, all sorrows –frustrated hopes, the corroding sense of failure, the weariness of constant struggle. To lose myself deep within the shadows of the forest, to hide, to wander aimlessly, to find a new life by a stream in a deep valley; build a cabin, fish and hunt, become a part of nature, a friend of wild animals–to dream in utter peace, never again to be a part of the world I abandoned. Perhaps it was not too late. I was not too old to begin again–to live alone with the animals of the forest.

I felt the spirit of adventure. What would Maplewood be like? Did I care? I knew what I would do: fade into the group, say nothing, do nothing, answer no one, read only what I pleased and leave the grounds to explore the forest whenever possible. Just to wander among the trees, young saplings, scarred and ancient pines, towering above me, their swaying limbs whispering their secrets to the wind, would be balm to my soul. I envisioned that there would be paths that led to adventure, places to discover, a stream in the valley, a mountaineer's cabin long deserted; other scenes, the wild animals and changing landscape–the utter peace of being away from everyone, from all routine and all responsibility. No one would bother me.

"How much farther, Art?"

"About fifteen miles, I'd guess, or a half hour's drive. The winding roads are slow."

I settled back and mixed the last of the Vodka and orange concentrate, amused at how well I had gauged the drinks; the last drink would be finished just as we arrived. How amusing everything seemed. It was madness coming here. Sick? Alcoholic? Why, I was utterly content, strangely happy, at peace within–no conflicts or confusion–all forces within me were in harmony. The world was serene. Without enemies or enduring problems, I was capable of meeting life head on–indeed I welcomed the challenge. What was I doing in this car anyway?

I was surrounded by fanatics who saw the specter of alcohol under every bush, behind every stone or twig. They saw it only in their fantasies–that was all. They were sick –not me. I could see through and around all of them! My vision was crystal clear as I read their thoughts and saw what they wanted more clearly than they realized themselves. If recently my behavior had been occasionally erratic, well, why not? Who had greater problems? Who could enter into my skin, feel, as I did, the pain–the searing pain–the confusion, emptiness, futility and long endless nights of growing despair? Even to move had become an effort. A grey ceiling had been over the world, but now, for this hour, that hopelessness and despair had ended. I would hold it, this peace, hold it forever. There was hope after all. Liquor was meant for men like me who needed it to function well in a difficult world.

My reverie ended as Art turned off the main highway and began driving along a narrow road through the trees. I was watchful, waiting for (I didn't know what) as the car turned right and left following the curve of the road. We came to a clearing in the trees.

"That's it," said Art. "We're here. See the building among the trees?"

Half hidden from view were three vine covered brick buildings, one larger than the other two. As we approached I could see that one housed the heating plant. Another, somewhat larger, was near a river– with a bridge across into the forest–and was probably used for recreation. Already I was making plans to explore the river and the forest beyond during the hours I had to myself.

As Art stopped near the main entrance, several men and women standing nearby looked up. They had been drinking coffee and talking. One or two seemed to smile as I climbed out of the car, but they quickly lost interest and continued talking. One lady appeared to take an interest in us.

"Coming in?" she asked. "Oh, you'll love it here! My name is Mary. Everyone is so nice, and we have the greatest time together. We are so happy."

Her enthusiasm amused me. She appeared elated in this remote place (certainly not the setting that most people would choose) isolated from the world, the activities to which people grow accustomed, and from family, friends and daily haunts. Loneliness and strange faces were what I saw. Turning to face Mary I observed she continued talking unaware that I was not listening

Art deposited my baggage, wished me well, and departed.

At the sound of my name, I turned.

"Mark. Your name is Mark," Mary said. "Come over and meet Bill. And this is Gene, and here is our famous Admiral, Raymond. And Dean. Dean—come here! He is such a dear man."

They smiled, murmured a few words of greeting, each telling me how much I would like Maplewood. No one looked ill to me. Bill, as an example, had an easy laugh, and a deep voice. He appeared to be a polished gentleman of some education. Later I learned that he had a Ph.D. in music.

"I see you have a box of books," he said. "Don't let Dr. Neilstrom see that carton, or he'll want to put them away for the duration."

"Anti-intellectual, is he?"

Bill smiled warmly. "No, not that. Just dedicated. Consumed with a total interest in the welfare of each patient. He doesn't want anything to distract you from his teachings."

"Sounds like a school to me."

"In a way it is. We hear the truth about alcohol as it affects us: the chosen ones." He laughed. "Men like you and me."

His charm was appealing.

"Speak for you," I said. "If I am chosen I'd prefer not to be selected as an alcoholic."

I felt uneasy about my books. Someone taking my books. How ridiculous!

Looking about, I became aware of a striking young lady looking at me with dark luminous eyes. Bill, following my gaze, remarked. "That's Lucy. She's been here several weeks. Doesn't say much."

"Attractive," I said, "and young. Too young to be here."

"You might be surprised to learn that alcohol is no respecter of age." Nodding toward Lucy, he added, "Or respecter of beauty."

Seeing a redheaded woman approaching, I asked, "And who is that determined woman?"

He chuckled. "You are about to be initiated into Maplewood. Now you will see what a haven of rest and solicitude you've come to. Stella has much to say here."

"Mark? Which of you is Mark?" a strident voice inquired.

"I'm Mark," I replied.

Her gaze was bold, direct: in a sharp glance she appraised me. She laughed. When she spoke, there was a ring of sarcasm in her voice.

"I see you've come to us in fine shape. Would you come with me?"

As we moved away from the others she turned and asked, "How much have you had to drink?"

"Is it that obvious?"

"You are obviously drunk," she snapped. "You are here to be helped, to do exactly as we say. To listen. To follow instructions to the letter. You are a sick man–far sicker than you realize–who needs help at once. Now–how much have you drunk today?"

I resisted this approach.

Stella led me from the yard into the long, low building to our left. As we entered, the screen door slammed behind us, and I was then ushered into a utilitarian, plain walled office.

"Sit down," she said, indicating a scuffed and much abused red Naugahyde chair. "You may smoke, if you like."

As we sat down in her office I was confronted by a woman who still retained her youthful beauty, who happened to be very hard and determined and endowed with a no nonsense approach to alcoholics. She was without a glimmer of humor.

"You say that I am drunk. The amount, then, is irrelevant," I said.

Her eyes widened, and then narrowed. They seemed to glitter and harden. She took a deep breath to speak, paused again for a moment, then measured each word.

"You'll find it tolerable here–some even find it pleasant–if you cooperate. If not, your stay at Maplewood can be as unpleasant as you choose to make it."

I sensed the threat in her voice. Less than one half hour was gone and already I had alienated Stella, who I learned later was the counselor in charge. The liquor was wearing off. I looked around the room and wondered if anyone had hidden liquor. Why hadn't I thought to bring a supply? She caught my wandering gaze; a shadow of a smile came across her face. Did she read my mind? I wondered.

"I want you to answer a few questions for me," she began. "We haven't much on you. How many years have you been drinking? How much do you drink each day?"

I thought for a moment. When did I begin? "I began drinking about twenty years ago," I said. "Five years ago my drinking increased. Some days I drink a fifth, some days none at all–but those days are few."

She continued, on and on, with a long list of questions. Occasionally she looked up, studied my reaction to a question, watched my movements, and listened to the inflection of my voice. One question seemed to interest her especially.

"Do you have black outs?" she asked.

"Sometimes," I replied. "That is, if you are asking if I lose parts of a conversation, or forgets that I met someone, or can't recall parts of an evening. Yes–that has happened to me."

"Mood changes?"

"Yes." This was a sensitive area she was probing. "Sometimes I lose control, become unusually elated or depressed, sometimes very angry. Afterwards, I wonder why."

Of course, I was understating my case. The truth–what actually happened in recent months–was that anger often consumed me so completely I did not know myself. At other times, my elation carried me to the mountain peaks, and I soared like an eagle, in wild flights of fantasy. So real and alive I felt on these transports, that the world seemed small–so easy to conquer. All problems diminished, and nothing seemed impossible for me. Afterwards, I felt so foolish that I cringed and writhed and blushed with shame.

"Do you have fears?" Stella continued.

"Doesn't everyone?"

She put her pencil down and fixed me with a level gaze. It was obvious that I had left any previous identity or vestiges of prestige behind me when I entered into the care of Maplewood.

"Don't fence with me," she intoned evenly. "I am here to help you. Cooperate. You are here because you were sent here. We accepted you only because we know we can help you. But our ability to help depends upon your cooperation. We can't help you unless you cooperate with us."

She stopped speaking and continued to look directly into my eyes. She toyed lightly with her pencil, but her attention was solely on me. My slightest movement was recorded in her eyes, and I could see that she was waiting–waiting for some sort of commitment from me.

"Yes," I sighed, "I have fears."

My God, I thought, do I have fears. My head–my arm–what pain! Uneasily, I began moving about in the chair.

"Am I different?" Forcing myself to smile, I continued. "Businessmen and my associates said I was fearless. Yet I feel fear."

If she only knew how much.

"In a few weeks," she said, folding papers, stapling others together in my file, "you are going to see things in another light. A revelation will awaken you. For the first time you are going to see the truth about yourself."

She smiled broadly to my surprise. She was hard but still attractive.

"Have no doubt about this–you are an alcoholic. You look like an alcoholic and talk like one. Your responses during our little interview gave you away. You have come to the right place."

She arose, indicating the meeting was over. She walked briskly to the door. Standing by the doorway, she told me (in a businesslike tone) where I'd find the nurse, the counselor in charge for the day, the rooms, and the daily bulletin which provided the schedule for lectures, meals, reading material, exercise, and stated the limits of the grounds– all necessary information needed by initiates to fit into the regimen.

Having already observed the buildings and the preoccupation of staff and residents, I felt I would encounter very little difficulty in slipping off, unseen, into the woods.

Stella wished me well, then turned and walked away leaving me alone in the long hallway wondering where to go.

CHAPTER 5

Someone touched my arm.

"Will you take a walk with me?"

Turning, I looked into the face of a young woman. Her hair was stringy and soiled, she was overweight, and she wore a plain dress which hung loosely over a shapeless figure. My curiosity aroused, I followed this strange figure down the long corridor onto the cinder pathway that wandered through the trees beyond the buildings and extended to the outer limits of the grounds.

As we walked along she talked incessantly.

"Do you know why I'm here?" she began. Not waiting for an answer she continued, "They put me here."

"Who? Why?" I asked.

"My family. I had money. My name is Bernice. They put me here to get my money." As she talked she turned her head close to mine and stared at me.

"How could anyone put you away?" I asked. "We are not living in a police state."

She turned her head sideways to peer scornfully into my face. "You don't know the professor. They need money–but don't tell anyone what I said. Promise?"

"I promise," I replied slowly, beginning to understand.

"You don't know what it is like here. There is no freedom. They tell you exactly what to do. Everyone is so harsh. They are cruel."

"But you were talking about your family," I said, feeling somewhat uneasy. It had been a long day and the trauma of my injured arm had drained all my energy. Could it be that I had lost more blood than I realized? The liquor, too, had worn off, leaving me depressed, restless, and with a raging headache.

Anxiously, I looked about as a gust of wind stirred the leaves. We bent our bodies and shielded our faces. The air was turning cold as the sun faded behind the trees on the mountains. My wandering attention was drawn again to Bernice, who continued talking, scarcely aware of my presence.

"Yes, my family put me here," she replied, absorbed in her problems. But there is a conspiracy with the doctor. He won't let me go. Others come and go with the changing seasons, but not me."

Feeling uneasy and irritable because of my arm and head and the lack of a drink, I asked bluntly, "Are you well?"

She stopped walking, drew back, looked me up and down and answered with scorn in her voice.

"I'm an honor graduate of Stanford University. I taught for several years, and I'm a linguist having mastered five languages. What are your credentials?"

My bad manners had wounded her pride. Would I ever learn to respect another's feelings?

"You are far smarter than I. I struggle with one language, and my progress would hardly make me the star pupil of your class."

She ignored my reply. "How long do you think you will be here?"

I shrugged. "Oh, three, four weeks, I suppose."

It was her turn to laugh. "Three or four weeks! You are going
to be here a long time. You are sick! I've been watching you! You're in
a daze much of the time. Don't you think they see that? They are going
to get you now."

How could they "get to me," I wondered, feeling even more
impatient and uneasy. Surely this mad woman was not a good judge.
Grimly I admitted to myself that she had taken my measure and I had
come up wanting. But Bernice was not my concern: what troubled me
was the thought that they could hold me here against my will. What
method could be used? Certainly not force. The doors were unlocked.
The forest (that was it!) extended for miles into the mountains. The
road to Maplewood was rarely traveled and it would not be easy for
anyone to leave here.

Bernice's touch on my arm caused me to start in pain.

"My, but you're jumpy," she said. "I've got to go, now. And
please–don't tell anyone what I said to you. You don't know about . . ."

I nodded my silent assent.

As she walked away from me, Bill, the Ph.D. musicologist,
approached. He was smiling.

You look," he said, "for the entire world like that cat that just
ate the canary.

Somebody just tell you not to kiss and tell?"

"Something like that," I said lamely. "Bernice has been here a
long time. She's finding that drugs and alcohol are a sorry
combination." Looking at his watch, Bill continued. "Shortly, you will
find what it is all about. Dr. Neilstrom will give his first lecture in
about twenty minutes. Come on into the lounge and meet a few more
of the patients. You must certainly meet the Colonel and Peggie! She's
usually dressed like a hippie, but looks are deceiving. She has a fine
mind and her candor, as I fear the Colonel is learning, is something to
witness."

As we walked along the hall a nurse stopped me.

"Mark, these are your pills. Take them now." She handed me several colored pills and a glass of water.

Without a word I took one.

"Stop by my station before each meal for your pills," she commanded.

Looking into her determined face, I asked, "What's in these?"

She gave me a searching glance. Without a smile she said, "You are here as a patient. The doctor decides what you need."

I swallowed the remaining pills and caught up with Bill who was by this time standing in the lounge watching the man whom I assumed to be the Colonel and the girl I took to be the hippie. Others were sitting or standing about obviously amused at something or other in their discussion. As I was casually studying the faces of the group, my eyes met Lucy's. She was watching me. She smiled sweetly and turned away! What was this? Why had I stimulated her curiosity?

Dismissing Lucy from my mind, I continued to peruse the group.

The Colonel was a big man, overweight, obviously self indulgent, in the prime of life: someone had said he was from the South. He had the confident, self assured manners of a salesman: he radiated confidence. When he spoke his voice carried the ring of conviction—a tone that also suggested that anyone who could not see the truth as the Colonel saw it, was either disillusioned or a dunce. At the moment all his attention was directed to a robust, heavy boned woman who could only be the hippie.

"You don't seem to realize, sister," he was saying, "that men decide the affairs of the world. In business and in politics we are the explorers, the adventurers, the great builders. Man is in the forefront. His is the vital, sustaining thrust of all activity and progress."

"Thrust all right," Peggie sneered. "You force a woman into the home, keep her with child, and like the hypocrite you are, tell her that this role is her duty. By such constraints—feelings of guilt, children, and the rules of men like you–she is unable to freely venture into the world to prove she is your superior. This, you call progress."

Unabashed, the Colonel went on. "A woman's place is in the home–providing creature comforts for her husband."

"Yes! Satisfying <u>your</u> needs, <u>your</u> appetites, and <u>your</u> ambitions, keeping <u>you</u> happy and contented. What an egotist! What about our needs? We are not just incubators. We have our lives to lead as well!"

"A good woman," said the Colonel, ignoring (or not hearing) her heated remarks, "Satisfies all the needs of her husband. Then, with confidence, he can face the real challenge of life, his mind free from the petty problems–the irritating, trivial matters that corrode life–enabling him to overcome, to meet his destiny!"

"You look upon a woman as a chattel," the woman snapped back, "like a car that gives good service, like a rug–a soft one–that you can lie upon."

"A Southern gentleman does not look upon his lady as a soft rug. She must be dignified, gracious, appealing, and above all, of good breeding."

"I know men like you for what you are," Peggie said raising her voice. "All you think about is using a woman, getting her into bed to satisfy your baser instincts. You are a chauvinist! No doubt you always want to be on top as well!"

The Colonel paused, looking slowly up and down her massive bulk.

"A man under you? Why, you're big enough to burn diesel oil!"

"Chauvinist pig! How many girls have you raped?"

The Colonel leaned back to consider the charge. Was he amused, or crushed by her vehemence? The violence of her invective appeared to have no effect.

"In the South the girls flocked after me. Why, I'd pull those little belles on like a pair of leather boots."

"You're too much! What do you do now? Someone said you were a factory representative, but no one seems to know what your product is or whom you represent. Likely as not all you sell is hot air. Is that what attracted the Southern belles?"

The Colonel showed the first signs of anger. "Listen, if I had a twig I'd carve you a beak–then you could peck corn and chase grasshoppers with the rest of the hens."

"You and your grand manners. Is this . . ." waving her hand in the direction of the rooms, "your idea of success? You have come a long ways. Near sixty or older, I'd judge. If you are so successful and intelligent why did it take you so long to find out you are a drunk? Did you discover the truth or was it your doctor who revealed that one-half of that belly was liver?–that you are going fast?"

I turned to Bill. "This woman is brutal," I whispered.

"You're a real barracuda, Peggie. It's a pity that the burning of witches ended in Salem." The Colonel smiled. "What you need is a lion tamer. If I had you for a month I'd make a pet pussy cat out of you."

Before Peggie could answer, a counselor announced that the first meeting would begin in five minutes. I'd heard enough, and I turned to leave the lounge for the conference room. As I walked down the hall, I began reeling from side to side. For a moment I feared my unsteadiness stemmed from the loss of blood. Bill, who was a step behind me, grasped my arm to steady me.

"Those drugs are potent. The dosage is on the evaluation of your condition when you come in." He laughed. "They must have thought you were in bad shape. Apparently they have had some poor experiences with patients cut off from the booze."

"What happened?"

"D.T.s–coming down too fast. They want to bring you down slowly."

"Thanks for easing my mind," I said. "I was sure it was loss of blood from this bunged up arm that was making me weave all over the place."

In a room bare save for chairs and a blackboard, our small group came together. No one said much as we sat and waited. Peggie was in the far side of the room reading a book. So far as I could see she was relaxed, absorbed in her reading: the bitter confrontation with the Colonel seemed to have been forgotten.

The Colonel, from all outward appearances, was relaxed, regaling Mary with the glories of the South before the Civil War. Her eyes glowed, hanging on his every word. She was wholly absorbed, each account a revelation. Such excitement! Such fascination in meeting a warrior, a knight, a noble descendant from that age of chivalry. Where Peggie saw the Colonel as someone who played a false role, a chauvinist, Mary saw him as a romantic figure–a living legend of the old South.

"Attention. No talking. I will give you enough to occupy your minds for the next hour."

At the front of the room I saw a lean middle aged man wearing glasses. He seemed intense and humorless, set upon having everyone's attention before he began. As he stood waiting, Lucy came over and sat by me. Stella walked briskly to the front, taking a chair near the doctor. She sat facing the group, her eyes turning from side to side studying each face. Her eyes fell upon Lucy sitting beside me. She stiffened. Her face grew hard.

Lucy–who did not notice Stella's reactions, or did not care– asked me if I understood alcohol as a drug. I was drowsy so I did not answer. The drugs I had taken had subdued the pain. I heard the sharp voice of the professor who now stood in front of the blackboard. Without a smile he began.

"All of you are here because somebody cared. Some of you came here, referred by businesses where management was enlightened–you were sent here as a last resort. You were worthless to them in your present condition even though their investment in you was great. You were worthless not only to them, but to your families and friends as well. To your families you were embarrassments and sources of pain. Unfortunately, your sickness is not self contained–you pass the deadly virus on to those dearest to you. They often become guilt ridden, neurotic, frustrated and deeply depressed, all because of you. They blame themselves because of your failure.

"Your behavior is destructive. In a few years, continuing on your present course, many of you will be dead through accidents, suicide, heart disease, cirrhosis of the liver, or a general deterioration of the mind and body. Statistics bear out all I say. These facts are irrefutable, and you will hear them repeated frequently by me and your counselors."

Looking at us with penetrating eyes, he continued. "What I require from each of you is total cooperation. Have no illusions: you are not here because you wanted to come or because you selected us. We accepted you at the urging of your families, your doctors, or employers with the understanding you would cooperate. We are not harsh; neither do we use tender loving care. You might call our method tenacious, and dependent upon the use of leverage and coercion.

"All of you have been avoiding the truth. In your present state you are more than just a little mad. You are destroying yourselves while bravely telling the world that you are like most persons–able to drink, yet able to control your intake. You protest that your obnoxious behavior is the result of many variables–your spouse, your boss, a lousy job, lack of mother love as a child, or a long series of problems due to bad luck. Whatever is wrong is not your fault–certainly not because of your drinking.

"When those about you–your family, friends, and employers– see your problem, it is usually too late: there is no turning back. All the

willpower in the world will not change you. You are alcoholic and
cannot drink again. Your metabolism has changed, now craving
alcohol rather than food. Alcohol becomes the nourishment, the source
of life. Paradoxically, an alcoholic functions better with it in his
system than without it. That does not mean that after proper care and
enlightenment an alcoholic, having stopped drinking, cannot learn to
live without it. Once detoxified, the arrested alcoholic may anticipate a
better life, and one more successful and harmonious. He should find
himself to be serene within, and no longer at odds with the world."

He stepped to the blackboard, picked up a piece of chalk, and
began writing.

Early stage - 5 to 10 years

Dependency - 5 years

After he had drawn the line under what he had written, he
tapped the blackboard sharply with his chalk.

"Beyond that line is alcoholism. Once beyond dependency and
into addiction, no man on earth–no drug, change in thinking or in
pattern of living–will enable you to drink normally again."

He spoke rapidly, intently, and seemed to be totally absorbed in
his ideas.

"If this science had been more advanced, some of you might
have avoided this disease by heeding early warning signs –although I
think this is unlikely. The disease is cunning, baffling, and powerful–
we don't see the symptoms. When others recognize them in us, it is too
late. We are already confirmed alcoholics.

"Life is unfair. It's childish of us to think otherwise. Everyone
going into the disease thinks of himself as a social drinker, because the
alcoholic and the social drinker drink for the same reasons: to relieve
tensions, to relax, to loosen the tongue, to speak more easily, to feel
important. They drink to celebrate success, to forget failures, to

overcome fear. They drink for the surge of energy alcohol provides. And they serve alcohol in their homes as a symbol of affluence, of having arrived, of being a part of the group. For all these and for many more reasons we drink. The more important the occasion the more likely drink will play a part in it.

"I mentioned that life is not fair–and so it isn't. If one is Jewish or Italian, the likelihood of alcoholism is remote to nonexistent, if North American Indian, the likelihood is eighty-five percent. The Irish, Danes, French, and Norwegians–all the northern water people have a high incidence of alcoholism. There are theories about all this, but they are hardly consoling to you.

"An alcoholic cannot recover without help. It is not unusual to see an alcoholic at a party refuse a drink by saying that he is 'on the wagon.' Social drinkers do not need to stop drinking periodically."

As he spoke I looked around the room at the sullen faces. Stella was watching all of us. Lucy nudged me. "I don't believe all this–do you?" I shrugged. The doctor continued imparting to his audience his intense feeling about the destruction alcoholism could bring about.

"The alcoholic may continue his charade for a week, a month, or many months until he has convinced himself–and others–that he can drink like most members of society. He cannot. In a short time he will be as bad as before–usually worse–for he must reward himself with added rations of liquor for the constraints he had placed upon himself."

"The doctor paused and looked at his watch. Nearly an hour had passed. "Are there any questions? Francis? What do you have to say?"

Francis began to stutter. "No . . . no questions."

This seemed to irritate the doctor. "Why do you stutter?" he demanded.

"I can't, can't help it," he began. Then he muttered something I could not follow.

"You are speaking now," said the doctor. "Continue! You have sat here for a month like an owl, speak up now, and show us what you have learned."

Francis struggled again for words.

A woman spoke up distracting the doctor. "Do you think," She said in a whining voice, "that one drink a night can make one an alcoholic?"

I looked at her bloated face and thought, "Oh, God! Does she believe that?" The doctor's voice softened. "You'll find after a few weeks when your mind clears that you have been drinking far more than ever you realized. Deception is a large part of this disease. No one recovers until he faces the truth. How much one drinks is part of the truth."

More like a fifth, I mused.

Lucy nudged me. "Let's go over to the recreation hall, there's a nickelodeon."

Why not? I thought.

Suddenly the doctor's eyes fell on me. "Mark? What do you think about all this?"

I began speaking. My words were slow, deliberate. It must have been the drugs.

"This is a great opportunity. Reminds me of Brutus' words, 'There is a tide in the affairs of men, which taken at the flood, leads on to fortune; omitted, all the voyage of their life is bound in shallows and in miseries.'"

"Are you an alcoholic?" Stella abruptly asked.

I looked up at Stella, startled and enraged by this frontal attack, especially since it had been made before the group, where I was attempting to make a good impression.

I spat out the words. "My mind says 'yes,' my heart says 'no.'"

"Yes, yes," the doctor cut in, "you have much to learn here. Put your books away and listen. Once you see what alcohol has done to you, you will be anxious to learn how to combat it. Our work is deadly serious. The lines of combat are being drawn up. If you succeed, you will find life–if you fail the loss to you and your family is incalculable."

For the first time I felt fear at Maplewood. Was he threatening me? What kind of battle lay ahead? Who were the contestants? I was alone–cut off from the world. No one knew I was here. Who would engage me in battle? Perhaps it was rhetoric, or worse, nonsense.

Lighting up a cigarette as I walked out of the hall after the long meeting, I sought diversion. Lucy–the nickelodeon? Why not? It all seemed rather foolish, but I knew my contact with her would be harmless. If my beginning to make friends did not set well with the counselors, that was their problem.

CHAPTER 6

Having Lucy at my side filled a need for companionship. It was an hour before supper. At that moment I did not feel like reading. The cold air of the evening overcame my drowsiness. The day was slipping away and the brown, yellow and gold of the falling leaves–the many shades from nature's palette–caught the last rays of the sun. The signs of nature –the chilling breeze, the gaunt appearance of the trees stripped of their leaves–foretold the coming winter as loudly as the tolling of a church bell.

As the sun dropped behind the mountains, dark shadows formed along the path that led to the outer building near the edge of the forest. The sky had changed from pale to dark blue. A bright star could be seen beyond the trees–great pines which stood silent. The dark towering mass appeared watchful, shutting us in, cutting us off from the outside world. And the path into the woods? If I followed it, where would it lead? Was there freedom, adventure, or the real danger of being lost in the deep recesses of the forest?

Feeling Lucy's hand I turned to see her eyes watching me.

"You're so serious. Did the doctor make that much of an impression?" she asked in a mocking voice.

"Not really." With a sweeping motion of my hand I pointed toward the trees and the fallen leaves all about us. "Just taking in the end of the fall season–wondering, too, what it will be like when the snows come."

Lucy shuddered. "Are you going to be here that long?"

Ignoring the question, I said. "So this is the recreation building. I see it has a suitable setting by the river."

She walked to the door as my eyes continued to follow the path that led over a foot bridge and into the forest. For a moment the only sound I could hear was that of the running water that covered only the middle part of the wide river bed.

Lucy stood silent; waiting. "Come," she said. You are slow! Are you always so preoccupied? You are such a dreamer. See, this is a meeting room. Over there is the gym."

The two rooms were spacious with high ceilings; large glass windows opened to the forest and the river. Darkness had fallen. In this emptiness a strange silence: I could hear only the rushing water and Lucy's footsteps as she crossed the room into the gym. She snapped a switch that flooded the gym with light. She walked over to an old juke box.

"Look," she said, turning toward me, "there's a lot of old records! Sinatra, Dean Martin, Ed Ames, Humperdinck. Let's try it. Let's dance!"

"Sure, why not?" I said. "Let me see if I can operate the machine."

No coins were needed. I pushed a series of letters and numbers; the lights flashed on in the machine; the selector moved along its track, lifted out a record, and the music began.

As I would have predicted, Lucy was a good dancer, gliding easily across the floor, her body pressed tightly against me. I wondered what effect her warmth and loveliness would have had if I had not been filled with drugs, my arm tender and sore, and my head pounding with a dull and painful throb.

Although I seemed alert enough, I felt no passion: just a faint sense of uneasiness that my actions might be foolish. But such a thought lasted only a moment. My feet seemed heavy to me, but she made dancing easy.

Looking down at her slender body, her relaxed placid features I remarked, "You don't show any signs of having a drinking problem. You're young and pretty too–at least to these old eyes."

She laughed easily. "You're not old. At least you don't look or feel old to me." She sighed. "No, alcohol is not my problem. Just confused–in the middle of a divorce. A girlfriend suggested Maplewood. My doctor also urged me to come."

"Rather odd, isn't it? Coming here, I mean. Booze is all they emphasize. So far I've heard little else–seems like they are fanatics."

"They do make exceptions," Lucy said. "Look at Bernice." She began laughing. "I saw you walking with her all the way to the main road. Her problem is not alcohol. My problem, like Bernice's, is– although not so severe–is nerves, frustrations, lack of purpose. So, at least, my doctor tells me."

"You have analyzed yourself well, it seems."

"With the help of my doctor and a few others."

"What has life been like?" I asked.

"I'm divorcing an attorney. We married young, we have two daughters, but I don't know . . . . "

Our shoulders touched and I felt her shrug. Her voice trailed off. "There must be more to life. We sort of drifted apart and no longer shared the same interests."

"Any regrets?"

"None." "Are your daughters as attractive as their mother?"

"Judge for yourself. They'll be visiting."

"When?"

"On Sundays. It's a long way from the city; a few come."

"Are we trotted out for inspection?"

"It's all rather informal. For now, let's just dance. Let's make the most of being here. There is leisure time. No one cares. We can go into the woods."

I glanced sharply at her. Was she mocking me? Was it laughter in her eyes? Was she actually suggesting we wander through the woods together? She could not have guessed that I planned to explore the river, to follow the path as far as it led into the forest. But she had not been a part of my plan.

Lightly I said, "We'll see how things go."

This seemed to please her. She was dancing very close now. I relaxed my arm around her as if to suggest she did not need to press her thighs against me. As we turned on the floor I caught a glimpse of the clock in the corner.

We'd better go," I said. "It's not long until supper, unless coming in late makes no difference."

She was silent for a few minutes. I wondered if she had heard me.

Suddenly she stopped, grasped my hand and said, "Okay, clock watcher. Let's go. I won't get you in trouble, if that's what you fear–not on your very first day at any rate!"

"All right," I laughed, "you win. Let's stay."

"No, no. It's all decided. The meals are checked carefully to see that everyone is present. Stella has a sharp eye."

As we walked toward the main building I could hear the water, a timeless rhythm forever hurling against the rocks, forever moving somewhere, perhaps to a silent lake where the still surface reflected the trees and the stars at night. Or the running waters might slow in a murky pond where cattle waded in among the frogs, tadpoles and the water bugs skipping over the surface only to have its vibrant force end in a swamp, like us, the inmates in this far off place.

In the cold night there were no other sounds, no cars or planes overhead. Just the tall trees, silent and erect, darker than the dark sky, creating a fortress, a wall that pressed in at all sides of the opening where the three buildings stood, making them even smaller at night.

Stars could be seen through the opening in the clouds. Without the stars the darkness would have been fraught with fear.

As we walked along, my thoughts turned to Lucy who was holding my hand, playfully. Scarcely aware of her in my dreamy state of mind I now felt like a fool. A cabin in the woods with her? How cozy, how simply charming. Was this the diverse pleasure I was seeking, I wondered. When we reached the entrance of the building Lucy released my hand. I opened the door and followed her into the hallway. For a moment I paused watching her as she walked toward her room. She was attractive, slim, shapely as a young girl–but sad, somehow confused. She stopped at a doorway, turned, looked back, smiled and entered her room.

The clock indicated more than a half hour remained before supper was scheduled to be served. The clock in the gym was set at daylight time. 'Well,' I thought, 'I can continue looking around. If I am going to be an inmate, I ought to be familiar with the buildings as well as the grounds.'

How bright the corridors were in contrast to the exterior of the buildings in their natural setting! Brown tile floors, dark mahogany doors, bright walls and ceilings. The decor was tasteless, apparently done with an eye toward efficiency, but without any sign that someone might have attempted to appeal to the aesthetic senses of the patient. How different from the outside of the building, where vines had grown unchecked, where the piercing winds of winter, the deep snow, the spring rains and summer sun had given the exterior a charm, sculptured by nature's hand. The nearby maple trees were barren, their leaves scattered; even the shrubs left untended and the overlooked gardens and lawns enriched the setting creating an oasis cut out of the forest in the mountains. But these brightly lit halls made everyone appear white like ghosts. We were dead enough. Why was it necessary to accentuate the death written by giving our skin this deathly pallor?

Where the hallways intersected there was a nurse's station and a recreation room with a few card tables and a cigarette machine. Bill was standing talking to Raymond, an anemic looking man. Seeing me he nodded, "Mark, meet the Commander. During the war Raymond was commander of one of our big Navy shipyards."

I looked at Raymond waiting for an acknowledgment. He did not appear to hear.

To ease the awkward situation I inquired half seriously, "How does a commander build ships?"

He looked at me. "Ships? I never built a ship. I sat at a desk and tried to keep the red tape from slowing those who could and were doing the building. I kept my wastebasket filled with foolish requests that would jam up the works. That was my only contribution."

Not a bad answer, I thought. Perhaps I had irritated him.

"We are going to play bridge after supper. Care to join us?" Bill asked.

"Thanks," I said, "but I feel a little out of it." didn't mention my throbbing arm or the dull pain in my head. "These pills tend to make me unsteady." As Raymond walked away I thought he looked like a very old and very sick man. Following my gaze, Bill remarked lightly, "If you played bridge with Raymond you'd understand brain damage. He cannot remember cards, has the attention span of a child, and sometimes cannot remember the playing sequence. Some of the others are almost as bad." I shook my head. "Has booze been the cause? Surely there must be more to it. Drugs perhaps?"

"In some cases drugs are involved. You met Bernice. She was an honor student at Stanford, a teacher–taught Spanish, I believe. Then she got hooked on booze and drugs–a near fatal combination for her."

"Which is worse? Drugs or alcohol?"

"They are both drugs. Alcohol is the most respectable drug in our society and the most abused. Dr. Neilstrom will tell you why most people gravitate to alcohol."

"Well," I hesitated, "I'm not sure about anything except that I have a roommate and I better go to see what he's like."

"Oh, Gene? You'll like Gene. You'll find him in bed, no doubt. He can't sleep at night so he spends all his free moments in his room."

"We'll make a great pair. Does he talk much? I like to read."

"In fits and starts."

Turning down the hall I said, "I'll look for you later." When I reached the room, near the far end of the hallway, I found the door open. I hesitated in the doorway.

"My name is Mark. I understand that we are roommates."

"Oh," Gene said, barely moving his head. He was lying on a narrow bed, a slim figure with white curly hair. He did not move again, just followed me with his eyes. His bed was against the wall to the right of the entrance where I was standing; to the left was another single bed with a small space between where a low window was cut into the outside wall. Across from the window, near the door, stood a double chest of drawers. Except for a small light over each bed and a small closet for clothes the room had no other distinctions.

"How do you like it here?" I asked. I sat down on the empty bed.

"Don't like it." "Is it pretty bad?"

"Can't get any rest. Someone is pounding on the door at six-thirty every morning. There's always someone wandering in the halls at night."

"Who is it?"

"Don't know. I hear cries. I'm not going out of my room at night."

Gene looked up at me. "Do you make noises when you sleep?"

I shrugged.

He continued.

"I come to this room to rest during the day–never sleep at night–and that nurse, Anne, is forever after me with pills or hauling me down to the clinic for a check up. Then we have exercises–or those talks. All they do around here is talk about alcohol. Just a bunch of fanatics."

"I take it you don't have a drinking problem."

"Drinking problem?" Gene rose up on his elbow. "Why, I drink, of course. Lost my wife a year ago. She did everything for me. Great wife. But I have no desire to drink now. My despondency caused me to drink a little more than usual and my friends finally put me in here."

"You loved your wife?"

Gene turned again on the bed to see my face. This small grey little man was suddenly very serious, very intent now on telling me all about his wife.

"She was so industrious! A great dancer, too. She could cook, took care of my clothes, did all the shopping, made all social arrangements." He took a deep breath. "She did everything for me. Never able to find another wife like her."

Gene continued on and on about his wife. Slowly I stretched out upon the bed, feeling weary. The drugs had dulled my senses. Lying there listening was better than talking with someone. Gene was totally absorbed in his recollections. For a moment I realization that Gene had failed to ask anything about me, neither had he shown the slightest interest in me. It seemed as if I did not exist: I was a voice that entered the room asking questions, stirring memories of the recent past–that was all.

"I was a barber," he went on. "It used to be that when I came home everything was prepared–my meals–the house was always clean and orderly. After dinner she always planned something–on weekends, a dance; during the week a movie; or we'd see friends. She became ill. I never knew she was sick until she began to fail. She was sick just a short time. Died a year ago."

Now very drowsy, I mumbled, "You'll find someone. You will marry soon. You will find a lovely widow who can cook and sew."

Answering the voice Gene responded, "Can't marry. How could I find anyone like her? She did everything. Where would I find anyone like her again?" He stopped talking.

There was movement in the hallway; men and women moving by the open doorway. Gene got up, glanced at me–as if seeing me for the first time–then walked out, closing the door.

My arm was no longer hurting. I sat up and snapped on the lamp, pulled out a book, then lay back slowly, skimming the pages for something to distract me–to keep my mind from dwelling on the day's events. I was unable to concentrate, and the book slid out of my hands and onto the floor. Through the open window I could see stars–then blackness–then stars again, as the clouds passed over, opening up the sky once more. How many pills had they given me? I wondered as I drifted off to sleep.

Someone was pulling at my arm, calling my name, telling me to come to supper. Through the drug induced haze (or was I having a dream?) I was conscious of a stab of pain as I lashed out with my good arm at whoever was tugging at my sleeve. The intruder then left me alone. There was silence.

Then it seemed that I sank into a dreamlike state (or was it real?) with the lumbering figure of Dr. Bogleman coming into the room and sitting on the bed across from me. I lay there with closed eyes in the dimly lit room, feeling his presence. Then I opened my eyes slowly–just enough to see him staring at me with a smile on his face. I had never seen him smile before. Why should he smile at me now?

His presence caused my heart to beat faster, then it began so slow at first I scarcely noticed: anger, rising anger. It crept slowly through my body, my arms and legs; I could feel the beating in my temples. He was not smiling. He was not laughing. He was mocking me. I could see it in his face. It was written there. Words were unnecessary, however I could see his lips begin to move, slowly emphasizing, picking, choosing each word. Every word seared my flesh. They rang in my ears. "You fool! You do not even know who you are or what you have become, yet you consider yourself intelligent and a success." His lips, his eyes, his heavy flabby features seemed to say; "You are a drunk–a drunk. No–you are an alcoholic. You will learn what that means soon enough. Also, without alcohol, you will see your divided nature. The struggle to heal your fractured nature, and to find your true self, while also trying to overcome alcoholism will be too much for you."

The doctor moved his head slowly up and down to emphasize this truth. His eyes and his smile appeared satisfied with these conclusions about me.

His features grew harder. He sneered, "You think life has passed you. You are wrong. You are a quitter, a cop-out, a coward, a weakling, and a fool–worse than a fool–a liar. You lie–how you lie– you live a lie and you will soon die lying to yourself. Why don't you face the truth? Turn around, look into your mind. No! Not your mind– your heart.

"See? It says you are a liar, because you refuse to hear its message. Blame a hard life."

Bogleman's face seemed to change ever so slightly: the mocking–the sneer–grew more and more intense."

You are the only one who has suffered. How much you have suffered, and so wealthy, too. What is there you do not have? Do you need a mistress? Well, buy one. You buy everything you desire. Oh, you say you cannot buy happiness. How sad! Is it your wife who causes your misery? Then blame her. You once had a solution. Remember? Kill her! Kill her! When they come for you–if you are alive–they will lock you up, mock you, laugh at you. When you are unaware and behind your back they will make signs indicating what you and I already know."

He was moving his head up and down. His inflated jowls quivered as each movement of his head emphasized his thoughts.

If I could only move or speak or spit at this inflated frog! Monstrous frog! Hideous shape! Villain! Vile mass of corruption gloating over me!

I could not move or speak. My heart was pounding and even leaping. Sweat formed, my eyes were open wide, but the saliva would not gather so I could spit. It drooled over my chin and dropped to the floor. I ground my teeth trying to move. Oh! To sink my hands into that flabby neck. The hideous mass was shaking, any moment his mask would crumble or slip off, like the cover on a tomb, revealing the corruption beneath.

No sound in the room but the beating of my heart. With the movement of his lips, with his leering smile, with the changing light in his eyes I saw clearly his thoughts. Wave after wave, like devouring locusts they fed upon my fears, turning them into anger. I felt a consuming hatred, a craving to seize and tear–to crush this monstrous creature that tormented me. There were no outward sounds, but nevertheless could hear his words ringing–growing louder–as he accused me of outrageous faults.

"Liar! Adulterer! Caught up in your wily machinations! You schemed and planned and grew rich. Where is your money now? Your health? You are mad! Look at you in this small room furnished with only a dresser and two iron beds. You don't even have a bathroom or a rug to cover the floor.

"So you don't like bright colors?" the eyes seemed to question. "Does this dirty grey suit your fancy? These filthy drapes to filter the sun? You are such an important man. Wait! Soon enough you will be cut to size. I heard about you at the meeting. The counselors are amused and Dr. Neilstrom is waiting for the right moment to set you straight. All the cards are stacked against you. There is no defense for your drinking. You see yourself only as an unhappy, miserable, misunderstood man. You hate my appearance. Even more, you detest me–everything about me–but have you looked at yourself lately? You are bloated; you drip with fat; you can scarcely open your eyes. If you could only see yourself walking about with that superior attitude you convey. Your head is raised, sniffing the air as though you detected some offensive odor. You are selective about your companions—only the select are favored by a few words in your low, modulated voice. You are so intelligent; so refined; a cut above the rest. This arrogance, your callous indifference and base methods have already been marked against you. They are itching to get at you, to sink their talons in deep to bring you down to size.

"Wait until you show your full colors. I see it coming: you don't but I do. You will step out of line. Your intelligence is only play acting—a show—you are in reality a blind fool, not even capable of seeing your own drunkenness. Everyone sees it but you.

"I overheard the nurse say that you are on the brink of madness—in such a confused state of mind that no one can reach you. But you are too intelligent to see that. You lie to yourself. Your manners, every mode of expression, say 'Look at me! At my success! Look at the problems I've solved. Has anyone done better with so many responsibilities, carrying so heavy a load? I rank among the stars!'"

His hand went up to show the greatness of my lofty achievements; to fully emphasize my towering arrogance. With this gesture he dropped his hands, rose slowly and shuffled out of the room.

Unable to move, I seemed to sink deeper into a nightmare state where one wild dream followed another. In every dream I was the pursued, always the defendant, unable to defend myself against the evidence that accused me of a frightful crime. After many nightmares the drugs and the alcohol wore off, then I became aware that all these scenes of despair and anguish were not real after all. At the same time I realized that I was lying in a cold room. The only sound was Gene's heavy breathing.

CHAPTER 7

When I awakened my pajamas and the bed clothes were soaked. Although the room was still dark, I realized that I had slept the night through. Outside my room, someone was pounding on the door and making a racket.

Gene spoke, "Coming, coming." The noise stopped. I sat on the edge of the bed shading my eyes when Gene turned on the light. He pointed to a towel hanging on a hook near my bed, mumbled something and went out of the room. Finding one of the bathrooms unoccupied, I shaved while drawing the water for my tub–there was no shower. I bathed hurriedly, wrapped a towel around myself, and went back to the room. Winter was near and the building was cold. I dressed and walked along a dark and empty corridor. In the distance I heard the sound of rattling dishes. I entered the dining room, and as I reached for a tray, a woman touched my arm and motioned for me to follow her. Out of earshot of the others, she turned on me.

"I'm Eva, one of the counselors charged with instructing you. Where were you last night? She demanded.

"I was tired." Attempting humor I said, "As you can see from my profile I don't need food. Besides, I really wasn't hungry."

"I didn't ask if you were tired or hungry. We have rules. They are not arbitrary, they are well thought out." Her voice was hard. She was making much out of a trivial incident.

"My arm was sore," I said, raising it to show the bandage.

She glanced at the bandage without interest, then looked into my face. She studied me closely.

"Don't worry about that arm; that ought to concern you least of all. You need help–our help. Get your breakfast and be at the morning lecture." She knew that I was late for breakfast, and as she walked away she said, "Be on time."

Having missed supper the night before, I was ravenous. I took a glass of orange juice, and filled my tray with scrambled eggs, toast, and bacon. I saw Bill sitting by himself at one end of a table so I joined him.

"Sleep well?" he asked.

"Bad dreams." I replied casually.

"Nightmares are not uncommon," he said glancing at me. "At least you haven't lost your sanity."

"Not yet, at least."

"How about you, Gene?" someone asked, having overheard Bill talking to me. "Did you sleep well?"

"Sleep? How could I sleep?" asked Gene.

"Well, isn't that what you do in bed?"

"Have you every tried to sleep in a dark room with someone groaning all night?"

"Not ghosts, surely?" It was the faintly mocking voice of the Colonel. "Surely you aren't suggesting that this place is haunted."

Gene was always serious. As if to dramatize his sleepless night, he then imitated what must have been the sounds which had kept him sleepless. In the bright light of morning, at a crowded breakfast table, his performance was eerie–as was the sound that came from his throat. It was a low, pitiful wail–a cry of despair, sounding like some animal in pain, or held captive. Or it could have been the sound of a man's tortured cry of fear. Gene's outcry was so authentic that the conversation and laughter at the table ceased.

Throughout the rest of the meal, no one again said anything to Gene–who, unconcerned and apparently unaware of the change his song of sorrow had wrought upon the others, continued to eat, as though nothing untoward had happened.

Only after a lengthy pause did the normal conversational buzz return to the room. I looked around. Peg was talking to Mary. Bernice was contemplative, and not speaking. The Colonel was consuming a large serving of bacon and eggs; in high spirits he was regaling several listeners with more of his tales of the endless glories of the South. Lucy was sitting next to the Colonel, listening, and I couldn't but wonder if she believed all she heard.

Someone asked Bill what he had done in the past.

I turned to hear him say, "Musician. Taught at City College, New York."

"You must be well trained to teach there," someone observed.

"A Ph.D., which, as you can see, didn't prevent me from coming here for more schooling." His tone was good humored, bantering.

"Do you play an instrument?" Peg asked.

"Piano and organ. I've given recitals on the organ. Now I play mostly in churches."

Raymond, the Commander, who had been only picking away at his food, looked up

"Do you play the organ as well as you play cards?"

Bill nudged me. "Commander–you weren't concentrating on your cards last night. You played right into our hands."

"My partner and I want to even the score tonight," Raymond retorted. "You have an edge on us." Pointing to Francis, he said, "I don't think he understands the game."

Hearing the Commander, Francis, the druggist, began to speak haltingly,

"You–you don't even remember hav–ing a partner. I had to–, to introduce myself after each hand so you'd remember who I was."

The dreamy eyed Commander stared at Francis while everyone nearby laughed. His reactions were slow. Was it possible that he had at one time held the top position in a large shipyard?

"You were thinking about pills, not cards," Raymond replied lamely.

Finished with breakfast I placed my tray on the rack, lit up a cigarette and walked down the hallway to the meeting room. The door was open. As I looked about the bare, drab room I decided to sit off to one side, near the back of the room. Looking about at the institutional gray walls, I was suddenly immersed in a deep depression. The battered chairs sitting in uneven rows on the brown tiled floor; the windowless walls which kept us isolated without the saving beauty and freshness of nature; and the silence relieved only by the pop and hiss of the steam radiator and the inane chatter of sick patients was enough to put a sane man out of his head. For the most part, the patients babbled on light heartedly, quite unaware of the seriousness of their sickness; unaware of the misery they (we) had caused. Unaware, too, of what could well lie ahead if this sickness was as serious as we had been led to believe.

What was it Dr. Milstrom has said to me? Something about "being prepared for the struggle ahead."

I could see that there might well be a struggle to overcome my illness–but I would not resist treatment–that was a certainty. If mine was a serious problem, then it must be confronted, dealt with, and overcome.

The ugly room was warm–filling with people. Most were, by this time, seated.

What's this? Eva? Dressed as a show girl–or worse. Her garb, emphasizing bare legs, and consisting of a short skirt, a mini-shirt, bracelets at her wrists and a chain at her throat didn't strike me as being particularly odd. She was simply hard–like many of the others at Maplewood.

Several men and women were standing outside the door smoking or drinking brim, absorbed in their thoughts and conversation. They stood without moving while Eva waited at the front of the room. As the group drifted into the room, Peg glanced at me, took a chair near the rear and began reading. The Colonel entered, talking loudly and apparently in jubilant spirits. Those near him were laughing at his remarks, and his presence commanded attention. He had many of the qualities of leadership: the commanding voice, assurance, self possession; his ideas, although neither brilliant nor unusual, carried the weight of edicts. Somehow no one would think to question anything he said–except Peg–and she seemed to have dismissed him from her thoughts. The Colonel and his followers sat near the front row. The last stragglers entered.

Lucy entered with Roy, the Boeing worker and shop steward. Short and serious minded, he had been in Maplewood for more than a month.

Eva spoke.

There was a rustling of chairs. She stopped. Silence.

I wondered if those in the room were staring at Eva's ridiculous dress, observing the short skirt, the bare legs, the high heeled shoes, the heavy belt, bracelets and chain. What she had she did not conceal.

Eva picked up a piece of chalk, hesitated, turned to face us saying,

"Several of you are new. Are there any questions before I begin?"

Peg spoke up. "Last night I did not sleep. Certain men," she said glaring at the Colonel, "were indulging in loud talk and raucous laughter in the lounge. I thought this was a treatment center, not some hangout for hooligans."

The Colonel, seeing he was being accused, smiled broadly at Eva. With a voice oozing with charm, he said, "With all those pills we take, surely there are sleeping pills for insomniacs or neurotics. Some patients are pretty sick," he confided in a patronizing manner.

Peg flared up. "That charlatan makes a mockery of the rules."

"Enough," said Eva. "You are not children; you are adults–sick men and women. You have a deadly disease. You are here to be cured." She looked at the Colonel, ignoring his charm.

"You are here for treatment, not a social hour. This is not a gathering place for old cronies to display their wits in conquests or to indulge in their seedy pasts. Vulgar stories and vain pipe dreams of what you've done or will do have no place here. You are at Maplewood to be cured: nothing else is important; nothing else matters. Accept what I say and make it easy for yourselves. The doctor will not be tolerant of any disturbances. Surely, Colonel, a man of your experience can find a more suitable time and place to tell your stories than after 'lights out' in our lounge."

The Colonel raised and lowered his hands in resignation, turning as he did so to give Peg a knowing smile. She moved her lips silently, and it was clear where she intended him to go.

Eva ignored the Colonel and Peg, and turning to the blackboard, she wrote in large print the letters A, B, and C in the form of a triangle.

"The trouble of an alcoholic," she began, "is caused by oversensitivity. Something happens–a traffic jam, an encounter with an angry boss, a loss–and we fall apart. In the normal course of events, something will happen to us (A); we might reflect upon the best course of action (B); then we react (C). That is, as I have said, the normal pattern. The alcoholic follows a different course. Driven by passion, anger, or fear, he rushes from "A" directly to "C"–bypassing "B" completely. In short, there is no pause for reflection, or to consider the calm, deliberate approach to problem solving.

"An alcoholic's wife asks him to be home early, to spend more time with the children. Surely, these are reasonable requests. He may promise to abide by his wife's wishes, but he does not: drinking rules his life. Or the husband may refuse at once, again driven by selfishness and unable to reflect. A confrontation invariably follows. An alcoholic's life is always in turmoil simply because the woman or the man is unable to face life. Alcoholics are immature."

Glancing at Roy, I saw that he was distracted and was gazing across the room. The Colonel, his hand cupped over the side of his face, was talking with Mary who was taking in every word. Gene–wide-eyed–was watching the Colonel. The Commander always appeared in a comatose state. From the corner of my eye I saw Peg, who was, like me, studying the group.

Eva's eyes swept over the patients. "Are there any questions?"

Silence. For several minutes she waited. Then she began a discussion.

"Roy, tell us. What is your reaction when your wife accuses you of being drunk?"

"It depends."

"On what?"

"How I am feeling. Sometimes I walk away. Sometimes we argue, or I tell her that my drinking is my business. When matters have gotten out of hand, I've called her a bitch."

"And then what happens?"

"Well, the next time she comes to visit me; I'll introduce you to Lillian. She is a big woman. I'll let you judge how she deals with being called a 'bitch.'"

"Did it occur to you to reflect upon what your wife asked of you, or why she was accusing you of being drunk–before you acted upon impulse?"

Eva walked back to the blackboard, drawing a line from A to C, saying, "Roy, this is how you react. This is your problem, not only with your wife, but in other areas of your life. You do not anticipate the result of your actions when you are controlled by emotion."

The Colonel, seeing me, made a slow movement with his hands, then rolled his eyes and nodded toward Eva. Several men close to him saw him make the universal gesture, and grinned. Eva who had been looking toward the simple equation turned in time to see the men smiling around the Colonel. Her expression changed. She pounced on the druggist, who was sitting, quiet and withdrawn, as if he had some heavy weight on his mind.

"Francis, do you understand all this?"

"I . . . I think so," he said. With considerable effort he continued. "We . . . we must al . . .ways think first."

"Yes, that is it," said Eva. "Think of our actions, control our emotions. That is maturity. All of you," she said, taking in the whole group, "have been crippled by this disease. To overcome it you must learn to live in control of your emotions–of all your appetites–to accept life as it is, not as you would have it. Emotional upsets not faced and dealt with reasonably lead to drinking. If there is a misunderstanding in the office or at home with your spouse or children, drinking solves nothing. It only makes matters worse; only leads to self destruction, and all because of immaturity."

Directing her full attention to the Colonel, she asked, "Is that clear?"

Before he answered she asked another question. "Colonel, if someone rear ended you in heavy traffic, what would you do?"

"I'd buckle his knees and lay him out gently where no one would run over him."

Eva threw up her hands. "Don't you understand what I have been saying? You can't live by impulsive actions."

"All right, I'll reflect. I'll even approach him and say, 'Friend, surely these are not the manners your Mother taught you.' Then, if he doesn't agree, I'll lay him out."

"Better, Colonel, much better. You can no longer indulge your emotions, unbridled, without certain constraints. Without these constraints you will reach again for a bottle."

The Colonel was watching Eva closely. Her short shirt and shapely legs drew his attention.

"Of course," he said, "if you busted the rear end of my car, it would be a different proposition. We could go somewhere and quietly talk it over. And if I had a stiff neck, you could soothe it."

Eva looked the Colonel over carefully, and showed not the least embarrassment. "I'm sure we'd settle matters at the crash scene. If your needs were not fully satisfied, I could give you a whole list of suggestions. You indicate a strong urge for indulgence."

"But all the problems you indicate can be settled amiably; that's what you are saying."

"Not all problems, Colonel, need be settled in bed. Did it occur to you that your life style may have brought you here? There are many routes to Maplewood. Yours would appear to be a consuming appetite for food, drink, and," she added with a sly smile, "the willing sex."

"A gentleman is not trained to hold back. It is a sign of good breeding to go after the fruits of nature."

"My God, he sounds like a Southern preacher!" said Peg, "and a perverted one at that."

"At least I've tasted life, not scorned or spit on it. What God gave me to use, I used."

"That's good, Colonel," Roy added. "Better to live and make a few mistakes, than not to live at all."

Eva stood listening to these exchanges. She appeared willing to allow anyone to express his feelings. She may have observed that now at least they were involved, thinking about their problems. As oddly as she was dressed, she was strong, in control: she was someone to reckon with and not easily fooled.

Roy spoke again. "How long have you been sober?"

Without hesitation she said, "Eight years."

"You were pretty young to be hooked," said the Colonel.

"You mean addicted, Colonel. Age is not a factor; the earlier you begin, if you drink enough–and I did–the earlier one is 'hooked,' as you call it."

"Didn't seem to hurt you," said Roy.

She looked at him for a moment. "There is no need for me to tell my story; not now anyway. My misfortunes were enough for me– enough, at least, to change my life. No one is a stranger to suffering– no alcoholic, certainly."

"You haven't suffered," scoffed the incredulous Roy.

"That's right," added the Colonel, "there aren't any boot marks on you. From where I sit, everything looks in order. I'll bet you sleep between silk sheets."

Eva looked long at the Colonel. "Some other time you can hear my story. Just now," she said, "we are out of time." She set the chalk on the board and walked briskly out of the room. Every man in the group followed her with his eyes.

The Colonel turned toward me in a friendly mood. "Now if anyone asked about you," he grinned, "I'd have to say you were one. You sure have signs of boot marks all over you."

"You've been around, Colonel, I can see that. Your opinion I'll hold high. And the next time you have an idea I'll run it through the ABC's."

"Don't be riled," he said, "this is an honest program; we're here to help one another. If we're going to be here for a time, we'd better get acquainted."

"You fit in well," I conceded, seeing his desire to be friendly.

"Say, I'd sure like to get that Eva alone. Maybe she'd go for a walk in the woods for a picnic or a nature study. She can be the subject!"

"Come on, Colonel. Surely there are more sporting ventures than chasing her."

"Name one!"

"Well, it is going to snow soon. We can divide up sides–the North against the South. You could be Stonewall Jackson."

"No," he said with mock seriousness, "my arm was crippled in the last skirmish–I was blown out of a tank by a German 88."

"Then a walk in the woods will refresh us," I suggested.

"No, long walks are out."

"Why don't we set up a still?" I asked.

"Won't be here that long."

"You're right. Let's try to convince them in a few weeks that we are cured, and, then get out of here."

"This may seem strange to you," the Colonel mused, "but I have no desire for booze. This place–being cut off from the outside, isolated in the wilderness–has taken away my desire to drink."

"Odd you should mention it. I feel the same way–but I've hardly been tested. These drugs keep me half out of it."

"They'll cut them out in a few days."

We walked down the hall to the lounge, had brim in the small room next to the lounge, then stood wondering what to do next. Hearing music I asked Lucy (who was standing by the coffee urn) who was playing the piano.

"Bill," she said. "Isn't he marvelous? He is so gifted."

I recognized Beethoven's Concerto No. 4. Indeed he was gifted, as far as my ears could judge. Everyone was silent, lifted up, for a moment, at least–carried beyond themselves into a timeless world of ecstasy, or enchantment. The listeners seemed to be caught up in dreams–dreams perhaps unfulfilled, and nearly forgotten in the mists of the past. Now, they came rushing back upon the wings of melody. Cherished hopes seemed to be momentarily again within reach, and it might have been that memories of childhood, of loved ones, of carefree life when the world was young and stretched on endlessly without grief, returned in a flood.

Now, shadows had passed over everyone's lives: the sadness that came when one lives long enough. There were a few moist eyes in the room. Bill was, indeed, an artist at the keyboard.

Few of us were young anymore. My youth was gone. I was not even aware when it slipped away. The music awakened feelings that I thought had long ago been put to rest–a longing for innocence and an open heart. The music caused pain, a bitter sense of loss. I knew what the driving force in my life was. It was ambition.

Ambition is but a dream. It deceived me; it confused and clouded my mind. Ambition had won over my heart a long time ago. Like a gossamer shield of finest webbing, ambition filtered a distorted light that clouded my vision. I saw fairy tales where riches were won without the scars of battle, where success brought joy and where I would continue–eternally young–never disillusioned or overcome. With my heart consumed by ambition, life had swiftly passed me by without ever sharing in the simple joys, the successes and failures of those near me.

I had to leave the room, and the fading music followed me down the hall. This place, the people in it, the strange sounds, the drabness; the pale white walls; the white lights that gave a death like pallor to our skin, all caused me to withdraw within myself. I felt nothing toward anyone. Only the blue sky, the fallen leaves, the bare trees standing erect and gaunt, ready to endure the long winter– waiting, forever waiting for another spring–seemed real to me. And the forest in which I was longing to explore (or was it more a strange compulsion) drew me as I was moved by an overwhelming desire for peace, feeling that it could be found only in nature because all else had failed.

Why was life hard? Why were good intentions not enough? Why did unknown forces always checkmate every effort, all worth while dreams and desire? Fulfilled, they became only illusions. The pleasure of life was so fleeting, the struggle so long, the fears so pervasive, the outcome so uncertain. Even when success was attained it was empty, and seemed futile.

My every success had demanded of me a price unforeseen. As pressures increased, I found alcohol to be the grand elixir. It supplied the energy; it alleviated pain, freed my mind of worries, and gave promise to my dreams. It was this discovery which sustained me.

Now I was shattered without it. Withdrawn, searching inside my heart, I had my first glimpse of personal decadence. Terrified at what I saw, I tried to control my mind and turn it away from the ruins I witnessed.

CHAPTER 8

As one day fades into another, all about me the movement, faces, and voices are as undistinguishable as the blurred scene of an impressionistic painting. People move, they talk but I do not feel their presence; only hear words that have no meaning. I feel nothing outside myself. My dreams are real, so vivid and intense they are consuming me. No longer am I aware of the outside world, the activities, the movements of people–everything seems so far away.

Someone speaks, and I do not answer. The voice speaks again, louder: I am startled. Slowly I come out of this haze–from another world–to see a face studying me, curiously.

Something is wrong. Fear rises within me. My heart begins to pound. Possessed by fear, with all my powers I strive to remain alert, in contact with the present. I study faces to see if they are watching me; try to read expressions, to detect a change in a voice to see if the speaker tests me to determine what I must do to conceal the struggle raging within me. I resolve that no one will see me slipping away again into another world that cuts out the present, where I feel no pain, where all is peaceful until the night comes. It is then that the demons are unchained. A hundred voices rise up clamoring to be heard: one saying I was a fool; another, "No, no! Follow me!" Still another assuring me that I am still in control–saying do not change my life.

But I sense destruction here.

So the struggle has begun: the lines are being drawn for battle. Yet, during the day, when I am exhausted, my faculties weakened, feeling withdrawn, there is at least a certain peace.

The building is still. Lights are out except for my reading lamp and a faint light somewhere down the hall. I sit reading, attempting to shorten the night. All alone–so quiet at night. I feel uneasy. My heart–slowly at first, then faster, louder, louder–begins pounding: shaking me. The fear, the unbearable noise is too much. The book slips away from my hand, and falls to the floor. My senses are acute. The room seems alive. Every object in the room is grotesque–made up of strange shapes which are enveloped in shadows and darkness. Alert, tense, aware of the slightest movement, my ears strain to hear any sound. My heart continues to pound, jumping whenever I hear an unusual noise.

My mind explodes with scenes of the past and wild scenes that never occurred. Waiting, watching, my mind races on. I have no control over the scenes that flood before my eyes–strange, grotesque images that haunt me, causing unnatural fear that tears at my vitals–growing, tearing, consuming like cancer. I am slowly being crushed, broken, sifted into countless parts, every part having a separate voice: each voice speaks faster, louder demanding a hearing–each voice saying it is I. I do not know who I am. Fear possesses me. One step further and I am lost–lost to madness forever.

Somewhere there must be relief. I must try to lose myself in nature. I hear the sound of the wind and see the trees warped, twisted but enduring. The clouds, grey or white, always changing, draw me out of myself, giving me a sense of permanence and strength–feeling and a reality I find nowhere else.

Why was life hard? Nothing was real anymore. All my ideals were gone, my dreams shattered. Nothing remained–there was nothing at all. Only disillusionment, the nightmares, the darkness: I understood nothing, felt only fear. Anger did move me–but then anger was the child of fear.

If anything meaningful remained to me that was nature: the blue, cold sky, the pale moon, the stars so vast in number yet so singular; every one a jewel never ceasing to illuminate the long nights of winter. The mysterious wind that came and went, that hid in the mountains, in the valleys, moaning early or late in the trees, bending them to its will–its presence felt, its power feared, its reign supreme.

There was some release of tension in the out-of-doors. Was the longing to explore the forest only a compulsion, like my consuming desire for alcohol? Was I being drawn further into madness with this obsession that nature held the key to my sanity? Would I reach the safety of the dark forest before someone discovered how mad I actually was and put me away? I could see madness in others, but my own I could neither grasp nor combat. To be ripped loose from my moorings, my identity lost, my past forgotten, a pawn to every wayward impulse made me shudder. At first I was shaken with fear, then, slowly, anger began to take possession of me. Why fear? I would resist! I had won many battles. This one would not be lost. Bogleman. Did he know that I was certainly mad? How much did he suspect? My wife had told him about me.

If I could but come to grips with the trolls and the witches–the dark forces of the night that haunted me in my dreams–I would survive. Unseen forces were standing–waiting. Now I suspected that they were confident, moving out of my nightmares and into the real world where I must grapple with them. I burned, now, to come to grips with them. How much hatred I felt at that moment! Maddening, consuming hatred! Fear reinforced my hatred. I would not go down easily.

Whenever I was confined in close quarters with bright lights; in grey rooms with serious faces; the empty eyes, the endless chatter filled me with gloom. Seeking diversion, some simple pleasure to distract me, I wandered about alone. Often, lately, I felt pursued, but saw no one. My mind–No!   It was my life that was wrong.   No!   It was seeking to fulfill my dreams–unreal dreams.   No!   It was middle age.   No!–My God. I did not know.

I knew nothing, except that my mind was going, that I was being devoured, shredded. A tug of war goes on; there are wild horses–dark knights, white knights, the screams of battle, the ring of sword against sword that I could hear. A violent struggle was pulling me in all directions and wild scenes were taking shape within my mind.

Who was I anyway? Which voice was strong enough to be called me? No one saw, no one cared. All anyone saw is what I saw when I looked into a mirror: an overweight man with a haggard face and weary eyes, who showed no unusual signs of suffering, only age and decay. Most of the time I felt nothing (if emptiness is nothing). When I felt anything it was anger and that exhausted me: but fear was there, too. More often fear those days–that gradually came over me and lurked about never far away. The anger fed on fear. But why was pursued? That's it! It was fear that pursued me. But fear was not an object, something I could touch and feel. (Even a ghost can be seen or felt). The dark forces of the night at least took shape in my nightmares. Where was my reason? Why didn't reason explode this myth and say, "Look here! This is all nonsense! Stop tormenting this man. Set him free, and let him play out his role in peace."

My fears! I would gladly have killed my fears. If reason could not, and if violence would, then violence I would choose. There would be no hesitation. With arms open wide, I would take violence and end this conflict.

The voices within grew louder. My instincts told me that a crisis was near. Would my own dark forces finally assume control? Did they have the power? Would I become their puppet, being allowed certain periods of peace and outward appearances of normalcy, then, when least expected, erupting like a volcano, spewing lava, vile obscenities, unearthly sounds, possessed–causing those about me to draw back? With open mouths, wide eyes, every voice would convict me of madness. The verdict: lock him up. Put him away where he can do no harm, out of our sight forever, in a room where he cannot be seen or heard, where no one cares. Put him in a place where no one comes to see him, so he can be forgotten by all. There, he can play the fool alone.

With my control slipping away, guided by a faltering will, and my faculties clouded by exploding voices, what ought I to do to gain

stability? What must I do to regain reason? What was I capable of?
Murder? Once it seemed possible. There must be a way out of this
hell. How did I get here? To become this? Who am I anyway?
Helpless! I feel helpless! I cannot admit that I am weak and afraid. All
of this must be a delusion or a nightmare. I do not belong here.

The ABC's. Such nonsense! I had always followed my
instincts. My fortune had been built that way. I would never follow
such a childish routine of reflection before reaction. A fox does not
think. Unerringly, he follows his nature. My instincts once were as
acute as any fox's. Now, I am confused, fears haunt me. Why can't I
come to grips with these fears? My mind races on. I cannot control it,
or I could control these fears, give the lie to those wild images that
cause my nerves to explode sending shocks up and down my body. I
am in danger. That's it. I am slowly being possessed. But why? By
whom? My pounding heart tells me this is true. My crawling skin is
evidence of fear. My mind is jammed, filled with colliding thoughts,
and is racing out of control like wild horses in a panic, racing toward a
cliff. And my cries, my reason, my force cannot stop them.

But why? Why me? Courage has been my strength. Others had
said of my success that it had not been my skill or special aptitude, but
raw nerve, a brazen defiance of all the odds, a callous indifference
toward others. A special brand of ruthlessness that either swings free
of all problems or finds a way to brush them aside, which had allowed
me to succeed where others would have failed. Still the wonder: how
could I sleep, avoid ulcers, or booze under so much pressure?

Now a hidden fault was seen, a splitting apart that I could not
heal. That these several parts which constituted me were to be shuffled
about–moved against my will–to be ripped and torn and bent by
unseen forces, shredded and consumed by an enemy I could not see or
touch, was maddening. I could not endure this much longer, nor could
I take my life: the thought caused me to draw back. To go naked into a
strange world, a coward, my problems unresolved, my failures coiled
about me like hissing serpents that pointed to every forgotten fault was
a journey that I feared more than the demons which besieged me. To

be judged mad is one thing; to be condemned is quite another. The thought of being lost forever filled me with trembling and fear.

Now, I see that madness is my fear. In all my dreams there is the realization, however faint, that I am dreaming. But of late, the illusion has become real: I return from another world. Only then do I realize that I have been dreaming. Filled with fear, in shock, soaked with sweat, the realization comes over me that I had been dreaming. Helpless, utterly weak and trembling I lie there suspended between sleep and consciousness as my mind slowly clears, unable to move, powerless to make a decision, wondering if I will be forever chained, or worse, fall into darkness where there is nothing—nothing at all but eternal loneliness.

What's this? A faint light in the hall. Leaning forward in the chair I peered down the hall. Someone had come out of a room, hurried down the hall, stopped, turned around—all the while moving his arms—then rushed toward the far exit and disappeared into the night. The cold would soon bring him back.

Another sound: the rustling of papers. What else could it be but the nurse in her office. Someone was on duty. No need to sit in the darkness when every object concealed by darkness takes on a strange shape—to sit here, to be my own prisoner while inanimate objects come alive. Surely, this is not real. It is my imagination that is threatening me, bringing to life that which never before had life.

I walked around the corner and saw Audrey, the night counselor, sitting by the desk painting her fingernails. Red nails on delicate pale fingers. Her pale skin, gleaming under the white lights, contrasted sharply with the dark shadows in the corners of the room. She looked up. Her grey eyes flashed, then she lowered her eyes and continued her painting. I stood looking at her in the darkened entrance. Her clinging sweater and skirt revealed her figure. There was no doubt that she was aware of her charms. The light alone gave her skin—smooth, translucent, without blemish—an almost deathlike color. There was a fascination about her. She was cold, indifferent, yet strangely appealing. I wondered if she could respond with emotion—or if she was lethargic and dull. She said nothing as I stared at her, fascinated, watching her breasts slowly rise and fall, taking in her charm.

Without looking up she said, "You're up late. You never sleep."

"A little restless is all. It's the change, I suppose." Admiring her nails I said, "With such shapely hands and long nails you must find housework a problem."

She looked at me with wide grey eyes which betrayed not the slightest expression or interest in me. Then she said, "On the contrary. I enjoy preparing food in the French manner. To me, cooking is fun."

She recounted the many types of wines she used in preparing salads, meats, fowl and fish. There seemed to be no end to the way wine was used to bring out delicate flavors.

"All those bottles of wine," I said, "within easy reach? You must have a strong will."

For the first time she smiled. "Eva once came to dinner. Seeing all that wine she said nothing, but afterwards, several days later, she called me into her office and asked me if I thought it wise to have all that wine in the house."

"What did you say?" She gave me an appraising glance as I moved to a chair near her desk.

"Well," she said, "I told her it didn't bother me. I was through with drinking alcohol, but not French cooking. Wine was essential so I wasn't giving it up."

Her coolness impressed me. She put the polish away and sat looking at me.

I asked, "Doesn't your family miss you, being on duty these late hours?"

She glanced at me and seemed to know instinctively that I was moved by her appearance. "I'm divorced," she said, "and my children—the five of them—are pretty well grown. Two daughters have been living with me."

"You must have married when you were a child," I told her. "You look so trim, so young. You're a most appealing young woman."

"I'm older than you think–far older. But," she smiled, "think as you will."

"How did you lose your husband? Through booze?"

"No, although it may have played a part. I married young, as you suggested. When we returned from our honeymoon, my husband was sitting by the unpacked suitcases, depressed and silent. I asked him what was wrong. He said that he felt our marriage had been a mistake. Right then I should have ended it–called it off–sent him on his way. Foolishly, I did not. Later, he became difficult, domineering, and unpredictable. But at first (I was young and inexperienced), I thought that love, and lots of attention would make him change his mind. I was wrong. Nothing pleased him. He demanded absolute perfection of himself, of others, and especially of me. In many ways, though, it was a good life: we skied, traveled, and enjoyed all the advantages of money. He was a skilled orthopedic surgeon, and rose quickly in his profession. And he did like the trappings of success– even then, in those early years; he commuted from our lakeside home to his office in his helicopter.

"On a skiing trip I suffered what at first seemed like a slight injury to my neck. But the pain soon became unbearable. My husband had not performed the type of surgery needed for a correction, but was sure he could master the technique with a little study. Together we studied his textbooks."

"Surely you didn't let him experiment on you?"

She smiled again. "Don't you see? I was young, and confident in his ability. He operated–and he failed. You've seen me with a neck brace. I wear it when I can't stand the pain. Any surgical procedure which holds promise of relieving the pain also carries the threat of permanently crippling me, and I'm just not willing to take that risk. So I have had to be content with reducing the pain with drugs.

Unfortunately, most drugs give me terrific side effects. All drugs except alcohol, that is. And of course, now I can't take alcohol either."

"What did your husband have to say about the failure of the operation?"

"Not much. You see I became a burden to him. I couldn't ski anymore. When my drinking embarrassed him we drew apart. And when I stopped drinking, he attended all social affairs without me. The end soon followed. I was provided for, and the two girls were with me until very recently."

"Are they gone?"

"Yes," she said, "They're gone now." Audrey spoke crisply, and her defensiveness at that moment was almost palpable.

"There were a lot of things, I suppose," she continued, "that led to their going. A man was living with me, and that caused some conflict, of course. And we'd come home and the house would be a mess. I was firm, and made some strict rules for the girls to follow, but they didn't follow them. So I laid down an ultimatum, they made their choice–and out they went."

"Tough going," I said.

"Yes–it was tough on all of us. But I couldn't take it, the way things were going."

"Where did they go?"

"To their father. He attracted them. It might have been the money, I suppose. He could certainly give them more things than I."

If she saw that I thought her treatment of her daughters was harsh, she did not show it. She probably cared little about what I thought.

She continued. "I have a life to lead. My daughters are growing up and must accept responsibility. I couldn't reach them–let their father have a try."

"What will you do now?"

"My days are active. I have been selling condominiums when I'm not working here–quite successfully too. And my boyfriend fills a need. I live from day to day not making too many plans."

She looked at me with her grey eyes, without any show of curiosity. She was neither hostile nor friendly, or seemingly in any way impressed by me.

I could not say that she did not affect me.

Restless, I got up to leave. "I'm going out into the night air. It's cold, but I'm not ready for sleep."

She made no comment about my strange hours. Instead, she said, "See you again some other night."

The hallway was dark except for the light near the exit. As I walked slowly down the hall I was aware of the small night sounds around me. I could hear the creak of the floor beneath my feet and someone's heavy breathing. I stopped, looked back to the end of the hall where Audrey sat behind her desk; then I stepped into the night.

The air was cold. I paused and listened for the wind: there was silence. I looked up at the trees outlined in the dark. Shadows formed, giving the trees strange, unnatural shapes: something about them was unearthly, something that challenged my senses and caused my skin to crawl, my heart to beat faster.

As I walked along the cinder path, I looked at each ancient tree and saw that they were not alike. One had twisted limbs so ugly and grotesque that it appeared to have been the prey of every storm yet it survived. Another, shielded by several other trees (by nature's whimsical choice) was straight, not so ugly or fierce, yet it seemed to lack the character of the one that faced the full blast of every storm. One tree stood all alone. In the darkness it loomed before my eyes as a defiant monster, its massive limbs were twisted and ugly like arms spread wide. As if defying winters' storms to do their worst. Let the night wind howl in anger, the penetrating cold, the suffocating snow and the burning heat of summer do their worst: the old tree stood scarred, but seemed secure in its power to survive.

I took another step–and stopped abruptly. A twig had snapped near me. I stood, slowly turning my eyes, searching the darkness. The only available light came through the branches of the trees from the stars. Someone seized my arm.

Pulling free, I recognized Bernice. "You fool!" I cried out. "Suppose I had been carrying a club?"

"Did you see him?" she asked. She was agitated, wide eyed, almost in a state of panic.

"Bernice, it is after midnight. You caused me to jump half out of my skin then ask if I saw someone. Yes, I saw someone–you!"

"No, you don't see at all. Someone has been running in and out of the trees near the building. I've been hiding–too afraid to go in."

"Let's go in before we freeze. Take my arm," I said, walking toward the entrance. After the shock of being grabbed in the dark the possibility of seeing another person did not frighten me.

"Do you think he will attack us?" Bernice asked, turning her head to peer into my face. She had just started to speak again when Francis stepped into the path near the entrance. I feared Bernice might scream and awaken the house which would necessitate needless explanations.

"Francis? What is it?" I called out approaching him slowly. Bernice dropped my arm and darted around us into the building, leaving me alone to confront the druggist.

"I can't understand," Francis said. "Someone is after me."

"I see no one. What don't you understand?"

"All of it. Nothing is clear. The ABC is . . . I am trying to understand the ABC's, I can't . . . "

He gasped, fell to the ground and began kicking his feet. His face contorted, and his eyes were wide, rolling. As I bent over him, I was sure he was dying. Feeling helpless I thought of Audrey. As I turned to follow Bernice into the long hall, I hoped that no one would hear my hasty steps. I wondered, too, why Francis in his great distress had not stuttered. No matter, he had appeared to be dying.

Audrey heard my steps and looked up as I approached. "It's the druggist," I blurted. "He's having an attack. I think he's dying."

Audrey picked up the phone, dialed a number and said briefly, "Francis is having an attack." She paused and looked up at me.

Anticipating the question, I said, "He's lying by the North entrance."

She repeated what I said and added, "I'll meet you there." She hung up immediately, pulled a flashlight out of her drawer, saying, "That was Anne. She should be there in a few minutes."

I led the way. At the door she said, "Wait with me until Anne gets here."

The druggist was lying near the door. He was no longer moving and I wondered if he were dead. I felt relief when I saw his lips move. He was trembling as Audrey bent over him. She did not turn the light into his face, but grasped his wrist and felt his pulse.

Within a minute or so the door opened and there was Anne. Audrey saw her look at me. Before Anne spoke, "Mark was up late talking to me. He saw Francis having an attack."

Anne nodded toward me and then knelt down beside Francis and loosened his collar. Turning, she asked for the light, and turned the full glare into his face. His eyes were wide, glassy; his face twisted. Out of him came a sound hardly human–a cry of anguish, the sound like an animal trapped unable to move. Or in fear of moving. What did he see? A beast? A crawling insect? Or giant reptiles, some hideous snake he was too paralyzed to elude?

In nightmares I often suffered such anguish. Did look like this? I wondered.

The nurse said something to Audrey, who turned to me, "Mark–you can go. I'll talk to you later. Thanks. You have helped." I thought she smiled.

Feeling fear and anguish, I went into the hall and walked slowly to my room. Gene, who said he never slept, was sleeping, peacefully.

CHAPTER 9

The next morning there was no sign of Francis. After breakfast and the morning conference I walked out into the cold air. There was no breeze, and no sound except the crunch of frozen grass beneath my feet. The maple trees, in the early morning sun, no longer appeared oppressive or malevolent, for now each twisted limb was clearly outlined in the sun. At night, they had appeared grotesque, threatening. In the dark, they had taken on strange shapes, and become alive, almost as animals are alive. On the night before, as I had walked among them, fearful, my senses had been alert, and I was fascinated– even compelled–to be exposed to whatever danger the night might have held.

I heard voices and turned to see Bill talking to the Commander, who stood erect, his appearance giving the impression that he was listening to every word. Dean, who I often saw stand alone, aloof from small groups was also listening. He appeared withdrawn, rather sad, and preoccupied with his thoughts. He was a kindly man, and to me, an enigma–a brooding, silent man I could not fathom.

Mary walked up to him and began talking. Animated as always, Mary began describing to Dean work she had once done in a cannery. The work had been hard and monotonous, and the hours long and tedious. Just hearing her describe the standing, bending, and sorting of fruit made me tired. This grueling routine, it seemed to me, would drain from a sensitive woman all sense of dignity and feeling of worth; yet Mary described these hard and dulling tasks with enthusiasm. Dean appeared to listen with understanding. He was drawn to Mary. She offered him companionship that was apparently lacking in his life.

I liked Dean, this strange withdrawn man–a soldier, who someone had said, had seen action, had been severely wounded, married an Oriental woman, had two children, and drank too much.

Drink formed a bond that joined us together. Our lives, in all other ways, were so different, our interests so diverse that in the ordinary course of events we would never have met. The world saw us as outcasts, the refuse of society: fools, weaklings, liars, full of deceit and self pity; unable to drink like men; always going to excess; and as being beyond hope; the despair of family, friends, clergy and psychiatrists.

Mary, seeing me, called out, "Come and join us. Dean and I are going for a walk."

Dean, as usual, had little to say. Mary was doing the talking, and to her, the world appeared fresh and exciting.

"Look," she said, pointing, "see the squirrel near the tree? Isn't he fat? He's looking for a handout." As we passed a fringe of trees and came into a clearing, she cried out, "See the sky? How blue it is! And have you ever seen whiter clouds or a paler moon? When I first arrived leaves were on the trees. They were brown and red, amber and gold. Now, see, the limbs are exposed, almost bare. So twisted, grey and ugly."

For days I had observed that fall was fading, that winter was in command: the leaves were almost gone, blown into the river and the forest; the air each day colder, all the mountain peaks crowned with snow.

Mary turned to Dean. "The air is so fresh. I'm so happy here. Don't you love it?"

He turned his sad eyes upon her, "Yes, Mary, I like it here. But I don't want to stay here forever."

"Wouldn't it be wonderful if only we could? It is so calm and peaceful, and we have so many friends. Such a nice group! And now we have Mark." Looking at me she smiled warmly, "Don't you just love it here?"

"It's a change," I said. "You must excuse my lack of enthusiasm. It is rather strange, this isolation–and it's hardly what I would call a vacation."

Mary did not seem to hear me. Dean always appeared interested in what Mary was saying. As we walked along the path that wound serpentine through the trees, I looked back to see Roy, the Boeing man, and the Colonel walking some distance from us, following the same path.

When Mary paused for a moment, I asked, "What will you do when you leave here?"

She looked startled–for once without words. "Why, let's not talk about that. I plan to be here for a long time. I see no reason to think about leaving. There are such nice people here–you and Dean, and that marvelous Colonel. Doesn't he thrill you with his adventures? There is Roy, that pretty girl, Lucy–she's rooming with me now–and I must not forget the druggist. Has anyone seen him? Peg said he was in some sort of treatment. I'll miss him until he comes back."

Mary continued on and on. Francis was mentioned and forgotten. Like a child, Mary was consumed by the events of the moment; nothing else mattered: there was no past, no future, just the joy of living now in this moment without tension or fear, free from the intrusions of that outside world that she dreaded.

Walking along, listening to Mary, I knew that her life could go on forever like this at Maplewood–no yesterdays or tomorrows–only the excitement of today. Dean, who was so often hardly noticed–silent, withdrawn, standing alone outside a group–was caught up in Mary's excitement. He laughed at her inane remarks, he showed interest in ground squirrels, in the fallen leaves, and whatever attracted her attention at that moment. He turned to Mary and said, "I'm good with a gun. In the service, my skill helped me survive."

Encouraged by Mary, he told us about his exploits. No incident was too trivial for Mary's interest: a minor skirmish became a major battle of heroic proportions. As Dean opened up, telling of his tales of battle, he grew larger in my eyes, for he was obviously sincere, recounting each episode with the simplicity of a child. To Mary he became a hero, so lifted up in her eyes that he ranked among the immortals. She appeared transported into the unreal world of Don Quixote, where she was witness to the tilting at windmills, saving a maid's honor, rescuing a princess, overcoming highway men—all accomplished with a faith and determination that brushed aside the realities of the world.

Heroes are made of unlikely stuff. Such courage in battle! The stamina; endurance; the will to survive (that made up a soldier, as well as a man) were not evident in Dean's appearance or speech. He was shy, uncertain; withdrawn (I knew nothing of the inner fire). Now, for one brief moment, he was shining in someone's eyes. Mary listened, wide-eyed, as he relived scenes of danger and hardship: being encircled and resisting; wounded in the stomach, but holding secure a position; rescued, almost dying from wounds; this was the insanity of war, now relived, that gave meaning to his life.

Listening, looking on as an outsider, I turned to see the Colonel and Roy only a few steps behind us.

"Say, you sure walk slowly," boomed the Colonel. "You and Dean are delaying Mary by too much talk."

Interesting, I thought. I had said scarcely a word.

We had come to the end of the road leading in and out of Maplewood. Where this road joined a mountain highway we stopped before retracing our steps. Roy leaned forward and peered up and down the highway.

"Roy," I asked, "do you think someone is coming for you or do you plan to hitchhike out of here?"

He threw up his hands. "No cars come this way. It's a jail—a prison. No! A nut house. I'm getting out!" Nodding toward the Colonel who now held Dean's and Mary's attention he added, "You can stay and console him."

"You are cured?" I asked.

"Cured?" he retorted. "I told Betsy when she was here that I'd never drink again."

"What did she say?"

"Not a thing."

"Nothing at all?"

"No. She just sat there and cried."

"You enjoyed drinking," I said. "Now your wife cries when you give it up."

"It wasn't all fun. I couldn't remember what happened sometimes. That always scared me."

Something amused him, and he laughed. His voice was harsh and cynical. "The last time I drank vodka," he said, "I decided to build a fire in the fireplace. As I was attempting to light a match, I apparently collapsed. Betsy found me stretched out with my head in the fireplace—just like another chunk of wood waiting to be burned. Fortunately for me I hadn't started the fire. Betsy let me lay there until I awakened. Convinced I needed help, she encouraged me to come here."

"You accepted your fate," I said.

"Fate had nothing to do with it. Boeing decided for me—either come here, or lose my job. Not much of a choice. Now I'm cured, and I'm looking for a clearance from Ralph so I can return to work."

"Ralph?—oh, he's the counselor Bill pointed out to me talking to Dr. Neilstrom. He looked pleasant enough. Can you count on him signing your release? It seemed to me Bill said he could be stubborn at times."

Roy shook his head. "There is no problem. How could there be? I'm fine. I won't drink again. All Ralph has to do is sign those papers–my release, saying I'm cured."

I stood silent, saying no more. In the darkness of my thoughts–in my utter confusion and isolation–feeling a sense of loss, always tense, living in fear, each day a long series of endless moments that made up endless days, I felt that I was going nowhere without hope of any change. In my present state any judgment I made would be confused at best. Would Ralph see Roy as Roy saw himself? Cured? No longer with a problem? After all it was a matter of judgment: Ralph could sign a letter saying that Roy appeared ready to resume work. Roy was a little man, direct and open hearted; he was determined; once his mind was set, it did not occur to him that anyone would challenge his judgment.

The Colonel was telling Mary how good the cold air made her look. For the moment she listened while Dean looked on. We had walked a long ways to the highway. Walking was our most refreshing diversion after each conference. Now, as if by a given signal, everyone turned and began walking again back to the sanitarium. Dean and Mary hung back and walked alone; Roy, the Colonel and I walked ahead.

A gust of wind blew leaves across our path. Soon they would be gone, lying beneath the coming snow, rotting, playing their role in the constant renewal of nature: giving back to the earth the life they had drawn from it; enriching the soil for the coming of spring. The fierce winter would run its course: the deep snow, the howling wind, the long nights would end; spring would come and flowers would bloom again and the entire world would be radiant with their color. All too soon the first flowers would fade, then the ancient trees around Maplewood would proudly display their green leaves, maturing under the summer sun. Nature would prosper, surging with new life–but not for long. Soon the golden colors of autumn would foreshadow the end of another summer: indicating the cycle to be complete–foretelling that winter again was near. With many signs–with harmony and precision–

all of nature served unerringly its purpose of birth, growth, maturing, fading, death and renewal.

It was left to man to begin with so much hope, drawing the praise of others at the first sign of success. Then the pursuit of that bright star of <u>success</u>; how it captivated the heart with thrilling, driving, burning ambition, always reaching higher, seeking to scan the loftiest heights. Hearing the roar of the crowd, overflowing with self esteem–this was life! This was living–the course I had chosen. Now there was a summing up. My life had run full cycle: after a long struggle success came and all too soon that star faded, followed by disillusionment and a nagging sense of loss and finally despair. My life became empty, without purpose or meaning and I felt helpless to find a way out of these blind corridors of the mind. Who cares for the alcoholic? Who can endure his arrogance? A few friends stay on, but they do not see, they do not understand. They are in one world; the alcoholic another: behind iron bars, shut in, lost, unable to find a way out, sealed as securely as if in a tomb.

I heard the Colonel's voice growing louder. Listening I realized he was telling how he came to Maplewood.

"You see," he began, "in the South there was class distinction, much the same as you found in England in the eighteenth and the nineteenth century. When I was a small boy, my uncle, who raised me, placed big Elnora, a young black woman, to care for all my needs. She was amiable, and strong, too. I would hook her up to my wagon, snap my little buggy whip, saying, 'gitty up, faster, faster,' and she would pull me around the plantation. As I grew older she became more self indulgent and would say, 'Colonel, you is surely going to live until you die.' She was a good woman." Laughingly he added, "Those were the halcyon days of my youth–on the plantation–with the servants– everything in abundance. You see, my uncle was a plantation owner who raised tobacco on a large scale.

"Later I went off to Virginia Military Institute where my career as a cavalry soldier began in earnest. I became an exceptional rider, competing in polo matches, and sometimes playing with George

Patton before he was made general. As you may have noticed, women are attracted to me." Seeing the scowl on Roy's face the Colonel hastened to add: "Of course there is an occasional barracuda like Peg. If I was marooned on an island with her, I'd join the sharks–they'd be friendlier."

Neither Roy nor I said anything. I wondered if the Colonel was so sidetracked, so concerned about Peggy and their differences, to continue with his story.

"I graduated as an engineer, got my commission and began moving up through the ranks. My ultimate goal was to become a general. I knew many of the leading officers: as I said I sometimes played polo with General Patton–before and after he was made general. Now there was a soldier: he was fearless, he understood tactics, the art of war, how to maneuver tanks in battle under all conditions–never panicked, always was in control. When the war came, I was commissioned to lead a column of tanks under Patton. We were in search of the enemy and moving up in formation. I was in the lead, standing with the hatch open–when we were fired upon by German tiger tanks. Those eighty-eights were deadly. A shell blew me out of the tank. I was fortunate in that I only lost the use of one eye, and my left arm no longer has any strength. The others in my tank were killed. That ended my career as an officer."

"Why?" I asked. "Once you said that you were determined to be a general. Could one tiger tank end all your hopes?"

"You don't understand," he replied. "For almost two years I was in the hospital, unable to see anything but light and darkness from one eye. Out of the other I could make out faces. Without help, I could hardly find my way about."

Roy spoke up. "Are you sure that was the way it was, Colonel? You didn't start boozing it up, getting in trouble with the nurses? Then they gave you a pension and let you go?"

"No, gentlemen! I'm a man of action. True–the nurses were very understanding, but I could never accept a desk job."

"So you say," taunted Roy, "but how did you get here?"

"Some of what you said was true. There was a long period of recovery. I was bored, depressed, at a low ebb in my life, and I looked about for consolation. And, as you suggested, for a diversion. The nurses filled that need. They were friendly and ever so willing. I was young, and a handsome war hero. As you suspected, there was whisky–an ample supply of good sour mash. I drank often, whenever I felt the urge, and my capacity exceeded everyone's. That was a danger I did not recognize at the time. When I faced up to hard competition in the world, I soon saw that I was a full blown alcoholic, so I quit. Quit for seventeen years, until I went back to Virginia to my daughter's wedding. Champagne was served. Drank only a few glasses. You know the rest of the story. It was all downhill. Three years later I found myself in your company."

"You are an alcoholic?" I asked.

"That's right–a full blown charter member of the club. To me, alcohol was life. The drive, the energy it gave. . . Such meaning and zest each day . . . There was romance, fellowship . . . Problems dissolved, grayness disappeared . . . the whole world changed." As he said this, he raised his hand with a dramatic flourish to emphasize the fulfillment he experienced while drinking. His eyes shone. It seemed that he was remembering when alcohol <u>was</u> life.

"Why stop then?" asked Roy.

"Because there was the other side–the black side–when I couldn't remember where I'd been, for instance. Waking in a room, finding someone sleeping beside me, not knowing how I got there. Or having someone tell me of some occurrence, a painful episode, that I could not remember. Or the anxiety I caused others–especially my wife. No longer able to depend upon me, she was in a constant state of apprehension, always fearful, never knowing what I was up to or what would happen to me–or what future there was for her. Something was going to happen, drinking as I was. I'd sometimes put away as much as two fifths a day. "

"Not long ago, I came home late. I could hear the TV in my wife's room. Sometimes she doesn't switch it off before she goes to sleep. With considerable effort (being drunk), I took off my shoes, climbed the stairs slowly (so the steps would not creak), walked down the hall to my room, closed the door and eased myself onto the bed. I lay there trying to remember how much I had consumed. I was drunk but I felt strange. The room seemed different. My mind was alert, and I felt tense, uneasy—wondering why the liquor had filled me on this occasion with the feeling of dread. "

"The room was very dark. As I lay there, unable to sleep, I tried to make out (in the dark) each object in the room. At first, everything seemed normal. I saw the outline of the dresser, my exercise machine near the window, a chair. Still, I felt restless, uneasy. There was a foreboding, somewhat similar to the apprehension I felt before going into battle when I didn't know the strength or position of the enemy. "

"I was lying on my back and the room began to move. As it began to turn faster and faster, I dropped my left arm over the side of the bed and pressed my fingers into the carpet near the bed. The room slowed and stopped. I laughed."

"Was this my foreboding of something unnatural? Why, in the past, I had felt the bed spin like a top. Then, with one hand I'd clutch the carpet, and with the other hand I'd hold on for dear life to the iron uprights at the head of the bed to keep from falling to the floor."

"As I clutched the carpet I thought I felt a creature—a soft furry cat—brushing its whiskers against my hand. Almost at once, I realized we didn't have a cat. For a moment that amused me. Filled with alcohol, I considered the problem, wondering what it could be. Whatever it was, it felt like numerous furry legs walking back and forth across my hand."

"Then it stopped."

"A moment later, I felt the soft legs coming up my arm."

"'Well, I shall see,' I said to myself–so I turned on my side to look down at my arm. It was then that my face almost touched a huge spider, larger than my hand!"

"I screamed and lashed out at it. It made a frightful crunching sound as I crushed its legs and belly. Red blood smeared my hand and the bed clothing. For some reason I couldn't rise off the bed. Giant spiders began running every where. One hideous spider lowered itself from the ceiling before my eyes. Others, in their excitement to escape, began to explode, their blood oozing down the sides of the wall."

"My wife came into the room, put her hand over her mouth and fled."

"I heard a siren. Men entered the room and fought with me. Then there was blackness."

"That's all I remember until coming here."

CHAPTER 10

For several moments there was silence. Heads lowered, we walked along reflecting upon the Colonel's story. Then Roy turned to the Colonel and said,

"Now you understand. You have been through this hell and you can control it. Your army discipline . . . an old warrior like you . . . you won't have any problem with the future.

Slowly the Colonel shook his head. "Discipline has nothing to do with it. Somewhere, perhaps, in the golden days of my youth, discipline, as you say, may have helped. Now I'm hooked. I know it. Peg knows it. She saw rightly that my liver is almost gone. I might get another turn at bat, or, he signed, "I might not."

"How are you going about getting back into the lineup?" I asked.

"By conditioning, not giving up, accepting the truth that I was a fool, a slave consumed by alcohol which controlled me, used me–like a puppet dangling from a string. All I need to do is look about me to see the results of alcoholism. Take the Admiral, for instance. Does he have a mind at all? Or Francis, who used not only alcohol, but drugs as well. And Peg and Bernice–one is strange, the other crazy. I know our counselors are not true professionals. After all, how could this place afford them? They are reformed drunks like us. Even so, there is merit in some of the things they say–the ABC's for instance. If I had reflected before acting, my life would not have come to a dead end in Maplewood."

He laughed. "Peggy, who is quick to see a weakness, would not have such a big target to shoot at."

"You must mean the hippie," said Roy.

"Whatever she is, she is one tough bitch."

"Colonel," I said, "you are too hard, not at all gentle. How else do you expect her to respond to you?"

"Gentle with that barracuda? In a tank of water with her I wouldn't last five minutes."

"Oh come, Colonel," Roy said, "she was disappointed. In you she looked for some of the grandeur of the old South. All she saw was the ruins. And, as you'll recall saying, she is a realist. I think she probably resented your pretensions, when she saw none of the greatness."

"Pretensions? Greatness? In this squalid world, she could not recognize breeding or quality. The old world of the South is gone, and its greatness–the chivalry, the refinements, the high standards of morality–were ground beneath the Yankee boot after the Civil War. For a time, some of the elegance remained on a few of the southern plantations that escaped the war. The wealth accumulated in land and buildings faced the supreme test in the crash of the market. Poor tobacco crops followed along with a poorer market. No one had money, and the plantation, without servants or help in the fields, fell into ruins. That was a long time ago. My problem is in the present. The solution depends on whether or not I survive."

Looking at me, he continued, "Mark, your problem and Roy's maybe different. Roy says he has his problem under control. I'm glad everything is resolved."

After a moment's pause, Roy spoke up. "My only problem is in getting a release from Ralph."

"You won't drink again?" I queried gently.

"Never! I've given my word to Betsy. I don't need booze any longer. All the desire to drink has gone out of me."

'So it has,' I thought. Why, I wondered? Was it the environment? Being cut off from the outside world, surrounded by counselors, seeing others who were not well, hearing the endless talks about the destructive force of this drug, or did it go even deeper? In a state of crisis, we were being forced to come face-to-face with the truth. There was nowhere to look but inward upon ourselves.

I wondered if the other patients witnessed a scene as revolting, as chaotic as the confusion that raged within me. All our lives were out of joint with what they were intended to be: sick, crippled; minds confused; subject to delusions, to anxiety; in high or low spirits, but never long on an even plane. But what was normal? Whose success was worth recording? Why blame alcohol for all our misery? Facing problems in our middle years, we had abandoned hope. Overcome by an indifferent fate, we possessed neither the stamina nor the will to survive. Or Nature had overlooked us: we were not equipped with the resourcefulness–that peculiar blending of talent, opportunity and desire to make our way in society. Alcohol made us shine, brought us to life (so we thought) all the while deceiving, consuming, destroying us.

"You are a sober one," the Colonel said looking at me. "Now take Roy–he's got his problem licked. Just a cracked head in the fireplace! All he needed was a change. A night in a motel would give you that–and be more exciting too."

Roy didn't smile. "Betsy is enough for me," he said.

"Colonel," I said, "surely your days of glory are past, the inner fire has cooled, so you live on memory, and no longer feel the heat."

"Come on, Mark, I've been watching you. I saw Lucy sit beside you at every conference. Mary let it slip (you know how she talks) that you were dancing with Lucy in the recreation center, and all alone at that. So don't give me any of your high and mighty talk. You've got good taste, though," he said, nudging me, "Lucy is a real charmer. You'd better watch yourself or she'll get you. Do you want me to watch out for you? Sort of play chaperone?"

Feeling uneasy, I laughed. "Don't bother. I'll make out all right."

Someone, it seemed, was always aware of what I was doing. Although it was not intended to be a warning I realized it would be wise to avoid seeing Lucy. Why should I bother with her? She was a harmless, simple girl–someone I met in a far off place: she would soon go out of my life.

At the moment all seemed peaceful. The sun was overhead in a clear sky, the few remaining leaves were crisp, and brittle, and brown, and breaking easily beneath our feet. They were scattered and blown everywhere by the fierce winds that ushered in the coming winter. Our little island, cut out of the pine trees in the mountains, was a lonely, isolated, almost forgotten spot, which, if neglected, would soon be overrun by the forest of tall pines that closed us in one all sides. The old brick buildings in the center of the grounds had weathered well. The ancient maples which surrounded them were sturdy survivors of many long winters. Stripped bare, with every twisted limb revealed, each tree presented a stark scene of defiance, strength and endurance.

As we reached the main building I stopped, as I saw Mary, exuberant as ever, talking to Dean. He was listening as if each word contained a world of wisdom. He appeared to be a lonely man, lost and unhappy; in Mary he found comfort; she filled a void: whatever she saw or heard excited her and this excitement flowed into Dean's somber life.

Mary, seeing me looking at her, said, "You must hear my sonnet. I wrote it while watching the birds. I was going to read it to Dean, but I know you love literature so you must hear it too."

She began: "My title is 'Resolution.'

With wide spread wings they skimmed across the lake,
Above waters whipped white by a raging gale;
Lifted up by unseen hands they seem to make
Their path across the sky a trail:
Chased by dark and angry clouds which I could see

From on the shore; where I could rail
Against my fate, for they are unlike me,
Enslaved by the conflicts of an alien world, so frail,
Not knowing who I am or what I ought to seek:
So often lost, so filled with fear I cannot stem,
Nor find a path to follow for I am weak.
But on this shore against all turmoil I will send
Not my weak limbs to match these exalted wings
But a spirit strong to surmount all earthly things.

How did you like it?" she asked.

The poem was out of character for Mary. Not once in the many days I had seen her at Maplewood had she expressed a serious thought of any kind. I was about to ask her if she wrote the poem, and if she had, how she had gone about it when I felt the Colonel pulling my arm. He was insistent as usual.

I praised Mary for her efforts saying, "At another time we'll talk about your poem. You know the Colonel–anything that involves him is of utmost importance."

"Mark, that's Ralph standing by the entrance, probably trying to clear his head for the next meeting."

"You interrupted my talk with Mary to tell me that?" I said.

"Well, you have such a way with the counselors, I thought you would tell Ralph what you and I think about Roy, or we could step up to him together."

"Colonel, that won't help and you know it," I said. "If we interceded for Roy, likely as not, Ralph would laugh at us saying that we had been here only a short time and now we knew as much as the counselors."

"Oh, you're too much of a pessimist, Mark."

"Let Roy speak for himself," I said. "I'll call him. He hasn't spotted Ralph. Roy! Over here."

Roy looked up and walked over to join us. I nodded in the direction of Ralph, who was intent on scrutinizing his clipboard. Roy upon seeing Ralph, grunted thanks and walked over to where Ralph was standing.

Roy's voice was confident, even commanding as he spoke. "Ralph, I'd like to see you."

Ralph looked like an outdoor man, tan, partially bald and muscular of frame. I'd heard he spent his off hours fishing. At this interruption he looked Roy over slowly before answering.

"Not now, Roy," he said.

"When? Roy demanded.

He looked at Roy casually, and then glanced at his watch. "I have a class now," he said. "I'll see you afterwards."

"I'll come to your room as soon as the class is over," Roy said. Ralph then turned and entered the building before Roy could say anything more. Roy just stood staring at the closed door. He seemed perplexed. Was he aware, I wondered, that Ralph probably already knew what Roy wanted; that this quick brush off was an indication that Ralph was not convinced that Roy was ready to leave. Saying yes would take only a moment's time. Saying no to Roy would have invited a confrontation which would delay the conference. Anyway Roy would know soon enough.

By the end of the conference, that began shortly, I felt that I would have formed some opinions about Ralph. I had an uneasy feeling about him. I hoped that I was wrong in feeling that he was opinionated and slow to see another point of view. On second thought, what basis did I have for my judgment? So far none whatsoever– unless my instincts were serving me well again.

The Colonel interrupted my wandering thoughts.

"Mark, did I overhear Ralph say that he was giving the next conference? I was looking forward to seeing Eva again. She gave me a great charge last time, just looking at her. Without that bourbon, I'd like to try her for a lost weekend," the Colonel said.

"Colonel," I said, "surely with your experiences–your many adventures–you have found more to life than your nocturnal exploits."

The Colonel gave this serious thought. "Every adventure has its peculiar charm. I'll follow my desires. They are basic, necessary, and on the whole, entertaining."

"Come on, you rogue," I said. "Let's go. Everyone has gone into the conference room. Let's not give Ralph a chance to single us out for attention."

CHAPTER 11

As we entered the class I saw that everyone was seated. I followed the Colonel to a chair near the rear of the room. Ralph began writing the word "Alcohol" on the blackboard.

"It is easy to spell," he said. "Being a fisherman, I think of Coho salmon. By adding 'al' to 'coho' and a 'l' to the 'o' I get alcohol."

Turning slowly I looked from side to side studying the faces nearest me to determine the effect of this spelling bee. The expressions were dull, sullen or slightly amused. Only Peggy had a look of utter contempt. My eyes fell upon a new and pretty face, that of a young woman, which for some reason impressed me as an oversized kewpie doll–innocent, dull, over painted and pretty.

"Who is that?" I said, nudging the Colonel and nodding toward the newcomer.

"That's Pamela. She's a former stewardess," he said in a loud whisper. "She has an eating problem." Looking her over boldly, he turned to me and added, "She sure looks good now."

Ralph, hearing voices, turned to us and asked if we wanted to contribute something to the class. The irrepressible Colonel spoke up.

"My friend," he said nodding toward me, "wants to keep up with the new inmates coming in."

As Pamela slowly turned her empty eyes upon me, Peg said, "The Colonel is a jailbird at heart. And he shows his background by speaking of 'inmates.'"

"Listen to her! What rock did you come out from under?"

Ralph's loud voice rang out above those of the two combatants.

"We are here for a reason. Confine your remarks to the problem at hand. Keep your opinions about each other to yourselves."

Pausing for a moment until the room was silent, Ralph continued.

"At this time you can't see what lies ahead. Your lives will be changed. Recovering from a deadly disease, as you are, you will be weak. Your recuperation will take time. To protect your sobriety, you must avoid any situation that causes undue strain. This includes avoidance of those persons who threaten your sobriety. Let me give you an example of what I mean: John, who is a recovering alcoholic, is married to Jane who drinks freely, who refuses to take any care, or reasonable precautions, with her drinking in John's presence. This leads to tension and the likelihood that John will return to drinking, because his wife is not supportive of his sobriety. In such a case it would be reasonable for John to leave his wife to protect his resolution not to drink again."

Pamela raised her hand like a schoolgirl.

"Yes, Pam," Ralph said. "Did you want to add something?"

In the voice of a whining child, she began talking about her husband.

"Charley works in the woods. He is gone a lot. With my flying, and all, we didn't see each other very often. Last week he called."

"What did you talk about?" Ralph asked.

"He said, 'Oh, I am so lonesome for you. My life is hard, it's just impossible without you!' As Charley talked, I could tell he had been drinking. He began to cry. I started crying, too."

"What came out of your talk?" Ralph asked with what appeared to me an unusual interest.

"Well, Charley said he needed me. He wanted his wife. He wanted me to drive to Williston for the weekend to stay with him. I said I just didn't know . . . I'd think about it. I had a few things to do. I'd try to get ready to come. He said he's call me back a little later. The phone rang again and again–I'm sure it was Charley–but I didn't answer the phone. You see–he was drinking."

Ralph smiled. "You are a brave girl, Pamela. My congratulations. No sense in going if he was drinking."

Looking about the room I saw several women smile. They appeared moved by this tragic tale. By the strength of Pamela and her apparent resolve to cut loose from a husband who drank–although it was not clear if he drank often or even had a drinking problem. I wondered if, like many loggers, he drank only when he received his pay check after a series of long, hard days in the woods. There was more here than Pamela's heroic resolves.

The Colonel gave me a nudge. "Wouldn't she make a fine wife? True blue and faithful to the end."

"That night," Pamela added, "I cried myself to sleep. I just couldn't go to see him. He was drinking."

"There you see a fine example of protecting your sobriety," said Ralph. "If your husband or wife or lover causes any danger to your sobriety, you must act. Pamela has shown courage and good sense in cutting clean from her husband."

I was confused. Wasn't Pam here for problems with overeating–and possibly with drugs, too? The Colonel's voice ended my speculation.

"Are you telling us, Ralph, that our partners, after putting up with God knows how much abuse with our drinking, be given the heave ho when we get out?"

"No, I did not say that." Ralph's tone was condescending. "Each one of you must make a choice. I will see some of you coming back once, twice, even three times after relapses. Each time it will be harder to recover. So often these relapses are caused by lack of support at home."

"Nevertheless, what you are saying" the Colonel persisted, "is that because I am a booze hound . . ."

"At least he admits it," interrupted Peg.

Turning toward the direction of the interruption, the Colonel snorted, "Who opened the windows and let that magpie in?"

Ralph threw up his hands, "All right, Colonel. Finish what you have to say."

Smiling at Peg he said, "I will. I intend to finish. You want my wife, Ralph, to tiptoe around the room when I return, never taking a drink, speaking softly, always patient, considerate, doing whatever is necessary to avoid tension. Once I am reformed, she must pay the price by changing her life to solve my problem."

"You put it in your words, not mine. Whatever it takes, sobriety comes first."

"No one in the house can drink in my presence?"

"Not if it bothers you."

"That idea doesn't ride with me. I'm the one who has the problem. So now that I am sober, everyone around me–my wife, those nearest to me–must suffer again. Once because I was a practicing alcoholic, and again because I'm sober."

"As I said," repeated Ralph, "others must make sacrifices, too. You are no good to anyone if you drink. Every lapse closes another door to recovery."

"Say what you will," the Colonel said, "I am not going to say, 'Mildred, dear, my counselor tells me you must not drink in my presence or ever have alcohol in the house. Forget all the grief I caused you, and remember that my comfort and sobriety take precedence before all.'"

Everybody smiled except Pamela, who was pouting.

"If you want sobriety," Ralph said sharply, "you pay the price. This is a selfish program. You are Number One."

"So–I caused much heartache–you send me out cured–now I look out for Number One. I bring suffering again only in a different form. Is that the formula?"

"If you want to put it that way."

"I do."

"What about AA?" I asked.

Ralph looked at me and his eyes narrowed. "What about it?"

"In reading the twelve steps it appears to me this is an unselfish program. Each step gives certain directions–self improvement, the rebuilding of character, is forged from suffering–from the ruins–the ashes of failure, if only we are willing to grow along spiritual lines. This implies generosity, kindness, opening up our hearts, overcoming hatred and bitterness and accepting life for what it is–a precarious journey without many sign posts or visible guide lines–a bold step into the darkness where not everyone survives."

For a moment there was silence, then Ralph spoke slowly, measuring each word.

"You are new here. How long? Several weeks? Now you are interpreting the AA program for us."

"That's no answer," said the Colonel, "it's a put down. Mark was telling you that AA offers a spiritual program, placing others ahead of self, and represents the opposite of selfishness."

Stung by Ralph's remarks, I asked, "Are you familiar with the twelve steps of AA?"

Ralph's face reddened. "I am familiar with AA," he granted.

I persisted, "The twelve steps are entirely spiritual: first by admitting our powerlessness over alcohol, followed by our calling upon a higher power to help, which means character building, rooting out old faults, getting rid of old ways–selfishness, resentments, destructive thoughts and habits– we approach recovery. Step nine speaks of making direct amends to those we have harmed. Step eleven tells us to deepen our spiritual life through prayer and meditation, seeking the strength to carry this out. Step twelve speaks of spiritual awakening and carrying the truth of AA to alcoholics everywhere. Also showing kindness in all our affairs. What you are saying, Ralph, is that anyone who threatens our sobriety is anathema: out they go, out of our lives. Either they live according to our terms, or they live without us. If their hearts are broken . . . well, as you said, it is a selfish program.

"All of us are in a controlled setting where alcohol, for the moment, does not tempt us. All too soon, it appears, most of us will be on the outside, in a world that is hard and selfish and without consideration for the weak or inept–a world that does not care a rap whether anyone here survives. We fit in or we perish–all of which means that if others accept our shortcomings, we accept theirs. Going without alcohol is not considered a virtue by many people. It is absurd that the ones closest to us must give up alcohol when they do not have a problem with it."

"That's telling him," said the Colonel.

Ralph regarded me for a moment in silence, his face rigid, his eyes fixed upon me.

"You come here to tell us how to run this program. After several weeks you do not see yourself as an alcoholic, yet you have the gall to instruct me. You even go so far as to interpret the twelve steps of AA for us."

I was not going to be intimidated by this man.

"I can read. I can interpret what the written word says. We have been asked to read the twelve steps. The rules are simple, clear, precise. Every step speaks of eradicating our faults and developing a spiritual life, the opposite of selfishness. It means helping others, not cutting them out of our lives because they are threats to our sobriety. To live without risk is not possible–that means not living at all."

"Yeah, Ralph," said Roy, who was listening, waiting to speak. "Maybe this Pamela hasn't been all she ought to be as a wife. Maybe she wants to get rid of her husband for other reasons. I noticed she didn't say how much or how often he drank. All she tells us is that he wept because he missed her. It appears a fault to love your wife."

Direct, honest Roy was not helping his cause. I turned slightly to see a look of offended innocence come over Pam's face. She was a good actress: she sighed in disbelief, slowly shaking her head, pouting at these harsh words, which questioned her motives and cut through her pretenses to reach the heart of the matter. I suspected her motives, but they were not my concern. Ralph was a hypocrite. His approach enraged me, and called for a challenge. He was setting up Pam as an ideal to follow–an ideal which I sensed, along with several others, to be phony. Dean looked across at Mary. She was absorbed in all that was being said.

Bill was sitting ahead of me, and I could not see his face. He began speaking in a low resonant voice.

"Mark was telling us about the twelve steps. How do you reconcile these steps with the physiological approach to this disease? Everything I've been told around here leads me to believe that I have a physical disease, not a spiritual one."

How would Ralph approach this question? Would he bluff his way through, or would he even understand the question? I wondered.

"We cannot cover everything at once," he began. "We must take one problem at a time. Dr. Neilstrom is able to answer questions of this kind–after all, he is the psychologist. My purpose is to tell you how to maintain the sobriety that you gained at Maplewood."

Ralph left me confused and with more questions than he answered. Was it true that my great tension and confusion was exacerbated by drinking? Was I an alcoholic? If I could see the hypocrisy in Ralph, his emphasis on discipline, his denial of spiritual growth and lack of concern for others, I ought to be able–by now–to see what drinking was doing to me. Was alcohol at the root of my nightmares, the fears, the disillusionment, the dreary endless days, the self loathing and contempt for life? To blame all my problems on drinking was a tall order. Of course, I was not a normal drinker. I needed alcohol to appear normal, to function in business and to face daily problems.

In his own eyes, Ralph could apparently justify his sneering contempt of me. Was alcohol the key that opened those dark, hidden chambers–the hidden recesses of the heart–where the demons lurked unseen: Freed, they roamed, possessing my mind. I could hear their voices, feel their presence in the darkness, see their outlines in the shadows of the trees, and in the dark halls and rooms at night. Even in the groaning of the buildings, when the activities of the day had ceased, I felt their presence. Then, my senses were alert, and my mind raced on in a babble of conflicting voices–madness so near, so certain, so inevitable. Madness, surely, unless there was a change, a solution, a new course to follow. Was alcoholism the answer? If this were true, why was I haunted now!

I had remained sober for one, two, three weeks. The idea that I had been sober for so long, and that so many days had slipped away (and I unaware of their passage) astonished me. Nothing had really changed except the signs of the coming winter. The sun rose and set, and the long nights followed: hardly a ripple in the stream of human events. Cut off from the world, there was no way to measure time except by observing nature; feeling the cold, raw wind out of the North; and being witness to a brown world. The vines that clung to the buildings were stripped clean of leaves, and the deciduous trees appeared stark and rigid, unlike the pines beyond the river, which were still green and untouched by the changing season. (But even they groaned as the northern winds bent them low in submission.)

Often at night, the windows clattered, the building creaked as the wind whistled and shrieked as if in defiance, through the long hours of darkness.

All at once it occurred to me that I was not listening to Ralph and that Lucy's eyes were fastened upon me. Where had she been for the last few days? I looked away as if I had not seen her. The Colonel was watching Pamela. Pam's eyes were following Ralph, who was absorbed in what he was saying–the 'party line' as Bill called it.

"This is a physical disease," Ralph was saying. "The body adapts to alcohol, craves it, functions better with it. Dependence is followed by addiction; then deterioration, a long, slow decline–until near the end, when deterioration is rapid and death is almost certain."

Already, I could see that much was left out of this formula. What about the strange aberrations of the mind, the soaring self esteem, the grand exaltation, the rapid descent into despair? These highs and lows were not physical–they were of the mind, of the heart, of the spirit as well. When I was high, I exalted in my mastery of all problems and felt equal to any difficulty. As the liquor wore off, my energy was gone and my elation changed to despondency. No longer sustained by alcohol, I entered into a black world where I was weak, without strength, and quite unable to face life. The golden shaft of light that pierced the gloom when I drank was extinguished.

When I drank, I prevailed under that glorious light. Those hours of total peace, the harmony within, the sense of power were what I sought. The great self esteem–was it only a state of mind? Had it vanished completely in coming here? If only this sense of unity and harmony would return; no price would be too high to pay if it could be sustained. Slowly, I was beginning to see that my happiness was an illusion. The wild swings of emotion, like a pendulum, carried me upward toward the heavens, into the clouds that shielded me from harsh reality. There, I perched for a moment upon that giddy height– only to be plunged into the depths of fear, anxiety, and hopelessness– into a world where I was lost.

Dull as each day seemed at Maplewood, where I followed the same routine and listened to the tedious and repetitive speeches, I observed a certain evenness of disposition and a feeling of peace. Accepting the routine gave me a hold on reality. Engaging others in conversation on trivial matters had a soothing effect, holding my mind in check, and stopping, for a moment, the wild, uncontrolled voices which had been leading me toward madness.

Once, I encouraged the proud dreams that accompanied the happier moments when I drank. Now, I desired only sanity. One step into this nightmare (by allowing my mind to wander into the world of fantasy) might tip the balance.

My problems were not the only cause of darkness. My blindness and my perverse will led me. I needed money, because it gave value to my life. It sustained me and helped those around me. Working, striving, planning, and taking risks gave meaning, a purpose to my life, and increased my self esteem. For years, I had realized that my real worth–whatever that might be–depended not upon wealth, but other qualities: the growth and development of the whole person. But ambition clouded my mind. My heart was seared with the desire for more.

The threat of losing everything was almost more than my mind would accept. Yet, this was not the only reason for my mind being cut loose from its moorings, to flounder upon high seas beyond my control. Was it suffering? Everyone suffers. I was no stranger to pain. Something has happened to bring me so close to destruction. I could laugh and say that I controlled alcohol and go on rationalizing forever. Even in an institution I could pursue the questions, seeking answers to my conflicts–knowing all the while that I was not right with the world.

This world might be out of joint with what it was intended to be, and not an ideal place in which to survive, but, nevertheless, there were many survivors. Many did adjust. I would. I would either find a way soon or madness would possess me. I had to find the truth. The time had come. Here, now, I would have to chart a new course, and follow it even though there was no light within me, nothing to guide me save for my faith–my weak faith.

Goodbye booze. Goodbye illusions, wild dreams, fantasies–and wealth, too. If I find sobriety, it might give a new direction to my life. I accept the challenge. Will this open for me a new world that I have not seen before? Will I see vistas of strange landscapes, envision new ideas, give birth to renewed hopes, feelings and sensations (so long lying dormant, buried deep by ambition, by hardness, by the cold realities of the business world)? I do not know who I am: determining that will be a new discovery–a challenge. I see things more clearly than those around me–or is that an illusion, too? Others say that I am a alcoholic which I never believed until today. To discover that I am alcoholic during Ralph's conference is ironic indeed.

When I listened to Ralph I saw that he was not clear at all, that he blurred all distinctions, and that he was unable to see when self concern ought to give way to a higher concern for someone injured by our drinking. In seeing his hypocrisy I suddenly recognized that I, too, was a hypocrite for I pretended to be what I was not. If, in this room, the light has broken through what changes are going to take place within me? Does it mean now that I recognize my alcoholism, that my mind, my will, and my heart will be freed from bondage? If I have been a slave to this drug surely I ought to be set free now.

But how my heart has resisted. I am at the brink of madness, yet so much of me has resisted giving in to truth. Ralph has made it all so simple saying that our addiction is mainly physiological which indicates that we are under a physical compulsion to drink. The appetites of the flesh did not drive me. Something else was consuming me. Something sinister was causing these wild aberrations of the mind–and these changes were not physical. The other changes, the rise and fall of my emotions, these violent swings, going upward–now elated, now filled with pride and confidence–then plunging into the abyss of utter darkness and despair. My superiority when drinking, my disregard of others, even the possibility of doing grave physical harm was evidence of deterioration far more serious than any physical addiction. That I am physically and mentally sick is obvious. But there is more than this: a battle rages as unseen forces struggle to possess my will, to set my future course, to determine my actions. With my will enslaved, my outward appearance would not change, but I would no longer be free.

But now I see the truth, the scales have fallen from my eyes. What a release of tension! For a moment, my spirit soared, and I felt free, light as a bird. I saw the answer. Surely this would not be a struggle. I wanted to cry out that now, at last, I was cured! The sun would shine again! The world was wonderful!

As I sat, joyful with my newfound peace of mind, my elation slowly began to slip away and reality reared its head. A still small voice was saying within me: "Wait. Do not be deluded. You have seen only a glimmer of light–a break in the clouds during a storm. Now your real battle begins. You are still blind. There is much to learn. Pray God you survive. There is no certainty you will win the battle. Your recovery is in doubt–the battle is yet to be won or lost. The real test is only beginning." I shuddered. What more could I endure?

Chairs were scraping the floor near me. Someone pulled my arm.

"Wake up! Are you going to remain in that trance?" I looked up. Ralph had finished and left the room.

I heard Bill laugh. "Did Ralph have that much effect upon you? Didn't sound to me that you were that impressed."

For some reason unknown to me I blurted out, "Ralph can chase Pam for all I care."

Bill replied, "Now, now, Mark. Anyone can see that Pam is a sweet girl. You heard how she weeps for her husband."

"And how she resists him, all on lofty principles," I added.

"She's not been a drunk like the rest of us," remarked Roy. "She has some sort of compulsion to eat. The protein diet, lots of meats, cheese and eggs, has done wonders. What a figure."

"Her figure? So you fellows did notice," spoke up the Colonel. "If I had her alone for a while she wouldn't be the same again. Her voice would be deeper, and she'd no longer sound like a 'baby doll.'"

"An old burned out soldier. What do you have to offer that Kewpie doll?" I asked. "At best you would disappoint her or merely arouse her curiosity. She needs a young man."

"Gentlemen, you do not know what this old soldier has to offer–experience, technique–and Southern charm."

"Well," I said, "we'll never know. I have a feeling that someone is already in line ahead of you. And that someone is here."

"You are a fox," said the Colonel.

"That I am."

CHAPTER 12

Roy caught up with Ralph in the corridor. Ralph, seeing him, nodded toward his office. They entered and closed the door. I walked across the hall and entered a room, hardly large enough for two people. Into it was crowded a refrigerator, a coffee maker and some supplies. Opening the refrigerator door, I saw various foods, fruits, cheeses, and cold meats. I took an apple to eat later, filled a mug with coffee and lit a cigarette. The coffee was hot. As I stood sipping the hot coffee, I could hear voices through the thin walls. Ralph was explaining to Roy why he was not ready to leave Maplewood.

Roy cut in, his voice rising. "How do you know all this? I think you know more about fishing for Coho salmon than alcohol. What is your training? You've been sober for two years, Ralph. Now you are a professional able to tell me when to reenter society."

"Not just me, Roy. This is not wholly my decision. I only recommend."

"How much longer do you expect me to stay?"

"Two weeks–maybe longer."

"Or longer, you say. Just like that. Didn't you, hear me, Ralph? I have a wife, a job. I want to get out of here."

"You are not ready, Roy."

As Roy's voice grew louder, Ralph's voice grew sharper: they could be heard up and down the corridor. There was no talking among those listening in. The Colonel, standing nearby, was smiling. Dean looked serious as usual. The Admiral wore a blank expression which caused me to wonder if he heard the angry voices. Even Mary was silent for the moment. The thought of another month at Maplewood distressed me. If Roy was not ready, what did they think of me? What were the others thinking? Mary, of course, would be happy–after all, this was home to her.

Roy began asking for a reason. "You know I've been here four, no, five weeks. What trouble have I caused you?"

"You are critical, argumentative and you do not grasp the program clearly. You don't yet accept that you are an alcoholic."

"Didn't I tell you I wasn't going to drink again?"

"You did indeed."

"Isn't that enough?"

"No."

"Why?"

"You don't understand yourself, your weakness, how frail sobriety is. . .

"But you do, Ralph. Is that it? You know me better than myself? You can't spell–but you are an authority on alcohol and fishing."

"Stop interrupting!" Ralph's voice was as loud and angry as Roy's. "You are sullen most of the time. You sit at the meetings, staring at whoever is teaching, defiant, having little to say, and showing no apparent interest in the questions or answers. When you do speak, you are arguing rather than seeking information about alcoholics. Now you feel that because you have put your time in, you can leave with our approval. Well, you can't."

"I was told–and my wife, too–that five or six weeks were enough. Now you are going back on your word."

"Often that is enough, but not for you. Every case is different."

"Damn you, Ralph! Damn the whole staff and this isolated prison. I'm leaving in the morning."

"You will not."

"Who will stop me?"

Ralph's voice came through low and harsh. "Will you read this letter?"

There was silence. I sipped on my coffee. As I waited for the explosion, I lit a cigarette. I looked at the set expressions of those standing in the hallway or seated in the nearby lounge. No one was talking–just waiting, listening.

Roy's voice broke the silence. "What's this, Ralph? What does it mean?"

"Just what the letter says, Roy. Only one word is missing–your name, where you see the blank. Here, let me read it for you.

'Dear Mr. Davidson:

'For six weeks Roy has been in treatment at Maplewood for acute alcoholism. Although there is evidence of progress, it is not sufficient for us to recommend his return to full employment.

'Not all alcoholics respond to treatment in the same manner. There are so many unknowns: the degree of physical dependency, the damage to the patient's system, the attitude of the individual, the stress of home life, the type of employment–these are a few of the factors that are considered. If Roy returned to work in his present condition, we feel he would suffer a relapse. Further treatment and indoctrination would improve his chances of a full recovery.

'Sincerely,

'Ralph Schneider, Counselor.'"

"You wrote this letter some time ago. It is a form letter."

"This letter is similar to others we use."

Indoctrination!" Roy was shouting now. "You have been filling me with booze talk for five weeks. That's all I've heard. What more can you tell me? Why don't you give me an examination? You have no basis for your judgment except your opinion."

"If you leave, this letter will follow the same day."

"I'm leaving."

"Have it your way."

I walked outside the building, not waiting to see Roy leave Ralph's office. Mary was standing in the path reading another poem to Dean. Absorbed in the reading, he did not notice me. Her talk was so unlike the poem I heard. Did she feel earthbound too? Helpless, in an alien world? Was she, too, lost, unable to cope with life? So unlike the birds riding upon the air currents, using the wind to carry them aloft. Like all creatures except man, the birds adjusted, without effort, to every condition of nature: so at home in the world, so content, enabled by instinct to survive in all seasons under all conditions–the harshest winters, the driest, hottest summers. Man was the alien. Adjustment to life, at best, was unceasing effort, with loneliness, with fear, with boredom, with constant struggle–these were man's lot in life.

"But a spirit strong to surmount all earthly things," Mary quoted. She was being romantic. She who could not surpass or overcome any problem in the real world.

Dean appeared to hang upon Mary's words. Except at the meetings (where she was strangely quiet) Mary was always talking, always exuberant. Everything to her was exciting and filled with promise. She saw life as an adventure, as a child sees it, and she was ready to explore new worlds each day: nothing was too trivial or insignificant to attract her attention. Seeing me at last, she acted as if I had been gone for ages.

With the excitement of a child making a new discovery she said, "Mark, I've been reading poetry to Dean. Poems about nature are so uplifting, especially in this mountain setting among the trees, and where everyone is so congenial."

Congenial? I wondered if she had overheard any of the talk between Roy and Ralph, or for that matter, between the Colonel and Peg.

Going along with her mood I said, "You have found what we are all searching for–serenity–that peace the world cannot give."

"Oh, you are making fun of me."

"Not really. I am more inclined to envy your good fortune. You have something I would give a good deal to possess. Even so, a few more weeks at Maplewood will be enough for me."

"You don't mean that, do you? You don't want to leave? Dean, you are not leaving, are you?"

Dean's face clouded slightly. "Mary, I have been meaning to tell you that I am going home. In fact my wife will be here tomorrow."

For a moment Mary's face looked sad–then she brightened. Following her gaze, I saw Roy coming toward us.

"Roy? Did you hear that Dean is leaving us? We were having such great times–now you and I must walk together."

Ignoring Mary, Roy looked at Dean. "So you made it. Good! But–I'm leaving, too. I'll be out of here tonight. That bastard, Ralph, tried to blackmail me into staying."

Mary grasped her heart. "Not you too, Roy?" Mary, for once, appeared lost and showed signs of fear. She looked at me. "What will happen, Mark, with everyone leaving?"

"Mary, Mary," I said. "This is not home–not the real world. We are here because we are sick. We are here to be cured. Aren't you happy to see Dean and Roy recovered? Now they are going to test their sobriety while we stand by in the bleachers cheering them on, waiting for the outcome. Dean will make it and Roy, too, in spite of what Ralph says. He's not God. He doesn't know Roy's strength of character. Ralph used Dean often enough as an example of someone who responded well to treatment. He felt so sure about you, Dean, that

I cannot see why he sees Roy in a different light. And Roy–you'll prove he's wrong."

Mary was not interested in what I said. After all, alcohol was not a problem with her. Losing companionship of the group was the threat. Seeing us leave, one by one; the eventual dissolution of the group, meant the end of her world –her life at Maplewood. I suspected that these were the only true friendships she had ever had: she would have difficulty in accepting the fact that these friendships would soon be ending, and would remain only as a memory–a fading dream of a time when friends once listened and treated her as an equal. In that world on the other side of the mountain I knew how hard it could be on someone as childish and simple as Mary.

Roy looked at me for a moment.

"Mark, you're too clever to let Ralph outwit you. Think you already know he doesn't like you. Watch out for him. Goodbye, Dean; goodbye, Mary." Saying this he turned abruptly and walked toward his room.

The three of us began walking. Mary looked toward me. "Lucy is my roommate. At night, if we can't sleep, I go to the kitchen and bring back pears, apples, and oranges–sometimes lunch meat and cheese. We have a picnic."

"How does Lucy like all this?" I asked.

"She says she is not hungry but I insist that she eat. Lucy is strong and lissome–swift as a cat. I wonder where she gets her strength? She eats so little."

Hearing the Colonel's voice, I turned to see the Colonel with Bill and the Admiral. "Seeing you fellows together does not auger well for someone," I said.

Bill chuckled. "The Admiral has been trying to convince the Colonel, without much success, that he is out of condition from overeating. The Colonel has just returned from seeing Mack, our cook."

"I told the cook we were not rabbits: that all those greens–beans, lettuce, carrots and celery and watery soup did not constitute substantial fare. We needed a big steak for a change."

"And what did Mack say?" I asked. "The insolent pup looked me over and said I ate enough to fill a regiment, and that this was not a pleasure resort. He had the temerity to call our fare a balanced diet!"

The Admiral, showing some life, pointed to the Colonel's large protruding stomach, and laughed.

"I thought an army traveled on its stomach. It looks to me like you have enough provisions stashed away to travel with a camel across the desert."

"All right, Admiral, it didn't take the navy long after the war to discover they had a surplus of warships–and officers, too. What did you learn about fighting, anyway, sitting out the war in a shipyard?"

"Which war are you talking about, Colonel? The South – contrary to your opinion–lost the Civil War. Or are you as confused as the Japanese soldier, found in the jungle, long after the last war was over, who was still searching for the enemy?"

Bill interrupted to announce, "Here comes Lucy. Let's walk to the road. A little hike will give us an appetite for supper."

"What's coming up tomorrow?" I questioned.

"Don't you know?" asked the Colonel, giving me a quick smile. "I look for the usual fare. Either Ralph will tell us that this is a selfish program, and how we must, if necessary, cut out wife or mistress or whoever threatens our sobriety. On the other hand, it might be Eva, with chain, short skirt and all, telling us how to control ourselves with the ABCs. The nurse has yet to be heard from. She could tell us about vitamins. Why not hear from that new girl, Pamela? She could tell her tragic tale–how to abandon a weak husband, the pain, the loneliness she endures, and what the future holds for a helpless girl cut adrift, alone, in the mountain retreat."

"But you overlooked Dr. Neilstrom," I said.

"Yes, that's right, Mark, you've only heard him once. You've missed Kiss and Tell."

"What's that?"

"We sit in a room, and the counselors are at the rear. Stella, and sometimes Ralph, are seated at the front of the room. The doctor is at center stage, and appears to be very much in command. His symbol of office is his clipboard and the sheaf of papers he has on each one of us. Our names are listed, and alongside are the remarks of the individual counselors who evaluate us, good or bad. It's just like being in military service, a factory, or a political rally–the man with the clipboard is the authoritarian figure."

"I don't see anything ominous about all that," I said.

"That is where you're wrong. The doctor will ask each one to give a talk. He insists upon each one speaking, and no one can slip by without giving an account of his progress."

Lucy added, "The doctor means nothing to me. I'll tell him what he wants to hear. That always seems to satisfy him."

For some reason I felt uneasy. "What about Stella? She seems in charge of everything around here."

The Colonel appeared delighted with the question. His eyes sparkled.

"She always sits next to the doctor. He doesn't make a move without her. Sometimes she sits throughout an entire meeting without saying a word. In special cases she sometimes takes an unusual interest. But with you, it will be different. She and the doctor want to humble you. They are waiting for this hour to cut you down to size before the group–to see you flounder and crawl. Your detachment, your self assurance–your air of superiority–has infuriated them."

"This is all very touching, Colonel. I don't fear them, although I do have fears–and I do see that I am alcoholic."

"Aha! You do recognize your problem. Maybe Lucy can help you with it."

"Mark is fine, just as he is," Lucy replied firmly.

"You see, you do have admirers," laughed the Colonel. "Stella will like seeing you sitting next to Lucy at 'Kiss and Tell.' You can describe for the rest of us how your relationship helps solve your drinking problem."

Lucy nudged the Colonel in the stomach. "You are such a wit. What we do is no concern of yours or the doctor's or Stella's or anyone's."

"More the point," I added, becoming uneasy at the direction that the conversation was going, "there is nothing to tell."

"We shall see," the Colonel said. "Everyone will be interested in hearing how you suddenly recognized that you are one of us."

"Come on," Bill said, "it is time to eat again. We have a long night to think about what we will tell the doctor tomorrow about our progress toward sobriety."

As we walked back along the path, Lucy began to question the Colonel about his life. She asked questions that I could see he did not like. She was deliberately attempting to embarrass him; to get her revenge for the direct approach he had taken with me. "Kiss and tell." So that was the game. I was to expose myself, and eat my entrails before everyone's eyes: tell about my fears, my disillusionment, my sense of loss, and my strange feelings which left me almost detached from reality, no longer exercising any sense of control over my thoughts or feelings. I was, I suppose, expected to tell them how I loathed those bright lights in the halls, the sterile, antiseptic rooms, the boring, simple, dull speeches given without learning or preparation. I should tell them how I dreaded the darkness and the deep shadows, and the hideous shapes that moved in and out of my nightmares, signifying, to me, some monstrous evil that I could never comprehend or control. And the sounds: my heart jumping, pounding; the electric shocks throughout my body; the movements of doors, voices so loud they were like the crashing of cymbals; the strange sounds in the building, and the shrieking wind that never let up, but howled and raged through the night.

Nor must I overlook the cries at night, and people going in and out of rooms. I would confide that when I could no longer bear the confinement of the building, I sought comfort in the cold night air, where I saw the mist or the dull light from a lamp or the faint glow of the moon and the trees stripped bare, still and watchful; their twisted forms, so enduring–their strength unlike mine. I would have to admit to my companions that I was frail, insignificant, and of no consequence when compared to the might of the trees.

Imagining myself before the group at "Kiss and Tell" I became frightened. I could see myself pouring out a stream of disjoined thought, trying to describe the changes taking place within me. As I talked, and my eyes met Audrey's clear, steady gaze, would her eyes tell me that my words had touched her? Eva and the nurse would surely watch me, and Ralph, if he were sitting there, would have his revenge (revenge for what?). As I thought of what lay before me, I could almost feel Stella's hard eyes upon me and the group's attentiveness as it waited and watched for any sign of change. Stella and the doctor would be judge and jury, who measured the progress of the sheep herded between themselves and the counselors at the back of the room.

I understood that in our speeches, we would be asked to measure our progress. In this unnatural setting, cut off from society, we would be asked to tell, objectively, "how far we had come." I would be able to say, I supposed, that I was alcoholic, and perhaps mad, as well. (Did it not help to be at least a bit mad to survive in this world?) Why not accept it? Embrace my fate? How I longed for peace! Giving in–admitting my alcoholism, publicly–might bring me the peace I so sought.

Someone nudged me. It was Lucy. "Dreamer, you look so serious. What goes on inside of you? You look so strange–your eyes glitter. I do not know whether you are surprised, happy or mad."

Lucy's word 'mad' was all that reached me. I laughed out of fear.

"Of course, I'm mad. You ought not to be seen with me. Not alone anyway."

She looked at me boldly. "I don't fear you."

Something in her smile, hidden, enigmatic, caused me to remark, "Perhaps, I ought to fear you."

As we reached the door of the dining hall, Bill spoke up. "If the two of you don't speed up supper will be over. Let's go in and see if the Colonel's complaints have improved our rations."

Lucy took my arm as we walked into the dining room and joined a larger group. I was aware that many eyes were watching us. I picked up a tray and handed it to Lucy so that she would release my arm.

The irrepressible Colonel, after telling the cook to go easy on the greens that Mack was heaping high upon his plate, said loudly, "Was that you prowling the halls again last night, Mark?"

"I'm glad you asked, Colonel. As a matter of fact I did see someone go into Peg's room. Someone large. Could that have been you?"

"No! Are you sure? That's one room I wouldn't go near. She might cry rape–or worse, pull me in."

"Of course," I said, "everyone knows you are irresistible. Your easy manner and your charm and regal bearing would turn any woman's head."

"True dignity is hard to conceal," said Bill slowly shaking his head.

The Colonel enjoyed this attention. His plate was piled high with peas, carrots and string beans, and with a large slice of roast beef and a generous serving of boiled potatoes with gravy. He concentrated upon eating from his plate for several minutes, ignoring our comments. After he consumed a portion of his food he looked up.

"The dignity and honor of a Southern gentleman must always be maintained. That is not always easy, when I find I must associate with you country folks from the North."

"Have no fear about your honor, or your innocence, Colonel," said Peg. "You lost that when you began chasing those little black girls around the plantation."

Before the Colonel could answer, we heard someone stutter. All eyes turned toward the druggist whom I missed seeing when I entered the dining room.

"Francis, I thought you graduated to the funny farm, or did someone say you had eloped with Peg?"

Peg, who was sitting with several women, spoke up. "Colonel, you not only disrupt the meetings, keep us up half the night with your immature antics and boorish behavior, but you belittle someone who is very ill."

"Now that you mentioned it, Peg," answered the Colonel, "since when did Francis receive the key to the door of the hospital? What do you think this place is? A health resort? There's not one person that I've encountered (certainly not you) that is not sick. Some of us are sicker than others, it's true. Now, I'm not capable of saying what stage of sickness each person is in, how far each person has deteriorated, or whether everyone will make a complete recovery. From my experience working with men in the service I'm convinced that some of us will not make it. Of course I was using heavy humor as far as Francis is concerned." Turning to Francis the Colonel continued, No intent on my part to offend you, Francis."

Francis nodded and smiled, "I . . . I always like . . . to listen to you, Colonel. You . . . you . . . console me like a bubbling brook."

Everyone laughed at Francis. The Colonel finished eating what was on his plate and then began spooning a large dish of plum sauce.

"Great plums. Helps a man to stay regular. Don't you think so, Bill?"

"Whatever you say, Colonel," said Bill, "but the way you pack the food in, I wouldn't want to be around if there was a back up."

"No problem there," the Colonel replied. "I want to be well fortified for the big conference tomorrow when Mark tells the doctor how he saw the light. That's going to be a scene that I don't want to miss," he said, finishing the last of his plum sauce.

"You know well, Colonel," I said, "that the doctor has heard my tale. There's nothing new for him. Anything I will say he's heard before."

"But I have a feeling, Mark," insisted the Colonel, "that you will make the meeting interesting. You are educated; you have that air of assurance about you that an intellectual like the doctor will notice."

"What you're saying is that I'm a challenge for him. I fear you miss the point. I came here to learn."

"Come on, Colonel," said Bill, "you must be fortified by now. Let's play cards." Looking at me, Bill added, "Don't let the Colonel worry you. I have a feeling that you will hold your own with anyone here."

"Thanks," I said. "I came to learn, not to challenge anyone." Rising from my chair, I looked at Lucy and the others sitting at the table and said, "I'm going to my room and read for a while before Gene comes in and turns off the light. Somehow, I feel tomorrow is going to be an exciting day."

Going to my room, I stretched out on the bed, turned on the lamp and began reading one of a collection of short stories. I could not concentrate. My mind was too concerned with the events of the day; each time I thought about Ralph I could hear Pam's baby doll voice. She affected such sweet innocence, but the way Ralph looked at her was not innocent at all. Pam looked at him so sweetly, she was not aware of those eyes—or was she an actress? There was noise in the hall as small groups passed by going to their rooms. Everyone seemed to be turning in early; perhaps they were uneasy about Kiss and Tell. The days were short. Gene came into the room, began to undress, looking at the book I was reading, but said nothing. He would be upset if I continued to read.

"Gene," I said, "I'm going out for some air. I'll take off my shoes when I come in so you won't hear me."

"Doesn't make any difference," he answered, "I don't sleep anyway, never sleep at night."

There was an exit door near our room where I let myself out into the night. The cold air cleared my mind. With the clouds gathering overhead it appeared very dark to me as I followed the path to the road. I walked briskly to warm myself. The night was still, the exercise I felt would help me rest; walking alone I reached the road much faster. Coming back along the path I realized it was not very late so I decided to cut off the path through the maples to the recreational building. Vaguely I remembered that among all those records there were a few that might lighten my spirits. As I approached the building shielded by the trees I stopped just short of the path, hearing someone's voice. It was Ralph.

"No one is up, Pam. We can go inside. We can spend the night and slip back to our rooms before daylight."

"Are you sure it is all right, Ralph?" It was the childish voice of Pam.

"Pam," Ralph said, "you need me. Trust me. We can leave here in a few hours. It is not unusual for a counselor to be up and around. I'll see you get back all right."

They moved on along the path, their voices fading more with each step. I stood still, and did not move until they entered the recreation building. Then I walked back to my room amused at the thought of sweet, innocent Pamela who was so concerned with her husband's drinking.

CHAPTER 13

There was silence at breakfast except for short bursts of nervous laughter. Unable to finish eating, I emptied my tray and walked down the hall. At one of the exit doors I stepped outside and lit up a cigarette.

The air was cold. I looked toward the pine trees and the mountain peaks where I could see clouds forming–black clouds that were heavy and ominous. It was too cold for rain. There was no wind. The mountain peaks had turned white; the thick, dark clouds might hang over the mountains, or later move over Maplewood. Anyway, now that I saw the danger of snow, I would be careful so as not to be trapped in the woods. The thought of a search party looking for me relieved my tension. I could hear Stella saying, "I knew he was a troublemaker the moment I first saw him."

I threw the remainder of my cigarette into the cinder path, and laughed at the thought of Stella being anxious about me, if she knew I was in the woods; especially if a snow storm was coming. My spirits lifted, I entered the hall and walked briskly to the conference room. For several moments I stood in the entrance. The room was arranged as I had pictured it: in the rear sat the counselors, the center the patients, in the front, facing the center and the rear, was Dr. Neilstrom with Stella at his side. All the faces appeared pale under the white lights. I picked a chair on the far side of the room where, by only a slight turn of my head, I could see the entrance and the counselors.

Stella was alert, watching every movement in the room as each entered, and looked about, bewildered, confused, and obviously nervous, uttering something to a companion before taking a chair. Lucy entered, and hesitated only an instant before her quick eyes saw me across the room. She walked toward me, ignoring the stares of the counselors, then seated herself beside me. She looked at me and smiled.

Turning to face the doctor my eyes met Stella's: her eyes gleamed and her face was hard. As she stared, unblinking, at me, I felt stripped of all sense of dignity. I lowered my head and turned my eyes toward Lucy. The sight of her chilled me. Her face was set in a mocking smile–she was defiant, leering at Stella–challenging her. I could feel the hatred that passed between the two like an electric current. Such strong emotion–such loathing! What was the cause? Was I playing an unrecognized role not even apparent to myself? Were the dark forces (with which I contended alone at night) now unleashed, spreading their confusion, dissension and hatred? Were they enticing a girl who was no match for their power? Were they, indeed, invading Lucy's mind? They would easily consume her if she was not aware of their presence.

As I reconsidered these thoughts, I saw them for what they were–utter nonsense. The two women hated each other because of jealousy or some indefinable reason unknown to me. And my "dark forces" had nothing to do with it.

The door closed, the chairs scraped the floor, and the tension increased as Dr. Neilstrom arose.

"Those of you who have been with us for a time know about this part of our program. It is helpful to your recovery to work with us in measuring your progress. We cannot form an accurate judgment unless we hear, from each of you, what you are learning–and know your attitudes and feelings toward the program. Sometimes what I learn from a patient's words is encouraging. Sometimes what I recognize is a destructive attitude, and only a vague knowledge, mingled with falsehoods, about alcoholism. A negative response from a patient combined with misinformation and ignorance leads to holding on to these old ideas, and this reluctance to 'let go' can precipitate a relapse.

"By now you must know what 'old ideas' are. Our society encourages drinking. Nothing begins or ends without it. We drink for many reasons or no reason at all. Our 'old ideas' tell us we must drink to escape reality, that life, without alcohol, is meaningless. So we wait, with increasing tension, for time to pass–those painful, dreary, endless hours–until it is time to drink again. For the alcoholic, drinking no longer requires a social occasion. Friends are not needed. He drinks alone. He drinks to fulfill his destiny. He drinks because he is compelled to do so. Alcohol is his life. Without it, there is a grey world where everything is dark and hopeless, where there is no joy or happiness. Without liquor, all of life is, for him, without meaning. There is no tomorrow–only a succession of painful moments that go on forever. Drinking ends this hell for a brief hour–and for that hour all the pain that will come afterwards is forgotten.

"None of you can drink, because your control is gone. You cannot win this battle against alcoholism if you drink, because your body can no longer resist the toxins of alcohol. You have no defense, and you are powerless over it.

"Believing the 'next time' (another of the 'old ideas') will be different is a fallacy. The 'next time'–and the next hundred times after that–will mean only failure, greater mental and physical deterioration– and eventual total loss of health, or death by accident or disease.

"How many times have you tried drinking socially and failed? As your mind clears and you reflect upon the past, it must become increasingly evident to each of you that you cannot drink again.

He looked about the room. From my vantage point at the side of the room I could see many of the faces. Everyone sat at rigid attention. Ralph was eying Pam. Turning my head slowly; I looked to the rear of the room. Audrey met my glance, and stared at me. I received no inkling from her of what was to come. The doctor's voice continued at a hurried pace.

"To live without alcohol you must transcend to a higher level of conduct. Hereafter, your stress level will be lower. Many acts of life (some trivial, hardly recorded before in your mind) will now become difficult and burdensome, and will cause pain and anxiety. Simply being polite at a party, as you listen to cocktail chatter, and the same story–punctuated with laughter–for the third time can be difficult. By living on this higher level, you show greater strength than some of those around you. This can only be done by making radical changes in your life. To succeed every effort must be made: grandiosity and selfishness and every vice must be rooted up. To do this requires determination and a lifetime struggle. This high level–sad to say— can't be reached and maintained in any other way.

"Some of you will make radical changes in your life. The one you are living with may threaten your sobriety by his or her drinking. To protect your sobriety, you will separate or get a divorce. Rest is needed. Any extreme is to be avoided. Any situation that causes stress, conflict, violent swings of emotion, confrontations, going too long without eating, improper diet–can lead to a lowering of resistance, and the reversion to active alcoholism. Following up with AA is essential. To survive long without it is impossible for many, difficult for anyone. For instance–and to avoid becoming just a dry alcoholic–serenity is found best by following the twelve steps of the AA program."

The doctor paused and turned to Stella. He hesitated for a moment, glanced at his clipboard, adjusted his glasses and slowly looked over the group.

'Kiss and tell.' Who was to be measured first? How would this group respond? Would every tale sound alike, follow the same pattern? Would each speaker learn (as the talks went along) what to say, what to hold back, what impressed the doctor, and what caused a reprimand? How many would accept the doctor's concept of measuring progress by exposing their innermost thoughts and feelings?

To me, all this seemed as confusing as the disease. How could anyone who drank freely for twenty-five years, addicted during the later years, measure progress in a few weeks in this controlled setting?

To attempt to do so was idiotic. To measure progress (something tangible, for every eye to see), to open a room long closed and forgotten, to let in the first shaft of light (and then among forgotten dreams and abandoned hopes find some marvelous ideal, a new concept as yet untried) and strut with this as evidence of renewal–this I could not do. No one would enter that forbidden city! Never would I allow anyone to see that heart or the conflict that raged there, nor what I saw or what I believed. Only bits and pieces–that was all. I mentally defied anyone to try to piece them together–to find the whole person– so they could say:

"Yes. That Mark. I knew him well." No one has known me, and no one shall. I fear that even I will never know who I am.

The doctor suddenly fixed his attention upon Francis. "Tell us, Francis, what have you learned? You have been with us for more than a month."

Silence followed.

The doctor's voice became sharp. "I am asking you to give us a measure of your progress, Francis."

Everyone looked at the druggist. He began to stutter. "I . . . I can't meas . . . measure any progress."

"Why not?"

After several false starts he said, "Everything is so confusing."

"Why?"

Again Francis suffered the same confusion of speech and followed with several halting statements, finally blurting, "I can't talk."

For some reason this answer infuriated the doctor. "Talk. Why can't you talk? You are talking now."

But the druggist remained silent. Quickly the doctor moved along, now visibly irritated by his encounter with the druggist. He called first on one, then another in the group to respond. The talks followed a pattern. Everyone was resolved to end his self destruction by following the program: never to drink again, to follow the proper diet supported by vitamins, to attend AA meetings, always keeping before his eyes what drinking had done and what the end would be if there was a relapse. All of these dicta appeared so simple to follow.

It was too much to expect that I would be overlooked. As I heard my name, I thought I detected an increase of tension in the room. Stella was looking directly at me. Her facial expression, her eyes–her entire manner conveyed hostility.

"Twenty years of drinking," I began, "and four weeks of sobriety. Five years of drinking for each week without alcohol isn't much of a yardstick by which to measure my progress. That brings to mind the river that flows near this building, which we can hear now, as the water rushes out of the mountains over the river rocks. The movement of the water, the wearing away of the rocks in the river bed has continued for centuries. Measuring my progress would be as futile for me as attempting to measure the wear of those stone in the water."

Dr. Neilstrom exploded. "We are not measuring river rock! We are measuring your quality of sobriety. Once before I asked you to forget about your books. You don't sleep at night like the others–you prowl the halls and the grounds and no one seems to know what you are about. You cause confusion and resentment in our conferences by your attitude. You challenge rather than accept. Your four weeks of sobriety hardly qualifies you as a master of this subject."

Stella had not taken her eyes from me. Her hostility ignited my anger. At least Neilstrom was consumed by the desire to solve a problem. His indictment was not personal. I opened my mouth to speak, hesitated, and remained silent. What was to be gained by making a fool of myself again? How could I outline, in a comprehensive manner, all the confusion within me? The conflicts, the struggle with unseen forces beyond my power to understand or control. As helpless as a rudderless ship among the reefs, I was not equipped to understand forces I could not see, to combat a riot of dissenting voices or to find calmer waters to sort out my desires and urges, so that I might cast aside those that did not fit and retain those which led on to growth, life, and hope.

While my mind was so distorted, my emotions were not to be reined in, and silence was the only safe course. I had little remaining will to resist if the doctor fathomed my present state of mind. I wanted out of there! The room was beginning to close in upon me. I could feel tightness in my head, and there was a pressure at the back of my neck. I could feel the eyes boring into me from all sides.

I was a fool! An angry fool, unable to offer a proper defense.

My voice sounded strange as I said, "You will have it your way. You are the doctor; I am the patient. It does occur to me that you asked a question. I answered you straightforwardly."

"Mark, you're not getting the message here," Neilstrom retorted. "Your progress is not good, although I don't say that you haven't made a start."

"I recognize alcoholism and my addiction, if that is what you want to hear."

"But you don't believe it!" Neilstrom challenged. "So you really understand what alcohol has done to you, and what you must do to change your life?"

I did not answer, for I knew I was not ready to leave Maplewood—at least not in the eyes of the doctor and his staff. My God, what was it about me that they resented so much? How late was it? As soon as this meeting was over I knew I would go for a walk into the woods. There was a feeling of a storm in the air, but I no longer cared. I felt desperate, and vowed that I would follow the path across the river and walk until sunset.

As soon as the conference ended, I hurried from the room (ignoring Lucy). In my room I put on a warm jacket, and slipped into a pair of walking shoes. I went to my door, looked up and down the hall—then walked out of aside door and headed toward the river.

In only a few minutes I was over the bridge and into the trees, among the tall, old growth of pines that cut off a clear view of the clouds that were threatening to open up at any time. I had seen these same clouds, in the early morning, over a distant mountain. Now they had moved toward Maplewood filling the sky above me–seemingly darker and more ominous than before. As I looked up I saw a flash of light followed by a distant rumble. I blew on my hands. My, it was cold, too cold to rain–but was it too cold to snow? I felt restless, tugged by a desperate urge to move on–to explore the trail wherever it led.

The fear of becoming lost was overcome by the release of tension, in seeing the trees clearly grouped. There was a feeling of permanence about them, and I felt a sense of grandeur as I stood for a moment, marveling at the mystery of nature: how each tree was alike, yet upon closer scrutiny, each pine tree was different from every other pine tree in the forest–massed together but their individuality preserved. I moved on and the sound of my feet on the path startled a bird. It cried out as it fluttered out of sight. Except for my shoes crushing the twigs and the pine needles, there was hardly a sound. The wind was still, and there were no signs of life about me. It was as if the forest had been abandoned to me alone. Once as I stopped to observe a tree which had been struck by lightning, I thought I heard footsteps not far behind me.

After I had walked a considerable distance, the trees thinned, and I stepped out onto an open meadow. What I witnessed recalled to my mind paintings of mountain scenes. Nearby stood an old cabin with a moss covered roof. I approached the cabin, and saw that it was deserted. The door hung ajar, so I entered. Once my eyes had become adjusted to the gloom, I saw that the former inhabitants had left no tangible evidence of their occupancy save for a tired, old mattress.

I was tired from my walk, and a quick appraisal assured me that the mattress was at least clean enough to lie down upon. It was inviting, so I stretched out, gratefully, on my back, and surveyed the interior of the cabin.

The walls appeared solid. Looking up I saw the open rafters, but there was no light coming through the heavy shake roof. Whoever built this cabin was protected from the heavy snows of winter. As I looked out through the open door I heard the wind begin to move through the trees. At the first sign of snow I would hasten back down the path. There was time. No need to be snowbound. As I listened to the movement of the trees I felt at ease, almost a part of the woods. As the sound of the wind increased, I knew the snow would soon begin falling. I was not alarmed. I savored the peace of that moment.

To get a better view I raised myself on one elbow and surveyed the meadow through the open door. It was at that moment that I saw Lucy enter the clearing. Instantly I thought of leaving the cabin, hoping to avoid being seen. My hesitation gave Lucy enough time to see the cabin. She walked directly across the meadow, through the wild mountain grass, toward the open door. She had, as yet, not seen me. I did not move. If Lucy was following me, hiding from her could be tragic; for she could continue along the mountain trail thinking that I was on ahead. I saw the first flakes of snow. I shuddered to think what could happen if this romantic girl lost her way.

Lucy stopped at the open doorway when she saw me before entering the cabin. She did not appear surprised.

"Mark, I saw you when you left. You seemed to be in such a hurry, T. followed." She turned and looked out through the doorway. Snow flakes were falling. "What a pastoral setting: a trapper's cabin in a mountain meadow; there will be so many wild flowers in the spring."

Lucy looked about the small cabin, studying the interior until something attracted her interest.

"Mark, see here. There must have been an old cook stove. You can see the markings on the floor where it sat; above, near the ceiling, there is the hole for the stove pipe. Over here," she said pointing, "where the markings are on the wall, were shelves. What a cozy cabin. What a marvelous place to be alone. Truly a lover's cottage—and the two of us alone!"

"Why did you come after me?" I asked. "If you were seen following me into the woods, there might be trouble."

"How Victorian!"

"Say it. I'm prudish. Oh, what foolishness! I'm human–a man–not insensitive to you. But I'm here to get well, not to create other problems."

It occurred to me that I should get up. Before I could lift myself, she moved with the grace of a cat to position herself beside me. She placed a strong arm across my chest and threw one leg over me so that I could not move. She was warm, her body firm. I could feel her thigh upon my leg as she turned to face me. The rise and fall of her breasts was distracting as she pulled herself closer to me.

"Mark, let's make the most of this. I want you."

I lay there silent–a misplaced fool in a lovers' setting. I was an old warrior with a young mistress, stirred by passion, yet my mind strangely calm. (There were no voices now or dark spirits. They were waiting, watching for me to abandon myself to Lucy. It was always that way at the critical moment.) The choice was mine.

"Lucy, you don't want a worn out old fool for a lover."

"You're not old or a fool. Why do you put yourself down? You are just different–everyone sees that."

"A real oddity."

"No. Only different–an individual."

"But what about you, Lucy? Where do you go from here? Do you think about the future?"

"I have no future."

"You will not if that is your attitude."

"I want you now."

"There is no future for us. I don't want you that way."

She began to draw even close. "Do you want me to take you?"

"Don't be a fool. Look. The snow is beginning to fall. We must leave here. We must leave here or we might be snowbound."

Now, lying on my side and looking over Lucy's shoulder through the opening, I could see the flakes of snow, curling, floating from side to side as they disappeared onto the ground. As their numbers increased, the wind blew them in the door where they fell on the floor and dissolved, leaving no mark on the dry floor. I looked up again at the dark sky and the swirling, white snow, which almost concealed the nearby pine trees.

It was then that a form suddenly filled the doorway. It was Eva.

CHAPTER 14

"What are you up to? Get up."

Lucy did not move. She had interlocked her leg with mine. Feeling like a fool, I struggled to free myself. Sitting on the edge of the mattress I watched as Lucy rose slowly to her feet. Eva was talking rapidly, describing our behavior as unseemly.

"You ought to be thinking about sobriety, not 'making out' in the woods. You were admitted for treatment, not for this purpose. . . ." Lucy challenged her. "Shut your mouth. I've heard enough from you. What are you, some sort of a cheap spy? Is it you who prowls the halls at night, opening and closing doors to see if everyone is in the right bed? Or are you a bed hopper yourself?"

Eva's face froze. She started to lift her hand, then hesitated. Eva wanted to strike. Looking at Lucy, seeing the taunting smile, her young body poised to counter any move which Eva might make, I knew why the instructor hesitated. Strong as she was, she sensed that Lucy had taunted her, and wanted her to strike. She showed fear of this girl who moved with such feline grace and agility.

Eva turned and stepped out of the door. Looking back, she motioned with her head. "Come on, the snow is really beginning to stick. We could lose sight of our trail–then we'd be in trouble."

As I followed Lucy and Eva I wanted to put that scene in the cabin out of my mind. We had been compromised lying on that mattress, with Eva standing over us, staring as if we had been caught in a foul act. Eva would tell her story and I would soon answer for it.

Surely no one would believe that I had lured a young woman into an abandoned cabin to seduce her when there were better ways. As I thought back, I realized that walking from the sanitarium, through the maples, over a bridge, one of us would have been certain to have been seen.

My feet slipped in the soft snow whenever I stepped upon uneven ground or fallen branches. The outstretched limbs of the trees were turning white. From the underside I could see the pine needles and the branches supporting the weight of the snow. The wind blew in sudden gusts moving the branches and causing the snow to break loose; some fell upon us. The wind hurled the snowflakes almost wildly in a swirling dance, and by morning all the forest would be white.

Lucy looked back and called out against the wind. "You look like a polar bear!"

"Or Bigfoot," I shouted. Eva appeared not to hear. She was moving steadily, looking from side to side, slowing her step to sight a familiar marking and assure herself that she was on the trail. I saw no danger in getting lost. Maplewood was below us, and if we missed the grounds, we could walk along the river until we found the bridge.

As we neared the river I could hear the water moving over the rocks. At the bank of the river I paused to watch the snow collecting along the water's edge. Lucy walked over the bridge while Eva turned, hesitated for a moment, then walked slowly back to me.

"You'll be questioned about what happened. Such things are not passed over lightly. I have one word of advice: start looking out for yourself. That girl is trouble. She is sick, and she can only cause you harm."

Before I could answer she turned and walked briskly across the bridge.

Near the main building I was jolted by a snowball. Dropped to one knee to avoid being hit again. "Fight, man, if you have the strength–or did you lose it in the forest?" shouted the Colonel.

Enough snow had fallen so that Bill and the Admiral and Mary were attempting to make a snow man; even Peg was helping. In the midst of so much falling snow, among the maples with the river just beyond and the pines encircling us, the world seemed like a fairy wonderland where children play. Someone distracted the Colonel, and I caught him squarely with a snowball.

"You make an easy target!" I yelled. "Officers should stay out of range." Snowballs began to fly. One hit Peg.

She threw at the Colonel, quickly formed another snowball and threw again. In the midst of the shouting and the flying snowballs I saw Ralph approaching me. His face was red with anger.

"Follow me," he said, in a voice one would expect to hear used against one convicted of some heinous crime.

He said nothing more as I followed several steps behind Ralph. At the clinic he swung open the door, and stepped inside, and then released the door, not once looking back to see if I was following him. Red faced and head erect, Ralph walked briskly down the hall toward his office. As we passed the several patients who were gathered there and those sitting in the nearby lounge appeared to sense something was wrong. Everyone stopped talking. All heads turned to stare at us. I caught a glimpse of Audrey at her desk, as she looked up from her work. In one long glance I saw all the faces before following Ralph into his office. Inside the door he turned quickly, slammed the door loudly, walked over to his desk and sat down. He did not offer me a chair.

"Just what do you think you are getting away with around here? What kind of lecherous hound are you, preying on a young woman—and a sick one at that?"

Remembering how thin the walls were, I knew that no secrets would be concealed from prying ears in this room. I could hear no movement in the hall; everyone, I felt sure, was straining their ears to hear what happened. Because, as Ralph indicated, a woman was involved there would be greater interest than his confrontation with

Roy. I was sure he intended to pick my bones clean before this silent audience.

"Ralph, I can hear you," I told him. "Don't shout at me. I'm no longer in the woods."

"You are a wretch, a miserable cur. You come here, take a young, innocent girl into the woods, do what you intend to do, then come back and throw snowballs, acting as if nothing happened—as if such behavior was normal and we ought to accept it." He jumped up from his desk and walked toward me jabbing his finger with each step. "You act as if you know more than the others. You have that knowing smile as you lecture me about the AA program. It was you who got Roy started criticizing that new girl, Pamela. I saw you looking at her with contempt. You are not good enough to even mention her name."

For one moment I felt the impulse to laugh at this fool and his absurd charges. His conscience was no doubt bothering him. He was a hypocrite. He wanted to justify himself in his own eyes and in the eyes of anyone who could hear his shouting at this moment. Seeing the color of his face, the intensity of his eyes, I wondered if this self righteous fool might strike me. I wanted to cut through that pink skin to expose him for what he was, a liar and a hypocrite. He'd not squash me like an insect beneath his boot I detested him.

"Did it occur to you that things are not what they seem?" I asked him. "What hard evidence do you have that something took place? You have nothing but your dirty mind."

"Eva saw you. She saw you—almost."

"Almost? I'm sure you above all men, Ralph, know how to copulate. And who has accused Eva of being a virgin? Certainly not me. What the hell do you mean, 'almost'?"

"Watch your tongue. You were lying together."

"So?"

He tossed his head impatiently. "Do you take me for a fool? Surely you didn't expect Eva to wait until you had completed your seduction of this poor girl."

What a hypocrite. As I recalled that conversation between Ralph and Pam that night outside the recreation hall, my contempt for Ralph increased.

"How do I know what Eva expected? As for you, Ralph, I shall withhold for the moment what I think of you."

I wanted to add that I did not know that Lucy had been following me–that I was in the cabin before I saw her.

'So he considered me a degenerate!' I thought. 'So indeed will the others!'

I was determined not to stand convicted by this hypocrite. Silently I watched this angry man who had by now walked back to his desk, and was sitting, glaring at me, hardly concealing his hatred and triumph. How he hated me! He relished his role as avenger, in making me out a whoremonger, someone to be watched and avoided if not thrown out of Maplewood.

I looked about the room. It was small, furnished with a desk and chair and, for visitors, two more chairs, a small table and an ash tray. A picture showing a fisherman fishing in a mountain stream hung on the wall. That completed the furnishings. Overhead were white tubular lights. The walls were white, and the worn floors were covered with brown tile. My eyes were drawn to the window through which I could see the white snow falling. The beauty of that sight contrasted sharply with the ugliness of the room.

I shuddered at the drabness of the room. I felt keenly the tawdriness of this whole confrontation with Ralph that now seemed to me so unreal–a foolish melodrama being acted out on a shabby stage setting. Ralph noted my reaction, and apparently took it for fear. He showed his contempt. How exposed and foolish I felt facing Ralph. Would anyone believe me if I told them that Lucy had followed me into the woods and to the cabin? Why involve her anyway? She needed help, and she might be forced to leave. I decided upon another tack.

Ralph was directing all his contempt and hatred toward me. There was certainly no professional concern for me. He was attempting to demolish me before his silent audience waiting in the hallway. They waited now, to hear my subdued voice, to see me come out a shattered man when the door opened. Did I imagine it? Or were my friends eager to see that pretender (who spoke in such a self assured, superior manner) reduced to a cringing coward?

Ralph was going about his task efficiently. Roy, after all, had been merely a warm up. Mark was the real prey who called up his entire wrath.

As I looked at his face, his thoughts and feelings came through to me so strongly that I fancied I could read them precisely.

Ralph leaned across the desk, belligerent, challenging me.

"Lecherous dog that sniffs about," he grated. "You found a girl almost half your age, played up to her–took advantage of her sickness and led her into the woods. If she had resisted, you probably would have raped her!"

His words were loud, and his manner contemptuous, sneering. It was obvious that he relished playing the role of my judge. He made no attempt to conceal his disgust as he delivered his verdict on my supposed vileness. And it was apparent that he took perverse delight in abusing me, adding fresh insults to earlier insinuations.

I had had enough. Ralph was a fool and a hypocrite as well. I would prick his balloon, cut into that righteous hide.

"At your conference, Ralph, you made an issue of sobriety–sobriety that had to come before all else.'Get rid of your husband or mistress or whoever comes between us and our sobriety,' you told us. You showed unusual interest and tenderness toward Pam who, it appears, has either discarded her husband or is unfaithful to him."

"What right do you have to mention her name?" Ralph exploded jumping to his feet. "What does she have to do with this business? You are a scoundrel! Pam refused to see her husband because he was drinking."

"Exactly. She wept. He wept. She refused to go. I witnessed that whole performance listening to sweet, adorable Pam with the stunning figure, the baby doll face, and the pitiful, baby doll voice. Rightly enough, you saw the amused contempt on my face. Honest Roy saw through the entire charade. You got Roy, perhaps even depriving him of his livelihood by refusing his clearance. What have you planned for me, Ralph?"

"You scoundrel! I'll see you are railed out of here."

"Oh, will you now? Your tenderness and sympathy for Pan was not professional interest at all. It was something else."

"What do you mean?"

I stood up and walked toward his desk. Standing in front of his desk I said, "I mean, Ralph," as 'measured each word, "you are a hypocrite pretending to be a virtuous man which you certainly are not. That makes you a liar as well."

"You'll not speak to me that way," he said, coming around the desk.

"You had better hear me out. You would regret the day you lifted a hand against me!"

"Get out!"

"Not yet, Ralph, certainly not yet. You must let me finish–and I have more to say."

"Say it and get out. I'm going right to Doctor Neilstrom with a report about you."

"Marvelous, Ralph! I hoped you'd say that. Include this in your report that Mark often walks late at night and that last night he was out walking the night before 'Kiss and tell.'

"You're mad."

"No, Ralph, just angry. Remember my superior, arrogant ways. Tell the doctor that Mark insists he heard voices about 10 P.M. outside the recreation building. One was yours, the other Pam's. Now I shall repeat for you, word for word, what was said, so that you can repeat these words to the doctor. These were your exact words I heard. . . .

"Stop!" Ralph shouted. Then he pointed to the door. "Get out You've taken up enough time. I'll make my recommendation to the doctor."

"Yes, Ralph, I'm getting out. When the doctor calls me in I'll build my defense around the example you set for me."

"Get out, you bastard!"

Stepping into the hall, I paused for an instant to glance at the many faces staring at me. They were curious–not hostile. Audrey was still at her desk. Her eyes, for the first time, appeared to appraise me with interest. Going down the hall I saw that the door to Lucy's room was open. I stopped, saw her seated on the edge of her bed, and stepped inside. She started to speak, but I interrupted.

"Lucy, I want to stay here until I am cured. I'm on thin ice. After this encounter with Ralph, they may ask me to leave. If I am to stay, I must avoid seeing you. You ought to concern yourself only with your sickness–not with me."

For a moment she looked helpless and sad. She sat there staring straight ahead. Rising from the bed she walked to her dresser, pulled open the drawer and began placing the contents in separate piles on the bed. I watched in silence. She looked at me as she picked up her suitcase from the corner of the room. "I'm going now," is all she said.

The sound of hurried footsteps in the hallway announced Stella's arrival. She was red faced and angry.

"Come out of that bedroom. What are you doing in there, anyway?"

"I thought it best to tell Lucy that I wouldn't be seeing her again."

Turning her head and shoulders abruptly in the direction of her office, Stella said, "Come with me."

As I followed her rapid steps, I felt relieved that the matter between Lucy and me was settled. Stella's office was also near the lounge. She marched with me in through the door of her office to her desk. Patients were watching, so I closed the door. I faced Stella.

"I asked what you were doing in that room," she began without preamble.

"And I told you why I was there."

"You were there for almost ten minutes. How long does it take you to tell someone you are not going to see them again? You are not the first one to involve himself with a woman on these premises."

I thought of Ralph and Pam. For a fleeting moment I was tempted to lay before her the actions of this hypocrite. Stella had just begun to unleash the full fury of her indignation.

"What sort of man are you? You wander all about, you go into the forest defying the rules and getting into trouble. You challenge the counselors, acting as if you knew more than they do about alcohol."

She looked at me with scorn, her eyes and face revealing her anger and disgust. From the disdain in her expression, she might have been looking at a reptile that repelled her.

"Your behavior is shocking. Aren't you a married man? While your wife was in Europe, you are cavorting about with a young woman seducing her in a log cabin in the woods."

Eva entered, closed the door and sat down behind me where I could not see her face. She did not speak. Stella's eyes darted toward Eva and back again to me. Stella continued, "I learned that Lucy is a very sick woman. Is that the sort of a woman you are drawn to? When she is defenseless, you win her over, and then use her to satisfy yourself."

She was not only censoring me, she was taunting me. She did not appear to show the utter contempt and loathing I saw in Ralph; she appeared enraged by what she saw as intolerable behavior–a middle aged man, proud and defiant, seducing a helpless, sick young woman. It appeared obvious that she expected more from me.

"You have done all the talking," I said. "You stated your case. Now it is my turn to say something."

"You and your words. How you love to use them. No, you cannot say anything to me. Get out! Out!"

She arose quickly and hurried to the door, opened it, and walked out, holding her head high.

I turned to Eva and said, "The bitch." Then I left the room. The Colonel, who was standing by the coffee urn, followed me along the hall and out into the grounds.

"Mark, if you are going to make out with one of the young ladies on these premises, you must be willing to pay the price if you are caught."

"You must think I'm guilty if, as you say, I was caught."

The Colonel ignored my comment, continuing as if he had not heard me. "Getting caught is one of the risks that cannot be avoided. Did I ever tell you the treatment I received from those army doctors? There was one, a Dr. Steinman, not particularly interested in virtue, but if you got a 'dose,' taking the treatment from him was worse than being caught by the heathens during the crusades. Sometime I might describe for you how he treated my case."

You've had a full life, Colonel. As a true soldier, knowledgeable in all these matters, do you really think I was intent on ravishing Lucy?"

"Whatever you tell me I would believe."

For a moment I looked at the smiling Colonel–hard, rugged, a dedicated soldier. In his day there was little he had not tried, few vices to which he had not succumbed. From the stories I had heard, his appetites were enormous. But he saw through sham. Even in his love of pleasure–the jesting, women, golf, polo, and long drinking bouts– there was courage and a straightforwardness I admired. He did not take life in mincing steps, but in bold strides. He was a strong man, a lusty man brought low by the consuming fire of alcohol. He accepted his fate, and there were no excuses. Outwardly, he appeared hearty and self assured. He did not know me, or that my life had come to the crossroads where I could not see where to turn or step. I feared each day more. I was certain that I was mad, or on the edge of madness, close to plunging over the brink into an abyss of total darkness. I saw before me the specter of a world where there was nothing, no hope, no consolation–only continued fear and despair. Once locked into madness, there was no return.

"You think a lot, it seems to me," the Colonel observed. "What do you think about?"

"About what you said. Your confidence is a help. I was not taking Lucy, no matter what Ralph or Stella think."

"You mean, after so much fuss you missed the prize?"

"They tell me she's not well. It seems to me everyone is sick except you, Colonel."

"Not as confused as some you see, but I'm here because I failed. Look at those people. They are subdued, they have problems with money, with marriage, with their health, and booze is at the root of it."

"So you look for something better when you leave here?" I asked.

"Anything is better than being drunk all the time. I am tired of being out of control. You know a man could kill someone when he's drunk."

"Yes, I know." "Or lose everything and do some foolish, violent thing."

"Like what?"

"Suicide."

"Rather extreme, don't you think?"

"I'm older than you. I know. There are men here capable of such extremes. Wait and see what happens to this group."

"How do you plan to 'make it' on the outside?"

"Through AA when I leave here."

"When do you go?" "I go home this weekend, and I'll stay for a few days. I'll be back here for two more weeks, then my stay is ended."

As we were talking I saw a car stop at the main entrance. Lucy came out of the main building. She had her suitcase in her hand. She looked for a long moment in our direction; appeared to say something, then turned and entered the car. It drove off swiftly and soon disappeared into the trees.

As the sound of the car faded the Colonel looked at me. "I wonder if she really cared for you?" he asked.

"Just a fantasy, nothing more. We were cut off from society, alone–there were no young men. She will forget me in a week."

"I wonder. For your sake I hope she does," the Colonel said, laughing. "Have you seen Audrey, the night counselor? Now there is a real woman for you."

I nodded, showing no interest. After my experience with Lucy, I was going to be careful in what I said. My actions, too, would be deliberate, and I would take care not to step out of line.

The fresh snow attracted everyone at Maplewood. The day was drawing to an end. Everyone it seemed was outdoors wandering about the snow covered grounds, cutting paths between the maple trees. The Colonel was the first to hear Bill's voice. We turned to see Bill and the Admiral a short distance away.

The Colonel appeared to forget about Audrey for the moment. Bill greeted the colonel and then looked at me. "I see Lucy is gone."

"So," I added, "are Roy and Dean. But haven't you heard? There is a dangerous lecher loose among you–preying on innocent young females and lusting after everything in sight. That is, if you believe Ralph. As for Stella, I really believe that she would never accept that any man could be alone in a mountain cabin with a young woman without there being trouble. She doesn't trust men–at least not me."

"Sounds like a bum rap to me."

"Thanks for the vote of confidence. Are you leaving, too?"

"No, not for a few weeks, but I think some of us are going home for the weekend. I hear the conference with the guest speaker, Dr. Bogleman, has been moved ahead."

"Say, Bill," the Colonel called out, who was now walking a few feet ahead of us with the Admiral, "will you help me explain tank warfare to the Admiral? You play cards with him. You must know how to reach him."

Bill chuckled. "The Colonel doesn't realize that the Admiral has forgotten how to play cards. He's out of it most of the time."

As Bill moved ahead to join the Colonel and the Admiral, I walked behind them, ignoring the Colonel's loud voice, as I became more engrossed in my thoughts.

So Bogleman wasn't coming, at least not soon. I felt relieved. The dark brooding face of the doctor, his black eyes, his uncanny insights, his casual even disinterested manner, opened up his patient. He probed the wounded heart with the skill of a surgeon. His voice was always low and well modulated; he asked penetrating questions in a casual manner; listened without seeming to do so, and fit the fragments and pieces of the puzzle together. Then, as if he held some psychological divining rod, he penetrated the entangled web; found the wayward strands that bound the patient in conflict, and sought to break those cables so that he might release his patient from their coils.

My present state of tension would not go unnoticed. If he came now, and sensed the agitation that existed yet within me (with all the confusing voices, pulling me in one direction, then another), it was possible that he would advise Dr. Neilstrom that I be moved to a private sanitarium, like Stiron, for further treatment. I feared this more than death. If those I saw at Maplewood were even half mad, what would it be like among the insane?

The instincts upon which I relied to sustain and direct my life no longer supported me. Yet among the shadows of my mind I witnessed vague scenes and a continued struggle between conflicting desires. Ideas clashed; resolutions were made and discarded. I was pulled one way and then another. But all the while I heard once again that new voice: a cry from within me (a faint but distinct cry), for unity, for harmony and peace–for that unity I craved, only vaguely understood and that I had never possessed before. But every resolve was stymied. I could not sift and unravel the wild, clashing flow of ideas that boiled up–that surged and tumbled –before my eyes and sapped my strength and any resolution I attempted to make. But this voice within me–this faint but determined plea–urged me to struggle, and never to cease struggling, to free myself from the demons of alcohol, greed, fear, hatred and ambition. With my emotions aroused, I resolved to change my life. Then scenes of peace and harmony filled my mind: a warm feeling of contentment flowed through me.

All too soon my strong resolves vanished. The appeal from within me to direct my life in a new channel could not be sustained. As my enthusiasm faded my resolutions and my dreams faded, too. Those hard realities dominated my present life–those surging, passionate, cravings for success that drown and consume (and in the end) had brought me to the edge of madness.

My nature was twisted and warped, like the limbs of the maple trees that surrounded me. But they followed nature's plan: they were strong and formidable, going on forever, it seemed, showing the scars from the long trials of winter and the heat of summer–yet they survived. My will directed my actions, not my true nature. Step by step, through an endless series of small, seemingly harmless actions my life had been sculptured by my hands. I loathed what I saw. There was no lasting strength or permanence, or beauty in that shape my life had taken.

My mind was trained to calculate; to weigh figures and tables; to make up schedules; to follow market trends with skill, knowing when, what, and how to buy, and when to sell. Timing always played a large role: no matter how skilled one was in perceiving trends, the future was always cloudy. Big risks meant big gains, or crushing losses. The pressures were enormous. A few survived in this world of business. Many failed. I survived–but failed. The fortune made consumed the man. Without alcohol, I wanted something else–to be someone I was not–someone I felt for brief moments I ought to be (even at times longed passionately to become), not knowing where that vision would lead me. This was the faint voice I heard calling me.

In the past I had shown so much hatred. Whenever I was crossed or my business threatened, I was overcome with a mixture of fear and anger and hatred. Fear always appeared cowardly to me; yet it seemed as I grew older, and more successful, fear increased. Sometimes I longed for that peace that I imagined death would bring. Was I drifting toward suicide, I wondered. If, at first, my nature was not repelled by the thought of death, what I envisioned that followed death caused me to tremble with fear.

In that still night of death I envisioned only a vast emptiness, falling forever into a void, with an ever increasing sense of loss, of isolation, of loneliness. It was not the act of dying, or decaying, or putrid smell, or staring eyes, nor bloodless lips that I feared. Nor did I fear the feasting maggot's that gorge themselves and dissolve into the clay. Nor did I fear the pain that sometimes accompanied death.

But in that dark night after death, all alone, separated, never hearing or seeing, or feeling the touch of a friend; cut off, condemned to wander forever in a fathomless pit without comfort, pierced with the knowledge that I had failed–this was the torment my mind could not endure. Gone, forgotten, unrecorded; without anyone to care, forever hearing the cry, "You failed!"

"Look! See" I cry out. "I am a creature. Someone who feels, who once had hopes, who once suffered, and feels only pain and loss and would love again if that mystery could be unraveled so that I could grasp it, understand what it means to care for someone, anyone. Direct your attention to me! See me as I am. (See me, rather, as I was.) See me as an individual who experienced life, who saw good days, who was not beyond caring; now I search for one word of hope–hope I know I will never find.

"Dr. Bogleman, you can bring light. You have the power to show me a way out of this darkness, this hell into which I am condemned. Turn away from me, see me as a fool, and I am nothing. Here I am consumed by 'nothing.' I cannot say 'I am.' It is not dying I fear. I fear living death, living on as nothing: being forever separated from life."

"You are pale, making gestures."

I was startled by these words from Bill. Looking about me I saw the Colonel several yards ahead of me almost shouting at the Admiral. Bill apparently had dropped back to see what had become of me.

"I'm sorry, Bill, if my reveries alarmed you. I often tend to drift off struggling with my confusing thoughts and feelings."

"Are you all right?" he asked.

"Oh, I'll make it somehow. I must. I need to be alone to sort out these conflicts."

"Well, you sometimes worry me. Good luck on your search."

"Thanks," I said as I turned and walked away through the snow.

CHAPTER 15

The snow felt soft under my feet as I walked through the trees. The snowing had ceased, the clouds had opened, and the light from the stars and the moon cast a silver light upon the landscape. The three buildings, the long rows of shrubbery, the maple trees and all other objects stood out clearly. The snow softened the rough contours and the twisted, gnarled limbs of the maple trees. I thought back to the moment when Bernice had startled me by seizing my arm. I looked about, almost expecting her to leap again from behind a tree.

Seeing the trees draped in white and the glittering snow covering the brown earth had lifted my spirits. Now, as I thought of Bernice, I felt drained and weary.

It was not unlikely that Ralph or someone on the staff would suggest that I be sent to a mental clinic such as Stiron. I wanted no part of such a place. Few returned to take an active part in society. How could anyone survive in that place? The inmates there were mad, every last one. Seeing them, being in their company would destroy all hope for me—it would drive me further into madness. They were so far into their world of darkness, of fantasy, of illusions, that no one could call them back.

Had Bogleman forgotten me? When he came to lecture us was he planning to see me? I supposed that he had planned to see me and was undoubtedly curious to measure my progress. He would have to evaluate my progress so that he could inform my wife what he saw, whether there was hope for a full recovery.

The night was turning cold. If I could not sleep after such a long day, I mused, when would I sleep again? Would Audrey be on duty tonight if I needed sleeping tablets? I could get them from her without the nurse knowing. Audrey would listen to me.

I felt a tingle in my left cheek; rubbing it I realized it was frozen. Even the skin on my face seemed to remember the past when I had frozen my face as a boy (who didn't take pains to turn his back against the freezing winds of the Dakotas), being too involved in a winter sport to care. As a boy I often walked a mile to the frozen river, laced on my shoe skates and then raced up and down the ice defying the icy wind to do its worst. Sometimes I skated when the temperature was below zero. At those times under a pale, lifeless sun, or under the stars, the wind was silent. But sometimes it blew no matter how cold. Then I laughed and defied the cutting wind, the piercing cold to do its worst. I heard the shrieking wind in full fury as I skated at full speed toward the north end of the river. I bent forward as I felt all my body strain against the resisting efforts of the wind. Sometimes the violence of the wind would be so great; I could barely reach the end of the river. I always won out, but one time I froze part of my face. After that it froze more easily. Now after all these years my face had not forgotten. The weakness in my facial tissue remained.

There was a sudden change in the texture of the night. Clouds sealed off the stars and the moon and the trees all but disappeared in a shroud of darkness. The only sound was the crunch of the snow under my boots. In the darkness the trees appeared strange and watchful. I could pick my way, for I could see lamps along a path near the main building. The snow glittered in small circles beneath each lamp, but total darkness lurked just outside these halos of light.

No one out tonight—no one but me among the trees. No Bernice hiding there. Bernice? Where are you? Where is your wild mind hiding? Are you hiding somewhere among the trees, or are you frozen in the snow? Where have you gone? Have they put you away forever, locked you in a cell? Have you found peace at last? Will I join you soon?

Drugs and alcohol did you in. No one will ever hear your story. No one will ever remember that young girl who graduated from Stanford with honors, who spoke several languages, taught successfully, married, and looked forward eagerly with the boundless joy and anticipation of youth to a rich, rewarding life. Something happened to you along the way. Was it at a gay party where someone said, "Try this, Bernice, a blue one–goes great with the wine–or if you want to feel really alive, try a red one."

I know nothing about drugs–only that I see what they have done to you. Drugs and alcohol, I am told, are often a deadly combination. You went down the road into darkness (where no one can see you; no one can bring you back), and there is no return. The Bernice I saw, and the voice I heard was not you. It was the sound from an empty shell, from your tomb. Your mind and heart were captive there, but someone else spoke for you. You are gone–gone forever from this world. You will never be heard from or seen again. Your end is worse than death, because at least the dead are mourned, remembered for some good, a show of kindness, of accomplishment. But the memory of you brings forth only the images of failure, pain and loss. You were cut down at that time in life when your family and friends expected much. You were a disappointment and a tragedy–no one wants to remember you.

No one saw you consumed by drugs. You were gone, over the line when your addiction was realized. Do you see yourself falling deeper into darkness, or have you found places in that blackness, in those depths where I tremble with fear to go? They put you here to get your money, you said. That I doubt. But of this I am certain: money is needed at Maplewood. I know business, and I know of the struggle here to survive. Trained counselors are needed, but without funds, they cannot be attracted to work here. Alcoholics are poor risks, and having wasted their lives, most are without money. The counselors here are willing, but they lack experience and training.

Accursed alcohol! It rots the soul of anyone addicted to it. A man using it all too soon does not want to know what he is. That would mean effort, sacrifice, a struggle to change, to become what one was intended to be—a new person, unique, unlike any other. So what is done? With alcohol, he reshapes himself into a new image: a buffoon, a caricature, an animated cartoon, who laughs and cries. Not accepting his real nature, he substitutes another, only to find that the new image is undesirable as well.

The artist sees into the hidden depths of the heart and catches a glimpse of the secrets which lie there. He records what he sees on canvas: the eyes show the passion; the face and the general bearing reveal the vanity and pride; every mood and every weakness is subtly detailed. If the artist has done well in recapturing the image of the man, a collector will exhibit the painting in a prominent space, and a museum will show it for everyone to see.

Suffering, failure, the pride of success, the many honors are all there to be seen by a keen appraising eye. The alcoholic is an artist, too: he paints for the world to see, becomes the opposite of what he wishes to become. He desires respect and honor and love, to be seen in high places, exalted among his peers; with alcohol sustaining him all dreams are possible, or so it seems.

You are at peace, Bernice. Be gone. You fell on the field of battle. I do not know of your struggle, how strongly you resisted, what you endured before succumbing to these forces that I fear are also consuming me. Must I go through it all again tonight? (These nights—they never end.) I am cursed with a divided self. One voice crying out 'fool! murderer!' the other self fleeing in fear, in eternal anguish crying, 'No! No!' Never fully possessed, being consumed slowly, each encounter with the pursuer feels like the tearing out of another part of me—one force against the other. A howl splits the quiet; startled, I look around. Then realize that it was I who howled in my anguish. Listening to the echoes of those sounds, I am filled anew with horror at the depth of my anguish.

At times it seemed that there had been not one feeling of depravity I had not experienced, or any decadent act which I had not been capable of doing. If I did not possess Lucy, or allow her to possess me, what was the merit? No one among the counselors, as far as I could see, believed me. They could not see that at the present I was dead to passion. Their words indicated they saw only a sensual man with strong emotions, with a sly, wandering eye; uncertain behavior–and they could not fit me into a common slot. Was I a ruthless, sensual, demanding, clever man after all? One to give a wide berth? On this point my mind was not clear. Eva and Stella were not to blame after what they saw. Ralph, however, was a hypocrite. I, too, must be honest: I did lead the girl on. Why they kept me here is a mystery. Was it money? The influence of Bogleman? I heard the sound of my laughter. Someone I was sure had already informed that good doctor about my interlude with Lucy. My wife was in Europe. She would know all about me through Dr. Bogleman.

Lucy, poor Lucy. You poor lost fool. Everyone who seems to know something about you says that you are not only sick but dangerous. I fear you are lost like me, but I will not add to your confusion. The physical coupling of two lost souls will shed no light, only increase the darkness. At best it might provide a release of tension, a conquest, some small comfort–but if I cannot give more than that I will give you nothing at all.

How dark it is out here in the trees. I can feel the cold in my feet and hands. There it goes again! My face is tingling, and I will have a rubbery cheek from having it frozen too often, like those early days in my youth.

What, I wonder, are you doing tonight, Lucy? Are you drinking? You said that you did not have a problem. Many say that, at least when they first arrive at Maplewood. You were not on drugs–of that I feel certain. Whatever is your problem it was not openly discussed. I'll never know. I'll soon forget you–but I wish you well.

Now if I had been lying in that cabin with you, Audrey, looking into your clear, cat like eyes, against your soft body, I fear that the constraints–the layer upon layer of respect and loyalty–would have been dissolved in one burst of passion. I would like your company. You are the only one who will make this night tolerable. The thought of you revives me. I must pull my face together, appear cheerful, act lighthearted. Is she, I wondered, interested in an old fool's struggle to find meaning and purpose at this stage of his life?

By a side entrance, I stopped to kick my shoes free of snow against a tree. As I stepped inside the hall, I stood for a moment to adjust my eyes to the darkness. The light near the exit door, and the light coming from the counselors' room at the far end of the hall provided enough illumination so that I could begin walking. I ran my hand over my face where it had frozen; my cheeks felt withdrawn against my cheekbones. I touched my chest. I could feel my ribs. While a battle raged within, my body shrunk. With every step in the hall I could hear the creak of my footsteps or, as I passed a door, someone breathing in deep sleep.

What was that?

Someone cried out, a pitiful wail; a nightmare. I was not the only one who suffered bad dreams. The heart cries out in the darkness, finding a release in those dreams that said, "See how I suffer? Life is hard, cruel, relentless, and often dreary with meaningless affairs and unfulfilled visions." It seemed so long ago when I first believed that life wasn't like this, when my life was young; when I was filled with hope; when every day was like the fresh breezes of spring enticing me to believe the promise of a warm and enchanting summer. But somehow no event or season fulfilled its promise.

As a boy when I reached those purple hills in the Dakotas I did not find the summers enchanting. The days were hot and dry, and the fields overrun by grasshoppers. The beauty of spring had already fled. The purple haze that hung over the distant hills, promising a new world of enchantment and discovery for a boy faded as I reached my journey's end. The hills were no longer colorful but burned brown by the sun.

I always sought more in everything, more than anyone could find. This penchant for seeking the ultimate reward, the greatest thrill, the highest high, manifested itself nowhere more than in my use of alcohol.

At first I found a release of tension, felt an enlargement of self. As the feeling of self importance grew, I became all knowing, all wise: arrogant, intolerant, unable to listen, heedless of the weak, envious of the strong. All this happened so slowly that I was not aware of the change. The more I used alcohol for stimulation, for energy, for special purposes, to function more efficiently in society–the weaker I became. In the beginning I used alcohol as a tool. Insidiously, the instrument gradually became the ruler–the master was unseated and replaced by the slave. What I sought for in life is not there, or if it is to be found, it is not where I have been seeking. Even as I rose in the world, my emptiness, my loneliness and feeling of isolation has increased. Wherever I turned I saw my divided nature. I felt cut off from life, from the real world.

Enough of all these reveries. I've searched; I've sifted all my memories. I'll let the dust settle. There is only pain in stirring up those scenes of the past: youth; innocence; the clear, eager eyes; the outgoing smile; the ideals. The natural warmth and generosity are gone.

As I reached the end of the hall, I opened the ice box and took out an orange. A long night was ahead. I saw Audrey at her desk working on some reports. She appeared absorbed in her work. I walked into her office peeling the orange. She glanced at me and continued working. I sat and ate the orange slowly. I dropped the peelings into Audrey's wastebasket, picked a book off the shelf beside me (by Lord Russell) and read a few pages. My mind was not on this book. Audrey worked on, ignoring me. I felt that I was unwelcome, so I replaced the book on the shelf and rose to leave.

"Mark," she said as I stepped to the door, "would you get me a cup of coffee?"

"Whatever is your pleasure," I replied. I walked around the corner and filled a Styrofoam cup. When I returned, she was sitting smoking a cigarette, her desk cleared, waiting for the coffee. She looked at me for several moments.

"My, you look different. A little wild. Look lean and fit, now that all the fat is gone. Have you reached the moment of truth?"

For a moment I sat sipping coffee and looking at her. She did not smile: she returned my gaze, her grey eyes fixed upon mine. Was that a sign of interest?

"Hasn't anyone told you," I said, "that I have not been drinking for three, four weeks? That a change has come over me? I'll let you in on a secret. Regardless of what Stella believes, I know this truth. As I stated at the last conference, I am an alcoholic. Each day I see this more clearly."

For a moment I thought she would smile.

"I wondered if you would see the truth. You are different. I'm not sure why they came down on you so hard. It may be the girl. Some girl! I'd stay clear of her."

"She's innocent enough–a lost spirit wandering about in the world."

"Lost? Perhaps. Innocent? No. You frighten some people, even a few counselors. But that girl, Lucy, frightens me. It is not my habit to offer advice or warn someone, but I am warning you to say away from Lucy. She's dangerous."

"How do you know?"

"I know."

"But how?"

"Let me just say 'I know.'" She changed the subject abruptly. "Were you surprised to see the druggist?"

"Surprised? That's putting it mildly. I thought he was dying or perhaps worse, going mad. Then I see him sitting calmly at the 'kiss and tell' stuttering as usual."

"You're bright. By now you must be aware what the body can take."

"And the mind?"

"That's the doctor's province."

She paused for a moment and looked down the hall. It was dark except for a few small night lights that caused strange shadows to form on the wall. I could hear the wind rising through the trees, moaning and sighing, keeping a lonely vigil over Maplewood and its dregs and wrecks of society.

"I only observe," She continued, "that for anyone who has courage and desire, if there is anything left of that person, change is possible. Sometimes great change–if, of course, that person is willing to pay the price."

Audrey was relaxed, looking at me through the smoke of our cigarettes. As she sipped her coffee her face seemed pallid under the fluorescent lights. She seemed inclined to talk. Having been duly warned about Lucy (who I was determined not to see again), I decided to ask Audrey about her lover, her future–whatever came across my mind.

"You find sobriety much better?" I asked.

"My life is better organized. I get along better with my boyfriend," she said smiling, "and my daughters, too. When I have time off, they often come to visit me in my home. They know they are welcome, and they are no longer fearful of my moods. All goes well when they respect my wishes."

"Sounds rather simple," I said.

"Not much is asked," she said. "In my home I set a few rules: call before coming, ask to use the kitchen and clean it up afterwards– and no guests can be admitted without permission."

"What is your boyfriend like?" I asked, losing interest in the mother daughter relationship.

"Oh, he's a real man–has a trucking firm and wants me to travel with him. His family is out of the way. He wants to set up an apartment for me in San Diego. Last week I found a marvelous antique

bed. The dealer told me that Napoleon had once used the bed. When I
told my boyfriend about the bed he said that he didn't know anything
about Napoleon or antiques. Being so old he wondered if it was a good
bed. But he said if Napoleon used it the bed must be all right."

Some use, I thought, with Napoleon's reportedly insatiable
desires for young women. At least they picked a bed that would suit
their needs if it was large enough.

"Napoleon was a short man," I said. "You are not small. And
your boyfriend? Most truckers are not small either."

"John is a big man. He can't spend too much time with me until
his divorce is final." She smiled. "I measured the bed. It will do."

Through the cigarette smoke, I appraised Audrey's grey eyes,
white teeth, and translucent skin. Her stunning figure was enticingly
revealed by a tight fitting blouse, and I found myself appreciating the
peculiar warmth her presence added to the room.

"Yes," I said, "I'm sure if you measured the bed, it will do.
What does the bed look like?"

"It has a high oak back with many carvings," she said.

"Sounds Victorian to me. A Napoleon bed would have a low
headboard of walnut with bronze carvings at each of the four corners."

"John checked out the antique dealer and found that he had
good credit rating and does an awful lot of business."

Good credit rating, I thought. What did that mean? He was a
good salesman? Good businessman? It sounded to me as if he dealt in
an 'awful' lot of junk–Victorian pieces and the like–with people who
had little knowledge of antiques.

"Doesn't matter, I'm sure–if you like it," I said. "The Empire
period that followed Louis VI showed the Egyptian influence. If you
saw Josephine's bed you would see this influence with gilt bronze
mounts in the form of swans, cornucopias and an eagle. Napoleon's
bed, showing similar influence, was simpler in design."

"You know a lot, don't you?" she added, smiling again.

"I've traveled. My wife likes antiques, so we visit the shops, the art galleries and the museums."

Not caring to pursue the talk about her Napoleon bed any further, I decided to ask about her work.

"Are you staying on when your apartment is ready and you begin traveling?"

She shook her head slowly. "No, I'll be leaving. If it doesn't work out, I'll be back." She looked at me. "Will you be here?"

"What a strange question," I said. "Would you expect me to be here after another week or two?"

"No, I guess not." Peering down the hallway I thought I could see a door opening and closing in the dim light. And I could have sworn that two figures moved toward the exit and disappeared. Was it Ralph and Pam, I wondered, or some other couple?

I turned again to Audrey and remarked, "Thought I saw someone go out."

"No one would go out on a cold, snowy night like this," she said.

"Unless there was a great passion," I said lightly.

She smiled. "You understand passion?"

What was Audrey hinting at? Was she interested too, like Stella and Eva, in my relationship with Lucy? Well, I'd evade telling her what that relationship meant to me.

"Of course you've heard all about that fuss in the cabin. Nothing to it."

"Satisfying passion is natural," Audrey observed. "Lucy is no innocent child. She is a match for you—more than a match, I fear."

"I'm frightened," I said in a mocking tone.

"You ought to be! She is sick. There is something strange about her–something deadly."

I glanced at my watch and, seeing that it was very late, decided to go to my room. Talk about Lucy disturbed me. That was one subject I did not care to discuss with Audrey.

Rising from my chair I said, "Thanks for a pleasant interlude, Audrey. Hope the rest of your shift is uneventful. It's time for me to get back to bed. It may not be Napoleon's but now I think I'll sleep royally."

"Sleep well, Mark," she said softly as I walked out of the small office.

When I reached my room I could hear Gene's heavy breathing. Quietly, I slipped into bed. Audrey's remarks about Lucy kept me awake. Why was she warning me? There was no situation I could imagine where I'd be seeing Lucy again. I saw her as a passionate young woman, confused, somewhat neurotic, and no doubt lonely and frightened after her divorce. But fear her? I never met anyone who I feared less.

Lucy faded from my mind. For a while I lay awake turning over in my mind the events of the day, eventually drifting off to sleep.

CHAPTER 16

My body was trembling when I awoke. The room was bitter cold. I glanced at my watch: there was an hour until breakfast. No sense in lying here freezing. Sitting up, I looked at Gene. As usual, he was sleeping, and when awakened would say to anyone who asked that he could not sleep because of me. Perhaps he would add the freezing cold to the list of reasons causing his imagined insomnia.

There was nowhere to go, so I took whatever clothing I could find and piled them high on the bed. Under the sheets, the blankets and clothing I lay wondering what was wrong with the heating system. Had someone carelessly shut off the steam (or more likely) had the pipes frozen somewhere? No, that didn't seem likely either. It was cold, but cold weather was not unusual at this time of year.

The hour passed quickly. I sat up and began stomping my feet on the floor. I could see Gene's face. Slowly he opened his eyes and stared at me.

"Elephant," he said finally.

Irritated, I considered pulling off his blankets, but decided upon another tack

"No, Gene," I said, "not an elephant, nor a kangaroo, or a water buffalo. Just me, Mark, your roommate, now rising after you have spent a sleepless night. After this exercise in this warm room I am going to take a cold shower before breakfast to cool down."

As I walked out with a towel around me to get to the bathroom before it was taken I could hear voices: they were mixed with excitement, anger, and even fear.

I mused over the thought that a few people realized that a breakdown in the heating system in this isolated, mountain retreat, meant real trouble. Cold water spurted out when I turned the hot water tap. I washed quickly thinking that the pumps were working and obviously the pipes were not frozen. Surely we could not be out of fuel. Very likely the coils that preheated the heavy oil were not working, or the oil burner itself might have malfunctioned.

Walking along the hall to my room, I heard muttered voices coming from the bedrooms. One alarmed voice was saying that it would be warmer to stay in bed. When I got back to my room I found Gene sitting up in bed.

"What happened?" he asked.

"The doctor is saving fuel," I replied.

"But it's cold."

"I know, but you'll get used to it. This may be part of our treatment."

"What are you going to do?"

"As you see, I'm dressing. Then I'm going to the kitchen to get hot coffee and breakfast."

While I dressed Gene watched. Without another word, he got out of bed, grabbed a towel, and stalked out of our cubicle headed toward the bathroom. I finished dressing and hurried to the kitchen where I saw Mack busily preparing bacon, eggs and toast. I felt relieved to see that the coffee was ready.

As I poured a cup, I asked, "What is the problem, Mack?"

"Don't know," he replied. "Maybe the boiler blew up."

"Mack, you are a cook, not an engineer," I said. I took a sip of the hot coffee. "You would hear the explosion if the boiler let go.

Certainly the pumps are working or we wouldn't have tap water. My guess it's the burner; it's either plugged, or broken down, or it could be the heating coil that warms the heavy oil to the burner. Anyway, Mack, what will happen now?"

"Mark, I don't know. I'm a cook." He looked around as if searching for an answer. "We can't go on like this very long. There are sure not many electric heaters. Not near enough to go around. Weatherman said there was a cold weekend coming. Somebody's sure going to be cold around here without heat."

"You gave me an idea," I said. "My wife is gone. She doesn't expect for me to return home for at least several more weeks. Bill and the Colonel are about due to go home for the weekend–I'll go along."

Mack looked at me. "You'll go too? Not a bad idea if you can sell Stella on it. Loss of heat–man that is a problem. Not too many can stay here. During the last breakdown–seems to always come during a freeze–it took four days to repair."

"What will you do, Mack?"

"Sleep right here in my sleeping bag. The women and the men will move their mattresses into the conference room. They'll make a divider in the room with plywood panels, set up them electric heaters, and get by pretty well–that's until they want hot water for something."

"Isn't it noisy?" I asked.

"No one rests very much," he agreed.

I thought of Gene. He was sure to keep a lot of people restless and awake with his snoring and heavy breathing, and was equally sure to be the subject of derision at the breakfast table the next morning. After being confined with him for just one night, no one would ever again believe that he didn't sleep soundly. After eating one slice of bacon, one egg, and a bite of toast, and downing two cups of coffee, I saw Bill and the Colonel come through the door.

Bill chuckled when he saw me. "Don't tell me you have been wandering the hills all night in this cold."

Before I could answer, the Colonel added, "Wasn't that you going into Pam's room at the end of the hall? I heard voices."

"Listen Colonel, that hurricane you generate at night would awaken the dead. No wonder you can't find a roommate."

"I like my privacy."

"Bill, the Colonel mistakes that sputtering and wheezing and coughing for voices. I think he needs further counseling. A session with Stella, with Peg assisting, might help."

"Wise guy. At least I don't take a girl into a cabin in the woods and then play innocent."

"Thou too, Brutus. You wound me deeply. I am lost, ruined, without a friend, my honor gone." Saying this I pressed my hand over my heart.

"Stop it, Mark," Bill blurted. "Colonel–forget about Lucy. We have a problem–or are you two, too well insulated to notice the cold?"

"Bill, I'm aware of the cold. I once trained at Fort Snelling outside Minneapolis in the winter. Coming from the South I thought I was in Siberia. Now I feel I'm back there again."

"Colonel," I said, "you were saying something about going home for the weekend. From Mack I learned that the conference room is divided and everyone sleeps there until the emergency is over. That's hardly large enough for everyone. I'll wager that Stella and the doctor would be happy to see us go for a few days. What do you say, Bill?"

"I say, let's see Stella before she gets too many requests. Are you ready, Colonel?" Bill asked.

"If the mountain pass is open, I'm ready," the Colonel replied. "You have to drive, because I don't see well anymore."

Mack turned his head to call out. "I heard over the radio that the pass was open."

"That settles it," said Bill. "Let's see Stella now. Mark–you can ride with us."

Mack called out, "Good luck. I'd wager that you three high powered fellows get your way with Stella. She needs the extra space."

Bill was starting toward the door. "Come on, let's go. Nothing will be gained by sitting here."

Bill led the way down the hall past groups of twos and threes rubbing their hands. A few persons were talking excitedly, others were laughing nervously, somewhat confused, or fearful, not knowing whether the loss of heat was a mild inconvenience or a potential danger to them. Mary did not see us as she was explaining to one group that everyone would keep warm if they helped build a snowman or team up to play a game. Mary was not a leader. She could lead Dean, but he was gone.

The Admiral was standing alone in the hall, watching the other patients, apparently unconcerned about all the excitement. I called out above the noise, "Are you looking for a partner for a game of cards?"

"I'm using the cards and all the magazines I can find for a bonfire. Don't tell the Colonel, but I've taken his bedroom set for fire wood."

"I won't," I said, "let him find it out for himself. When are you leaving?"

"Soon after the freeze."

"Look me up."

"I will," said the Admiral.

The Colonel did not hear us. He was at the door of Stella's office. Without waiting for Bill or me he walked in after two quick knocks on the door. Stella looked up at the Colonel, then toward Bill. When she saw me her face hardened.

"What do you want?" she asked, looking directly at me.

The Colonel didn't hesitate. "It's going to be a busy weekend coming up, and I'm about due for a few days at home."

Nodding toward Bill and me he continued, "These gentlemen are ready, too."

"I'll decide who is ready," she snapped at the Colonel. Ignoring Bill she spoke to me.

"Haven't you caused enough trouble? You amaze me having the gall to ask for a weekend at home."

My face felt flushed. There was a limit to these indignities. I restrained my anger, knowing that any outburst would end my chances of going home.

Even though Stella was harsh and self righteous and Ralph a hypocrite, and many of their lectures dull and confusing, my alcoholism was revealed to me at Maplewood. Whatever the forces converging, splitting wide the darkness of my mind, the truth was that I had learned of my addiction here, and thus far I had remained sober. I was sick, constantly attempting to mask this truth. I was so close to madness and despair that I could no longer endure the luxury of anger or any form of self righteousness. With all my patience and strength and wiliness I must hold on, so I remained silent, watching Stella for a sign. How much did she fear this breakdown? She had a problem to solve with those patients; many here like Gene who needed special care and guidance, and who needed someone to transport them. Because she had only a few heaters, the three of us going would lessen her burden. So I stood silent, waiting.

"What do you intend to do when you get home?" she asked. "You wife is gone."

Before I could speak I heard the Colonel's voice, soft and convincing, in honeyed tones.

"No reason Mark can't stay with me. In fact I'll insist upon it, if you think it is necessary. I'll make him my responsibility. Bill can help, too. Between the two of us we won't let him out of our sight."

Stella looked unconvinced. She was not taken in by the Colonel's confidential approach. His Southern talk sounded too good for her to trust.

Before she answered the Colonel, Bill said, "Mark can stay with me. I live alone. There is a fold out bed in the living room. I'll see that Mark calls you each day we are gone, if you like."

I saw the relief on Stella's face. She was either touched by their concern, or, as I suspected, the problem here was a serious inconvenience with a number of patients needing special attention. Stella was understaffed. She did not want to resist these two strong minded men who confronted her. She needed their cooperation.

Stella turned to Bill and the Colonel, ignoring me.

"All right. You can go on two conditions: call when you reach Seattle, and call once each day. Secondly, you heard me say Mark is alone. I want him with one of you until he returns here. Until the treatment is complete, I am responsible to your families."

I said nothing as we left the room. Outside I turned to the Colonel.

"Charm wins out. With Bill's timely help, you added another trophy. All the women who are interesting are drawn to you."

"Like Peg," said Bill. "She's the kind that ignites the inner fire in the Colonel."

"My success with women always baffles you Yankees, makes you jealous. As for you, Mark, it would have served you right if I'd left you here with Peg and Mary and Bernice—or is she gone?"

"Bernice is gone," said Bill. "She's in some asylum somewhere."

Feeling a sense of fear, I asked, "How big a step is it, Bill, from here to Stiron?"

"Hard to know. Each case is different—but if you're wondering about Bernice, there was never much hope. Drugs, booze, a bad marriage, no help in the earlier stages of addiction–this is what I hear happened. All of which says little: it tells us nothing about her willpower or her resistance to drugs or even how far she deteriorated before someone helped her."

"How far gone was she when she came here?" I asked.

"Only a guess," said Bill, "but I don't think she had a chance."

"Let's get out of here," I said, "before the Colonel's charm wears off and Stella has a change of heart."

"Or before Stella begins wondering if Lucy is pregnant," laughed the Colonel.

Bill started along the hall for his luggage. The Colonel followed him. As I turned to go to my room, I was aware of the cold that seemed to intensify the drabness of the hall and the open rooms that were much like Bogleman's office. Pale, grey walls, the tubular lamps gave every face a sickly pallor, the washed out, hopeless look of the damned: men and women who failed, who knew they were lost and were sent here by someone to find a new beginning.

Not one of us has measured up to life. For years, many of us had appeared stable, strong, secure, and had been involved in activities of all kinds. Now, by sorting out our lives, by examining behavior, activities and dreams, no one could say why we were addicted. Some of us were too long in selling, in merchandising, in working in a factory, in a life without challenge or meaning: the list could go on and on, and in the end would not reveal why we were addicted to alcohol. Some of us appeared as strong as the maple trees, which stood naked and still in the snow. Strong, that is, until life's forces converged upon us, and under the mounting pressures, some sudden jolt split us wide so that every curious eye could look inside and see what we were. Being unable to cover our nakedness, we were appalled at what others could see: that which we had attempted to conceal by lies and activity, always evading the truth, unable to face the truth until now. At Maplewood there was nowhere to hide.

Lost to reality, lost to hope, confused by wayward impulses, driven to achieve goals that (once achieved) had little meaning–this was my illusion, the life I led for so many years. Now, split wide, I saw the truth. Even though the vision was not clear, I was groping toward the light. Probing deeper, exposing my innermost self to the white light, I reached out and touched a nerve: a scream followed, a cry of anguish and soul wrenching pain.

Looking deeper, shading my eyes from the light that case a deathlike pallor over all it touched, I recoiled at what I saw: maggots crawling, moving in and out of the flesh, sapping my vitality, devouring my will, slowing eroding away my life. Despair, madness, a sudden collapse into a decadent heap–this was the end ordained for me. In the white light, for one long moment, I was allowed to see the work of my will. The sight repulsed me, forcing me to draw back and turn away.

As an outcast, cut off from society, unloved, unwanted, I somehow must be redeemed. I must rediscover myself. Like the reptile, I must shed my old skin, become a new creature, show the world that I was in control, no longer blown about by every passion or wayward impulse. To be in control would mean overcoming pride, and as pride diminished, the companion vices that pride spawned such as malice and envy and hatred would also lose their hold upon me.

Maplewood was unlike the world outside. There was no warmth or gay colors in the halls or rooms, no attempt to brighten one's life–not even cosmetics colored the faces or concealed the pallor cast over everyone touched by those white lights. Our appearance matched the dead lectures. The truth was served straight, without embellishment or any attempt to lessen or soften the impact. Cold realism–a bitter, tasteless gruel–was the main dish. "Take it, swallow it, choke and gasp from the foul taste–but hold it down you must." This was our law at Maplewood.

All the refinements of society were ignored here. The firm handshake, the warm smile, the easy manners were reserved for those on the outside. More and more I heard one cry echoing through the halls: "Hear the truth. Time has run out. There is no tomorrow. You are the victim and the thief. You are the pursuer and the pursued: the enemy that is driving your real self further into darkness. One more step and no one will reach you."

How strange, being pursued. Now I see that it never mattered where I was, for wherever I had been or longed to be, I was always pursued. If I turned right or left, or walked the hills at night; or sat in the parlor and listened–trying to fathom the voices raging within–or looked among the shadows half expecting those unseen forms to show themselves; or walked among the trees in the snow; or sought refuge and solitude in the forest, it was always the same. I was pursued and driven by forces I could neither comprehend nor resist.

Life's purposes were so broad and diverse, so vague and confusing, that reality–the truth–had never been grasped by me. All I saw was the shadows: for years I had been guided by those vague outlines of reality which at first gently pulled me and finally drove me toward success and into pride and a world where I am now a prisoner. This was the end of the line. I see where I stand. It is the edge of madness. The terror I feel night and day is because I am a prisoner bound within. I cannot see where to turn, what to do, how to break free from the raging conflicts within me. Often I feel that I cannot speak or move or even focus upon the person nearest me.

I want to come back. When my mind and my emotions rebel, crying out for release, my heart begins to beat faster and faster until it feels like it will explode within my chest. I feel I am breaking loose from my bones; my head is wrapped in steel bands and I can feel the bones breaking. Any moment I will leap out of my skin. So far I have held on.

When the raging conflict ceases within, I am exhausted, depressed, and hardly able to move. At such times I hear a new voice, hardly a voice at all–so quiet it is barely a whisper. I have heard it among the trees when I have seen the leaves blown by a gust of wind. The voice, so low, seemed to say, "Patience. Go slowly. Do not give in to fear or hate or anger. I am all you want to be. I am kind and caring. I love life and all its simple pleasures: the first sign of the morning sun, a songbird's song piercing the frosty air, and the books and travel that open new worlds. I enjoy friends and seeing laughter in the eyes of a child and living out the mystery of life with hope and the promise that it has an ultimate purpose. This is the life I want to live with you. Who am I? That, too, is a part of the mystery of life."

Seeing a vague outline of myself, as I was meant to be, I then walked in peace among the trees, no longer aware that any conflict existed within me. The feeling of peace and wholeness was so overwhelming I felt I had witnessed a vision of truth. When I pondered what I had learned, I saw that my vision was only a simple insight–that many men and women lived in peace and harmony.

Almost imperceptibly, at first, I felt a change take place within me. I felt the searing flame of anger. Why, I was no ordinary man! Not, at least, like the rest of men. At first, the voice was just a whisper. Then it was joined by other voices, and the solitary whisper became the thunder of a throng. Then I felt my real self, the man I had been for so many years, slowly take command. My thoughts flowed easily. Like a servant, I listened to the one dominant voice rising above all the others."

I am you–not you! I am the real Mark, not you who feels harmony with birds and trees and flowers. I am the brilliant one, able to see all that others do not see; the crafty one that has given you the insight into business, made you wealthy, made you a name, made you feared and respected among your peers in that world outside of Maplewood. Surely you cannot leave me now?

"I am what is, what exists. I am your identity: what you think, feel–most of all–what you will. No other existence, for you, exists without me. The thrill of being supreme, of sharing the throne with me–seeing life as I see it–was made possible only by yielding yourself to alcoholism. It has made us one, you and me. I become you. You become me. Hereafter, we are one, just you and me. Ha, ha, you will see!

"You have come so far. What a pity to go backward now. What do you care how others look at you? In their eyes, you see what they fear—that you are a strange, unnatural person. Perhaps, we are, you and I. It will be our little joke, but no one can enjoy the joke like me. In time, of course, you will see.

"You resist and twist your nature into an unnatural shape. You have endured much—your wife leaving, your long struggle to excel and now listening to these fools. True, you have overdone things a bit, but that is no reason to become a fanatic. If you feel hatred, frustration, and no sense of warmth toward anyone, well—that is the price you must pay to be a leader. Their minds are set along a narrow line thinking evil of you and me. How dare they threaten you with the accusation of making love to that girl and lusting after her? We have no desire for anyone, you or I. Soon you will be yourself again. Even without alcohol (we do not need it any longer, you and I) we can live in harmony. No need to resist any longer. I am you, I have you: for now we are one—you and I!"

Not so! Even in the darkness of my mind, and in my heart, I can hear the sound of battle: the ring of steel as swinging swords clash; the screams and the anguish and mortal terror as white chargers fall, knowing now, as I felt the intense pain, why the battle was fought. For one instant I saw the dark forces that were consuming my will. As each resolution fails, as hatred rises up within me, there was only darkness. But I had seen for one brief moment another life. The struggle for wholeness and freedom had begun. I have resolved to break out of these chains.

No one can be bound and chained by ghosts. No one can be a slave to monsters which do not exist or cannot be seen or touched, that reside only in the fantasies that arise within a distorted mind. Oh, if they were not so real, so loud, so possessive, so determined to have me see them as me! My resignation—what would it bring? Submit myself fully, completely, without any turning back, to the strident voice that filled me with pride and ambition—that is what's being asked! Then, at last, would peace and harmony follow? Strongly I sense that this is true. All I must do now is allow one dominant voice to reign within me, to guide me once more, as I have been guided for so many years in the past—only this time without alcohol. I would be strong again, far stronger and more capable than ever before. All confusion would end. My mind would be clear again. I would have reached an exalted level. The battle would be over: the victory complete. No other cry would ever again arise within me saying there is, without alcohol, another way of life: a simple way that first called for the abandonment of pride and ambition and then a dedication to the care and concern for others— to a life constantly changing and growing in richness with every new experience.

But the desire to continue following pride and ambition is overpowering. I can hear the promise: surrender you will and you will be different (unlike Bernice who wanders about Stiron in her dreamlike state entertained by her illusions). Make little of the hatred and malice and resentment that burns within me; rather, accept their presence as a positive good, as much a part of me as my eyes, ears and mouth. Alcohol is no longer needed; it has done its work: my will is ruled by pride. I will find peace and harmony within by being unmoved by any living creature. Then, I can pass freely among men untouched by their needs or wants, their disappointments or failures: their tragedy and pain will be forever sealed off from me. Without concern for anyone, this will give me an objective approach to life; enable me to see every opportunity; being above caring there is an advantage that will allow me to wring from every situation whatever is fortuitous for me. There is no price to pay really, except to be forever separated from the rest of men. For the most part am I not that already?

So little change is necessary to find my destiny. I sense that with this resolve (this abandonment to the strident voice that has already sapped my will) even the desire for alcohol will never trouble me again. My habit of life had been set up while drinking. Now, all I am doing is giving up the alcohol while making no other changes. The sacrifice does not seem to be very great after all. Perhaps, if I saw Lucy again, I could explain all this to her. She need not change. Just stop drinking.

CHAPTER 17

Along the hall the faces were tense. There were sudden bursts of excited talk and laughter. There was fear; patients appeared confused, helpless, looking for someone to assure them that there was no danger of freezing. Doctor Neilstrom was patiently explaining to several of the patients why there was no heat.

Nearby Mary was talking. Mary was always the same, living in the eternal now. With her, there was no past or future–only the excitement of the moment. Dean was gone: lonely Dean, wandering about somewhere out there. With whom does he share his thoughts? Does Mary remember him? To Mary's credit, he seemed to draw some strength from her.

"Mark?" It was the Colonel.

"Yes?"

"Get your things. Have you been standing there outside the room all this time? We've been waiting in the car for you."

"All right, Colonel, I'm almost ready. Sorry to hold you. I thought you might be going around saying 'goodbye' to all your lady friends–especially Peg."

"Forget her. I hope she's gone when I get back. The others will appreciate me more."

"Spoken like a considerate gentleman," I said turning into my room.

Getting ready was a simple task. I placed my books in a box and pushed them under the bed, stuffed my clothes into a grip, reached for my topcoat and looked about the room to be sure I did not forget something. Gene, lying on his bed, fully dressed, and with a blanket covering him, was watching me. I quickly picked a blanket off my bed and tossed it to him.

"The elephant is leaving," I said.

"Are you coming back?"

"Of course," I said. "Surely you don't want to lose me."

He stared at me, not speaking. I left the room and hurried down the hall after the Colonel. When I caught up with him he was lighting a cigar and talking with Mary. I passed him without a word, and wondered if he saw me. No man had his capacity for immediacy: one moment he was saying he must leave at once, the next moment, distracted, the urgency forgotten.

Outside, the morning air was bitter cold. My breath turned to frozen vapor. The soft snow was covered with a thin crust and made a crunching sound as I walked to the car. I climbed into the rear seat, knowing that the Colonel with his long legs would preempt the seat next to the driver. I preferred the rear seat anyway. Sitting there would give me an opportunity to reflect, to enjoy the countryside, and to enter into or ignore the conversation between the Colonel and Bill.

"You made it I see," said Bill. "I knew if the Colonel went looking for you, we'd end up waiting for him. He's forgotten about us. Why can't he keep his mind on one thing at a time?"

"I'm afraid I was at fault," I said.

"He's so restless. He didn't need to go after you. If many officers were like him, how did we win the war? Once he plants his feet, sets his jaw into action, he is as immovable as one of our Sherman tanks," Bill said.

"Yes, he's hard to stop," I added. "He has a great passion for life. I've heard as much about the joys of love, the glories of the South, and desert warfare the past month, as I've heard about alcoholism."

"Passion and the joys of life, you say. He's probably rubbing some maiden's knee about now to keep her warm."

"When I passed him in the hall he was talking with Mary and lighting up a cigar."

"Good God, we're lost! She'll allow the Colonel the first ten minutes then she'll begin talking. After twenty minutes the Colonel will get a chance to answer."

I laughed. "You do think Mary is safe with the Colonel?"

"Oh, sure. He talks a lot, but I think he's fired his last cannon. I've heard, though, that he was a good soldier. A silver star from General Patton is a tribute to his courage. I've heard the general made sure that each medal was earned."

"I'm not surprised about the Colonel," I said. "I felt that beneath all that buffoonery there was something solid and tough."

"Are you anxious to get home, Mark?"

"Not really. I'm just beginning to sort things out."

"Good for you. Recently you have appeared to be more relaxed. Often you've seemed far away, as if you were involved in a struggle of some kind. At times I thought you were fighting a war."

"I am."

"What kind of war?"

"For me—to determine who and what I am. Off of alcohol I have come face to face with myself for the first time in years. I can't describe clearly what is happening within me. For brief periods I enjoy peace, followed by intense conflict—a struggle between two forces for my will with each contestant pleading his case. I often believe that my life took the wrong course. You might say that I am trying to wrench it back again into the proper channel."

"Sounds strange to me, Mark. You are a strange one. I like you as you are now," Bill said with a laugh. "Hope you stay that way."

"What would we do in society, Bill, without the patina of manners? You see only the outside, the facade, the studied behavior. You do not see my motives, what has driven me to do the things that I have done. Over a long period this has shaped my life–most of which is hidden from everyone, even me. Anyway, Bill, I see my alcoholism. Whatever I do, however I change, I cannot go on drinking. At least I see that much."

"Good! You'll find yourself. The doctor thought you were a hard case. Do you like him?"

"Not certain."

"Do you like this Bogleman that I hear is coming here?"

My heart leaped. "A little," I said.

"What's he like?"

"A deep one. Sees a lot. He's penetrating, slow moving–rather ponderous–and guesses well."

Bill had been watching the front door while we were talking.

"Here comes the Colonel," he said.

Seeing me in the rear seat, the Colonel growled, "Where have you been? I've been standing in the hallway waiting, Mark. You always keep everyone waiting at meals and the lectures; the doctor is always after you for not understanding the program. You want to get out of here, don't you?"

"Good speech, Colonel, but we have been sitting here for twenty minutes. You are now standing outside the car. Doesn't that tell you something? Did you win battles by talking?"

"Come on, Colonel, get in. You and Mark can discuss your differences going home."

As the Colonel settled into his seat, Bill headed the car toward the main road, giving his full attention to narrow, snow covered road that led out of Maplewood. When we reached the highway the Colonel spoke up.

"Mark, how did you get by me in the hallway?"

"You were talking to Mary."

"I think she has a problem," the Colonel said.

"Doesn't everyone?"

"She doesn't want to go home. She lives alone, her husband is dead, and her mother doesn't approve of her. I think she would be happy living here."

"Then she is really sick," I said.

As the Colonel began repeating what he had said, I thought of Mary. She appeared interested in every one at Maplewood. She had like Dean more than all the others. Surely, he had revealed to her all his secret hopes and his disappointments and how his unfulfilled dreams might be realized now that his alcoholism was under control. She was a warm, friendly companion. She encouraged, she flattered, and she built upon his self esteem. She was sincere, and when Dean left Maplewood, she never mentioned his name again. She was the same with anyone she contacted: reviving their confidence, enhancing their diminished self esteem, helping them to overcome their self loathing and self hatred. The pity was that Mary had no substance. She was as ephemeral as a white cloud or the fog that dissolved in the morning sun.

She deceived, not knowing that she deceived: she was as lost as those she tried to console. She hid her fears or ignored them, or, perhaps, did not see them at all. She submerged herself. She became totally involved in the fears of those around her. In her presence I felt her emptiness, as she talked on and on, deeply serious, rarely smiling. I heard her laugh only once: a strange laugh, not rich and full, but empty, as if she were unsure that she existed as an individual. Mary lived for the moment, ignoring the past, making no commitment to the future. Dean was gone–and forgotten.

The Colonel's voice interrupted my thoughts. "As soon as I get home I'm going to get a good piece of baked Virginia ham and some grits. Have you eaten grits, Mark?"

"No, I thought only your slaves ate grits."

"Mark, you spent too many years in that deep freeze. Where was it? The Dakotas? Bill, when we get through these mountains, stop at the first Baskins and Robbins you see."

"You know what we were told about sugar," I reminded him. "Sugar lifts you up like booze, gives one a false high and then drops you with a crash. You'll get all the energy you need in a high protein diet."

"Don't lecture me, Mark. Remember, Stella entrusted your care to us. Now you are preaching."

"Spoken like a true alky," Bill said.

"Bill, you and Mark are jealous of the Colonel. You don't have my charm and stamina, or my appeal to the fair flowers, which are as tantalizing as the magnolia blossoms of the South that I once plucked. I can hardly wait."

"You are a poet or a dreamer," I said.

While Bill and the Colonel carried on with their talk about the merits of the different flowers, their shape and appeal (in contrast to the charm and poise and inner beauty of more mature women), I looked out the window at the countryside. The highway was open; snow was piled high on either side of the road. The trees were tall and still and held fresh snow in their branches. Bill was a fast driver. Within the hour we would be descending from the mountains.

Looking up at the grey sky, I knew there would be rain falling near sea level. The fresh fall of snow in the vast forest and the pine trees that stretched endlessly from valley to mountain peaks, always had the same effect on me. I felt a sense of mystery, of adventure; felt a strong desire to explore the deep recesses of the forests and the valleys. Searching–having always looked beyond the present moment– I saw now that my real life, the only life I possessed, was here in the present moment. Was I then, like Mary, heedless of the past and its lessons and unconcerned with the future and its promise of change and growth? Not at all! I feared. I lived in fear. I was often driven by desperation, yet was able to face my demons. Mary became hollow and empty by acting as if they did not exist; by never coming to grips with her feelings–by ignoring them, avoiding conflict and thereby becoming a stranger to herself. She was ruled by impulses. She did not know their source. She was the tool and the instrument of whatever force dominated her at the moment. She saw nothing, learned nothing– and emptiness became her.

Still, I was aware that my life, too, was now in this present moment. I was living, breathing and feeling, sensing pain. Whatever was to be gained, any change to be made, must be made and changed now, not in an uncertain future. Delay–always waiting to attempt what ought to be attempted now–was a sure course to failure. But now, I must shape my life into a new life, moment by moment, with each ticking of the clock. If I am what I am because of false decisions, because I was deceived by overweening pride and ambition, then I will change. No one is forced against his will to remain what he has been.

As the clock ticked away (giving evidence of my mortality) my thoughts were directed toward new goals, toward forming new habits that would change the shape of my character. A new man then will emerge, strange and different from the old, but still wearing the old shell. I will build today what I will be tomorrow–and tomorrow I build, adding refinement and strength to that new life, on and on, always living with intensity, and the full awareness that all my life exists now in the present moment. Certainly from the past I have gained knowledge and experience. This will be retained. The sufferings and joys, too, are not lost. They are a part of me. The future does not exist but I still live in hope: I look for fulfillment and growth and change in my life. But the future, with those nagging, haunting fears of impending doom, will no longer be allowed to cloud my mind

and prevent me from living out the present moment–each moment of
the clock–with the full involvement of all my faculties. The new man
will not be like the old. But I will look the same; feel the same except
the fire of ambition will be extinguished. Once freed from this
bondage, all the other vices will topple.

Anyone can live for one moment at a time, no matter how
severe the pain. Whenever my mind turns backward, I will wait in
patience, remembering that the past is gone beyond my reach.
Powerless to change even one failure, my will, in time, will come
around and accept this truth, then the pain will grow less as I accept
the fact that the present moment is all I have, and all I must give an
account for. As clear as all this seems to me, at this moment, I know
the struggle within my heart still rages.

How strong is that proud voice within me that cries out saying
that my character is formed and set, as if it were chiseled in stone; that
insists that all decisions and actions, no matter how destructive, have
cast me into a mold that neither lightning nor earthquake can break.
The voice is deafening as the cries grow louder.

"Level the mountains and dry up the sea," this voice
challenged, "and still you will not have the power to change or break
the habits and patterns of thought that are as much a part of you as the
marrow of your bones."

To distract myself so that I would no longer hear this
destructive voice I searched the mountain side. As the car rounded a
curve I saw a deer near the river bank; farther on I looked up and saw a
break through the clouds and the open sky–clear and blue in sharp
contrast to the grey clouds. My spirits lifted. The ugly voice ceased.
The thoughts that I was chained to the old habits and old vices faded
away when I saw the clouds break, the sky open and the clear, deep
blue of the evening sky.

Without alcohol I am free. My mind is clear once more. The
past cannot shape my future, not if I allow myself to live only one
moment at a time, cautiously taking each step forward, always aware
of past mistakes so as not to repeat them. I will not morbidly dwell

upon these failures: they will be relegated to a deep recess of the mind to be drawn upon when decisions are made. Then their voice can be heard; "Beware," the voice will say, "do not repeat this action. This decision is making you ambitious, and your ambitions eventually will lead to your destruction as surely as if you began drinking again."

Suddenly my reflections wearied me. Examining them, turning my thoughts and resolutions over in my mind, they seemed so dull, so insignificant and foolish. Of course, anyone can live for a series of endless moments. After all, isn't that of what life consists? The sensations, the constant bombardment of stimuli of sound, speech, heat and cold that call forth our responses. Are my reactions any different from those I have witnessed in others? Are the wild aberrations of my mind so wild after all? Are my failures any worse? My struggles greater? I fear that I fancy myself to be unique, when in truth I am as common as a pine cone buried in the snow.

In a moment, if I don't take care, Bill and the Colonel will hear my laugh. Me unique? What nonsense! The flowers of spring are rare and delicate and they squander their fragrance and rich color in an unseen meadow or a dark forest. Wild animals pass by, unaware of their beauty. Only a few eyes are privileged to see such splendor. Yet such lavish color and such radiant beauty thrives unknown and lasts but a few short days. Nourished by the melting snow, the early rains and warm breezes, these exquisite flowers are the delight of spring and the glory of the mountain meadows. Their reign lasts only until the summer sun grows weary of them.

From somewhere it comes back to me that I am worth more than song birds and the wild spring flowers. But how can that be true? I am not unique. I am a babble of voices, a form, a solid mass that contains within it a battlefield where knights are pitted one against the other. I have never been in command. My life consists of passions. One day I am consumed by lusts; then envy follows; then hatred. But ambition is always near at hand, waving its banner of triumph.

No one cares. Why should they? Who am I to think that anyone should waste even a moment wondering or caring about me? No one will ever look at me again. If I have dried up like the spring flowers, choked by the sun or consumed by the beasts of passion; that is my struggle and my loss. No one has witnessed my struggle. Scant attention will be paid to the shell that remains after I have failed.

What is this price of peace? "Surrender! Give up your free will to me," cries the strident voice within me. "Accept the knowledge that you cannot drink again, but go no further. No other change was necessary after you stop drinking. Hardness, hatred, ambition, pride and avarice are as much a part of you as the snow covered rocks are a part of the mountain side."

Give up my freedom, my true identity, become one with you? Never! That is not the answer!

If I also refuse to listen to that other voice, that has been silent all these years, that is now attempting to help me discover who I am: if my pride refuses to hear the low, pitiful cry that is appealing to me for recognition and encouragement, then I will not see who I am. Refuse to hear this gentle, but firm offer of help, crush these inner feelings of tenderness, concern and affection; ignore them, call the unfamiliar feelings by their true name (instability and softness and emotionalism) then I shall remain as I have become–a hard and driven man.

As I listen once more to that faint cry within, calling for recognition, I am stirred by memories of my youth. Now that I no longer drink, I am, in the silence of the evening, and, in those hours before dawn, hearing this call that I once remembered as a child. Follow me, it keeps saying; let me grow stronger within you, and nourish you with kindness until I can be clearly heard. As I grow you will see a new reality, a new person: an image like me, your true nature, is what you will become. Feeling strength from this voice, and peace too, I know instinctively that for the first time in many years I am hearing the truth. I resolved to follow this voice. There will be, at last, peace and unity.

Fear. Why does fear come over me? I know why. Any radical change in my nature will cause confusion, a babble of dissenting voices, and from this chaos only failure. Drink and forget. Drink and all conflicts end. Only peace and serenity remained. In those early days of drinking only one voice caressed me. It nurtured me, saying, "We are one, you and I. You die but not me. Do I confuse you? Remember we have grown together. Your change is complete. We do not need alcohol any longer to remain as one, you and I."

My weak nerves will no longer tolerate alcohol, but I can have other gratifications. Like a proud eagle I can stand alone with money, prestige, and influence and in the knowledge that my efforts were crowned with success. Never will I ask myself again of what that consists. How foolish to ever call such success an illusion when, from its glow, I feel such warmth. Such feelings of importance are not an illusion. They have sustained me all these years.

After all, what would the world by like without ambition? Greed and avarice and envy have filled more men with fire (and thus sustaining the world) than all the caring and tenderness since the dawn of history. I am one of those men. I performed well when driven by ambition. My nature does not need to change. All I need do is stop drinking.

Of course that is not easy. No voice needs to tell me that. Nothing, after all, is easy. My life, if it is to continue, must be without alcohol. What a life! (Not much of a life–but all I have). Laugh at myself, pity myself–weeping and wailing, looking about for someone who cares–then turn bitter and cynical and order myself to bear up like a man. Turn hard, then cold, and harder still. Mock the weak, or even better, ignore them as if they did not exist at all. How fresh, then, will be the morning air. What a thrill to laugh in the face of the howling wind; to ignore the heat of the sun while my spirit glows with pride and soars upon the wings of ambition that has already carried me so far.

But now I recognize that my nature is divided. Without alcohol to help sustain my old vision of reality, I did not expect to be confronted with a new vision of the truth. With the ambitious, calculating side of my nature (that had for years encouraged me to follow my own ends) and pitted against the idealistic and creative side of my nature, which I hardly knew existed, there was bound to be an ensuing struggle.

My soaring egotism no longer holds me aloft. There is no lightness or gaiety or laughter in me. I see only darkness in my heart. The darkness outside at night seems bright and full of light compared to the darkness within me. I search my heart: I see nothing; nothing at all–only emptiness. When I roam the empty regions of my heart I feel utterly alone.

Often in the night in a dreamlike state my mind or spirit seems to wander in another dark region. At such time it always seems that I have been led into a black world where all light was gone, and emptiness and despair reigned. Although there was no sound, no visible presence, only a black empty space, I was still aware of my own existence. I sensed that I was in a region ordained for me. I sensed a presence and that every intimate detail about me was known. I felt shame, intense shame as I realized that all my feelings and motives were understood. Even worse was the loneliness and the isolation. Fear increased–a terrible lonely fear.

Faintly at such times I heard this cry, "Turn back, turn back. Call out for help. Call out to me before your leaden weight carries you so deep into this void that my power can no longer carry you back. Then they will come and shut the door of this great vault, and you will not be able to come out again. You have wandered in and out of the dark side of your nature. Once your internal life is controlled and completely shaped by another power, your humanity will disappear, and my voice will grow silent. You will then be locked in this vault, you will be a part of that dark world that you dread–and all you will ever hear forever in that lonely darkness is the occasional laughter of someone mocking you. For you will be lost, mad, and utterly consumed by that power with the strident voice that has waited so long to have you."

Such confusion within me. Such dreadful thoughts. I felt great fears. I did not know why I should suddenly be fearful. Yes, I really knew. My life had reached a turning point: giving up alcohol was not enough; now, I must face reality and make other difficult decisions which meant changing my life. My God, if there was one person that I could turn to to express how I felt. If I had one person to stand beside me who understood my split and torn nature—I could endure anything. Would Bogleman understand me? His insights were penetrating. He was coming to Maplewood. I must speak to someone . . . . .

"Say Mark, what are you doing? Haven't heard a sound from you. I have an idea."

"What is it, Colonel?"

"We are not far from Seattle."

"Yes, I can see the rain."

"Let's stop off and see Dean."

"That's all right with me, but as you can see I'm not driving."

"Not a bad idea," said Bill. "I'm not going anywhere but back to Maplewood."

"There's an ice cream parlor in the shopping center not far from Dean's house," I added.

"That settles it," said Bill, "the Colonel had that in mind all along."

The Colonel turned his head slightly as he leaned back in his seat. I could see a sly smile on his face.

CHAPTER 18

Dean's house stood at the end of a lane outside the city. We reached the house by threading a course through fir trees. Looking at the house I saw that it was the same size and shape as other houses we passed among the trees. Only the facades differed among these homes to conceal from the buyers that they were tract houses and all alike. The roof treatment alternated between hip and gable, with a shorter or longer overhang; some had garages, others carports; front entrances varied slightly with minor window variations. The colors were different. By such artifice the builder concealed the monotony of repetition, giving the appearance of originality to each home, while passing on a considerable savings to the buyer. This was one of the many skills of a merchant builder.

"There's Dean's car," said the Colonel.

He was out and up the front steps as soon as Bill applied the brakes. Dean saw us through the front window and came immediately to the front door. As I walked up the steps I looked up at Dean who was more outgoing than usual, wringing the Colonel's hand.

"What a surprise seeing you fellows. This is great. Come in. I was sitting in the window thinking about you and then I saw the car drive up and the Colonel run up the steps."

Inside I looked around the living room, which was orderly and plain with that sort of modern furniture which is seen everywhere; furniture whose purpose is utilitarian without having any appeal to one's esthetic tastes. At the dining room table a young man with oriental features was studying. He looked up and smiled. Down the hall I saw a girl, somewhat younger, and attractive, with the same features as the young man. They looked very much like their Oriental mother whom I had seen only once at Maplewood.

As I settled into a large chair, Dean told us that his wife was attending a meeting at the church. The Colonel listened while he ate candy and nuts from a dish by the sofa. To this point, Bill had been sitting, silently smoking a cigarette, watching Dean.

"Is everything going well?" he asked.

Only then did I look closely at Dean. My pulse quickened. His face was flushed; he was agitated; his excited, talkative manner was unusual for Dean. I looked at the Colonel. Hearing Bill's question he hesitated (while reaching for nuts) and looked at Dean

"My stomach has been troubling me," Dean said. "Colonel, you're an old Army man. You were injured and know how these old wounds act up at times."

The Colonel, who now listening attentively, replied, "I know what you are saying. I have a purple heart, too. But not even the Silver Star kept me from becoming a drunk. Are you trying to tell us something?"

Dean did not answer at once. He sat looking at the three of us.

I admired the Colonel. He was hard. At times he could be mean—a tough one to cross—but there was nothing wrong with his heart. Corrupt, perhaps, but in his corruption I found the warm flow of humanity. If I wanted consolation or needed a friend to stand by me, I would not hesitate to seek his help—at least for anything except my strange aberrations of the mind.

"Dean," the Colonel laughed, "you are not going to try to fool your superior officer. As civilians we are equal now, you and I, and you have a problem. Admit it. We are friends. You are not talking to one of those uninitiated out there who doesn't understand a real drinker. I've been around the horn many times. I didn't get off the pickle boat yesterday. You've been drinking. Say it."

Dean lowered his head. For a moment I thought he might become emotional; then, he raised his head and looked directly at the Colonel.

"I was coming home from work. It was raining and snowing, and it was dark. I turned on the radio and heard this song that brought back old memories of happier days. I felt so miserable, so filled with longing to be happy again. If only for a moment I could recapture something of my lost youth–the vitality and zest for life that had left me. The longing increased. At the stop sign I noticed I was low on gas and pulled into a station where, by the odd hand of fate, I saw an old army buddy. He invited me to have a drink at a nearby cocktail lounge. I couldn't say to him, 'I'm an alcoholic.' I went in, determined not to drink."

Dean threw up his hands. "You know the rest. I can't get off of it. I never dreamed that I couldn't stop."

I heard my voice. "You are a veteran, Dean. Make use of your rights. Go now; go today, if they will take you."

"Mark's right," said the Colonel, "go now."

Bill spoke up looking toward the Colonel. "Where do we call for veteran's services?"

"I want to go," said Dean, "but I'm afraid that if I take much time, I might be cut short on my pension. With all the time I spent at Maplewood my firm is getting impatient."

"Let me take care of that," I said. "I'll go to see your firm the first of the week. They'll listen. They are not going to let you go over this problem. You are a veteran. You have a crippling disease and you are trying. You are also a gentleman in my book."

"Thanks. That helps. You fellows give me a real lift."

Bill left the room and walked down the hall to the kitchen. I could hear him dialing and talking to someone giving them a brief resume of the facts. While Bill phoned, I watched Dean, who was listening to the Colonel tell how he was blown from a tank, which accident left him with only partial use of his left eye, and impaired use of an arm. From war casualties he drifted to describing some of his nurses–particularly one he met while he was recovering. His tale was lurid. He described her size and shape and all her revealing merits between bursts of laughter.

"She was a little thing," the Colonel said. "I would pull her on like a pair of boots. She almost killed me off. I wonder is she might have been working for the enemy."

Dean displayed nothing unusual, except a slight nervousness, and a seeming desire to please, which I attributed to a feeling of guilt. I wondered if Dean felt lonely and isolated. I had met Dean's wife only once, but I liked her immediately. She was of slight stature, and had clear golden skin and lovely, soft almond shaped eyes which seemed to express understanding and kindness. Dean may have felt abandoned because of lack of communication with his oriental wife; or his children, who appeared respectful, had other interests; or because of his alcoholism which may have caused estrangement. He needed a friend. He needed to release his feelings, to let go, to examine freely, without constraint, his anxieties and fears. He could not recover alone– this had been made clear to us at Maplewood.

Among the maple trees, the scarred veterans of many winters, I had often seen Dean walking along a path with Mary. Always his head had been bent as he talked earnestly to her. But Mary? I wondered if she listened? Did she hear anyone, even herself? She talked, appeared to listen, and then talked some more. But it appeared to me that, in all of her earnestness, she never reflected upon her own chatter or retained anything she heard. Life was the excitement of the moment.

For me to blame Mary for not being more help to Dean was unjust. Blame her? My God, why not blame myself? I was immersed in self; in mortal combat, fighting to hold onto something. I was far too involved with myself to go for a walk with Dean, to draw him out and encourage him to continue his struggle. While I was battling for my life, why had I assumed that Dean, who always appeared so sad, was not involved in a similar conflict? If I had taken the time to listen to Dean and had encouraged him to recognize his own worth, he might have hesitated over that first drink. Now, it was easier for me to blame Mary, because she had appeared to forget Dean the very day he left. So she acted upon impulses without sorting out her thoughts. At least her world (small as it appeared to me) included Dean while he was at Maplewood. If I had spent a few hours with him during those long days at Maplewood, he might have not felt so abandoned, so isolated and so lonely. Knowing he had the warm support of friends, he probably would not have fallen at the first temptation when an old buddy offered good fellowship. The thought of this drink was undoubtedly tempting, but he probably wanted the fellowship more. He feared offending an old friend–so he drank and undid himself.

For the first time I saw something in Dean's manner and in his eyes that alarmed me. He appeared frightened. It was not fear, entirely, but something else as well. He had a crazed, haunted look, and clouded eyes–the kind of reflection I sometimes caught of myself in the mirror, when, unexpectedly, turned a corner or opened a door to see my face suddenly in a mirror, staring back at me. Seeing myself (as an outsider would have seen me), I was shocked at what I saw: the despair, the frustration, the wild eyes of the damned. Quickly I turned my eyes away from the mirror pondering what I had seen, and feeling then that I was really lost; that happiness and peace and caring for anyone was gone forever, yet the memory of my loss would always remain to torment me.

In Dean's eyes, and in his manner, were signs of desperation–not ordinary signs of depression and despair but something deeper–something dark and sinister. I could not fathom the depth of his feelings. I could only sense that he was disturbed and that the pain and confusion he was experiencing was threatening to overcome him. All I had to go on in judging Dean's present state of mind were these vague signs, and the agony of my own experience at Maplewood. I might be projecting: seeing alarming signs in Dean's behavior that did not exist; judging him by a mind which had been warped by my own bizarre behavior. Like the patient who analyzed his own symptoms by reading a medical journal, I was, with limited knowledge, becoming unduly

alarmed. I would do well to calm myself. My feverish mind was not
trustworthy.

Dean turned toward me. He was aware of my silence; his
expression indicated that he understood I had been observing him
closely.

"How is Mary?" Dean asked.

"She is fine now. At first I thought she would pine away after
you were gone. She sends her best. She said she hoped to see you
again soon." None of what I said was true. I excused myself thinking
that Dean needed encouragement.

Dean smiled. "I liked Mary. She always listened to me, and I
always felt good in her presence. For me it has always been hard to
talk freely with anyone. With Mary it was different. I love my wife but
she is Oriental and so quiet. We don't talk much. You see how it is."

How could I see or know how it was? His wife was Korean.
Their two children appeared well adjusted. At the moment they were
studying and certainly showed no signs of tension. Dean was not a
man who sought out other women. Why he could not communicate
with his wife was beyond me. There could be numerous reasons: a
falling out caused by Dean's drinking, as so often happens in
marriage—they drifted apart, eventually seeing one another as
strangers. Struggling alone against alcoholism presented frightful
odds. I feared for Dean: the battle for sobriety was not won alone. In
my present state I recognized my limited knowledge, but I was also
acutely aware of my painful encounter with a divided self, with forces
beyond my comprehension and strength to overcome. If Dean was
waging a similar battle he needed help to win out.

"Dean," I said, "you surprise me. You have charm and wit and
surely all that was not reserved just for Mary. She's gone. She was a
gay and sympathetic companion, but like the others at Maplewood she
has gone out of your life. You have your wife, and you can surely talk
as freely to her as you talked with Mary."

204 MY DAEMON   MULLALLY

"That's right," said the irrepressible Colonel. "Mary was crazy anyway. One of these days she will follow Bernice; Mary is only one step behind her. Whenever I saw Mary she was ten feet off the ground. I don't think she ever got off the booze. Do you, Mark?"

I shrugged. Although I knew that Mary was unbalanced, I did not want to disillusion Dean. The Colonel appeared unaware of Dean's dangerous state of mind.

"Oh, Mary is fine," I said. "Colonel, you don't understand her. You like those big lusty girls who don't talk much and are after your body."

"What's wrong with that? They know a good thing."

"I'm not passing judgment, you old devil. I'm merely saying that some men are different. Dean and Mary developed a fine friendship."

"Mark, save your idealism. Mary never remembered anyone ten minutes after he was gone."

I looked hard at the Colonel, trying to give him a sign that Dean needed encouragement, but the Colonel was set upon giving us the truth about Mary. In his mind she was a chatterbox, a shallow, mindless creature, always high: a woman without sensual appeal, without any qualities worth discussing and, above all, a poor choice for Dean. Looking across at Dean, I felt he was waiting for me to defend Mary.

"All right, Colonel, you've told us that Mary doesn't measure up to your standard. I like Mary because she happens to like Dean. She saw something good and fine and noble in him. She saw a man who fought hard for his country, who endured much. And now–like you and me–suffered a setback with booze. She saw heroic qualities in Dean. Is that bad?"

"Save your sermon, Mark. It's not Sunday. You're right about her not being my kind of woman. Wooing her would have as much appeal to me as attempting to court a noisy chimpanzee."

"We are not all made alike," I replied as Bill entered the room.

"It's all set, Dean," he said. "You can go in the first of the week. Just bring your V.A. records with you."

Before Dean said anything I added, "Don't worry about your job. If you like, I'll go in and see your employer."

"No, that won't be necessary," Dean said, shaking his head. "I prefer to do it my way. I've been with the company for more than twenty years. I'm near retirement. The worst that could happen is that I'd be retired early."

"Whatever you say–but go," I urged. "Look at the Colonel. If he can make it, this ancient warrior, surely you'll make out."

"Who's an ancient warrior? I'll match you at any game, Mark. You're too burned out to catch a maid in the woods."

"Colonel, you assume too much. Lucy has gone out of my life."

"Don't be too sure. She wanted you. I know women."

"She was a simple, sick girl."

"You are simple and naive if you believe that. I'll grant you that she was sick, but she was not simple and innocent."

At the mention of Lucy's name, the Colonel seemed to become lost in thought. And had the truth been known, this was very much the case. Thoughts of Lucy brought to mind another girl in another place, another time.

The Colonel had a faraway look in his eye when he continued.

"That Lucy sure stirs up the memories. There was this girl that I met at a little resort hotel I used to go to. Her name was Tessie. We'd get a case of good sour mash, and I mean to tell you that she could drink any man I've ever known right under the table. And still be able to go all night.

"'You sure is a nice gentleman,' she'd say. 'You be kind to Tessie. And you sure are some kind of performer.' Then she'd giggle, and take another drink."

"Here we go again, Dean. I think alcohol has softened the Colonel's mind. If half your lurid tales are true, Colonel, you'd be gone by now," I said.

"Colonel, did you ever get a dose?" Bill asked.

The Colonel ignored the jibe.

"Jealous, that's it! You're all jealous of my success."

"Colonel," I said, "we came to see Dean to help him with a problem, not to listen to you entertaining him with X-rated tales of your lusty youth."

"There is nothing wrong with Dean. He is an old army man, a soldier. The problem he faces will be taken care of in a veterans' hospital. Is that settled?"

I watched Dean. He had brightened as he listened to the Colonel's lurid tales. Dean seemed to be drawn out of himself by the Colonel's vigor and hearty zest for life.

There was a moment's silence when everyone made the small moves preparatory to leaving. Dean's eyes turned clouded and wild and the lines seemed to be more deeply etched in his face. His shoulders slumped and he appeared to sink deeper and deeper within himself into that sanctuary where his feelings and motives were hidden from us.

His voice, when he spoke to thank us for coming, carried a false ring of courage. I sensed that he was possessed by guilt, fear and loneliness, but I could not act. My senses alerted me to a danger–but what danger? What I could not see I could not attack or defend. I felt helpless in Dean's presence. I felt as if I was standing at the foot of the scaffold and could not lift a hand to save a friend from the gallows. He could be led or dragged up the steps and after the reading of the sentence, blindfolded; his hands tied, legs bound, and a noose around his neck. At a given signal he would be plunged into eternity–and I was constrained from uttering one word to save him.

When the doors of the car were closed, I looked back to see Dean standing alone, watching us as we drove off into the night. When I turned around in the seat of the car to face the front we had reached a stop sign. Bill, aware of my silence, glanced at me.

"Mark," he said, "when we left the house you looked sadder than Dean. There is no need for you to be alarmed. His setback is nothing. It happens all the time. You are the one who alarms me when you fall into one of your melancholy states. With your wife gone, the two of us must watch you closely."

"I'll babysit him the first night, Bill. Our houses are in the same area," said the Colonel.

"You gentlemen are so kind," I said, "but your help is not needed. You put on a good show for Stella and I appreciate it, Colonel. You can save your nursery rhymes for your grandchildren."

"Is that all the thanks I get for getting you out?" said the Colonel.

"Come on, Colonel. You know I'd only get in your way. You have my number. I'm as close as the telephone. You're right, Bill, about one thing. I am concerned about Dean."

"He's depressed, that's all," said the Colonel, "but he's a real combat soldier. He feels guilty, I suppose. The doctor told us this would happen if any of us suffered a relapse. He fought in Africa and the south of France, and spent some time in Korea. If he was able to get through those battles, where they were shooting real bullets, he ought to be able to get through this little skirmish."

"If you are sure, Colonel, I won't think about Dean any more. You ought to know your soldiers," I said, closing my eyes. I tried to drive all thoughts of Dean from my mind.

CHAPTER 19

As the car neared my neighborhood I became restless.

"Bill," I said, "let me out at the next intersection. I'll walk the rest of the way."

"You're not a duck, you'll get wet," the Colonel snorted.

"I really want to walk. It's not raining that much. Windy and wet–that's my kind of weather. Clears the mind."

"You're crazy, Mark, and I'm supposed to be responsible for you," said the Colonel.

"I know, but let's keep that a secret between the three of us."

As the car pulled over to the curb, Bill turned and asked, "Are you all right, Mark?"

As I got out I said, "Everything is fine."

The Colonel called out as the car began moving, "I'll call tonight and in the morning."

I waved and began walking along the dark street. A light rain was falling and the bare trees hardly moved in the wind. The stars were sealed off by the clouds. The night was cold and very dark.

As I walked along listening to the wind rise and fall, I wondered what I would do in an empty house. No one knew I was coming. No one would hear from me. Catching the light from a street lamp I glanced at my watch, after eleven. Could it be that late? I was a creature of the night, I mused.

The darkness invaded my pores, slowly penetrating like the cold air, until I could feel a presence. The assaults upon my mind were always at night. There was a babble of voices and then the many voices grew silent as one strident voice confronted me. The cry was always the same; a steady, relentless onslaught, a wearing away of all resistance in the attempt to convince me that any change, except to stop drinking, was needless, even harmful to my well being.

I mocked and taunted the voice within saying, 'At last you concede that alcohol is no longer good for me. Now that I recognize this truth you state that alcohol served me well for many years, and shaped me into a desirable man, admired and envied and looked upon as a success. Damn your lies! Alcohol has almost destroyed me. Exalted ambition has carried me along a painful course to success—but at what a price! My nerves are shattered. My marriage almost gone. My total interest in life for years has revolved around business which in the end has insulated me from friends and art and beauty in every form: the wonders of nature, the laughter in the eyes of a child—all the ordinary, simple pleasures enjoyed by anyone who is not driven and enslaved by ambition.

'So now you are calling out to me! I can hear you, but you no longer will control my actions or my thoughts. Call me a milksop? coward? weakling? You will not drive me back into your arena—that is your game. You have said it all before; that you are the master—not me, but you. But who are you? Come clean just once with me. You desire to absorb me, to have my will, to direct my thoughts and actions; to possess me, all of me, except my consciousness: there must be something left of me to torment.

'You are the power of the night. For too many years you have deceived while leading or driving me. You are untiring, relentless, a ravenous beast. Your weapons are formidable: you consume with ambition (calling it zeal or necessity); and you offer soaring, exalted pride that blows darkness into the eyes and into the heart, so that all decent feelings are dried up. You would have me shaped into someone like yourself and in your power: someone you could possess and ravage and torment at will; someone you could consume again and

again without destroying–to your delight. With my nature split I could
be a shallow and empty chatterbox like Mary; or mad like Bernice; or
further weakened and confused by alcohol like Dean; or burned out
and beyond reach like the Admiral. Each of us bears your mark:
somehow you have led us, consumed us, possessed us, so that we no
longer direct our own lives.

'Thankless idol, whoever you are, to whom I have given my
allegiance for so many years–release me! For too long I have obeyed.
You encouraged my meaningless struggle to soar upon the wings of
pride like an eagle; you created for me an illusion that I could outstrip
my very nature. Forged into something I was not meant to be, I have
lost the very feelings and the simple joys and kindness that make me a
man. Release me! Come out into the night so I can see you.

'Show your face now. Is that you over there behind that tree?
now behind that shrub; no, in the tree–are you everywhere? Did I see
your flared nostrils, the gleam of your eyes? You are not fearsome
when I see you. It is when you run at will throughout my mind,
holding my will in one hand while you stir up all your allies–lust,
ambition, fear and hatred–that you are formidable. Now that my
independence and self worth has increased you grind your teeth, for a
new life to me is death to you. I see you in the dark. How ravenous
you are! You are not in a closet now. I can see those teeth that are
always consuming; that have drained away so much of my life, so that
now, not much more than a husk remains.

'You want more than the empty chambers, the halls and
passageways of my mind where your voice rings out, and you run
rampant; where I cannot enter to fathom the depth or the height or the
width of this unchartered region. Somewhere within this vast cavern
you reside all too near my heart and my will. You have the advantage.
I cannot go into myself and scan the terrain or measure the boundaries
where the battle is fought.

'What is this roar I hear? Have you released the wind? Or is
this howling I hear your voice? For years I did not recognize your
presence or even hear your voice. Together, as one, in perfect

harmony, we were unified by alcohol. My will was your will–the cunning, slyness and ruthlessness was your gift. Now recognizing your presence, there is a great division within me, as my true nature rebels against your possession of me. Your solution for ending this struggle within me is ingenious: stop drinking but make no other changes in my life. After all, my character is already formed, you say. Cease struggling to change your nature and then a kind of peace will follow.'

My mind was now feverish with excitement. I hurried along the street at a faster pace. I could see the dark outline of my house in the trees. I walked across the street and along the tree lined walk to the steps that led to the entrance. I stopped at the top of the steps by the glass door that opened into the house and stood for a moment fumbling with the keys before finding the right one: but I did not enter the house.

Slowly I turned as if to confront the night. I heard the rain dripping from the eaves, I saw the fir trees moving back and forth along the walkway–and all about me the once familiar forms shrouded in darkness. In every strange shape I looked for the enemy. It was all a fantasy. Yet, my heart longed to see in the darkness something real–to see the enemy come out of my nightmares into the open. Standing in the rain, slowly unlocking the door, pushing it open, and moving cautiously into the interior of the house, I realized that I would welcome a contest now, alone in a closed room with my enemy. Let him assume the shape of a foul beast, a giant reptile of spider–let him take any form–and I would still accept the challenge. What I have suffered through division, being split apart; with every jagged edge subject to pain! Any contest would be worth the price if I was then rid, forever, of the conflict and the confusion and the division within me.

No price would be too great to pay for the strength to change; to be able to put an end to ambition and its fruits that only create an insatiable appetite for more. Peace is all I seek–that inner harmony and contentment. That desire I place above all others. I have had enough of the foul taste of success and all that goes with it.

Crossing the room, I pulled up the drapes allowing the dim light from the gas lamps to filter into the room. My eyes adjusted to the feeble light. Nothing had changed. The details of the portrait, in that weak light, were not clear, but I could make out the smiling face. Its features were fixed in my mind because I had studied that face so many times. What was I to do with the next few days? I felt no desire to see anyone or to drink. As I walked about the room I stared again at the portrait. Such a handsome man: complacent, well fed, well dressed, contented, just as I last remembered him that fateful night that now seemed so long ago. At least he had not changed.

The rafters creaked in the arched ceiling. I listened. There was silence in the house. Outside I could hear the wind. I felt a vague sense of uneasiness and a premonition that something was about to happen. I looked yet again at the portrait and turned away. The dead picture of a young man no longer interested me. To speculate about his past was meaningless.

Restless! How restless I was! It was too late to go to a movie. The room was cold. I was hungry, so I looked for something to eat. The refrigerator was empty. I snapped on the light in the pantry just long enough to find canned tuna, English cheese and crackers. Standing at the counter while I ate, I looked out through the glass doors at the pool, the rain falling, the gas lights, and the trees bending in submission to the wind. I preferred the semidarkness that enabled me to look out through the windows. My hunger was satisfied. I dropped the empty tuna can in the compactor and washed my hands. I felt a chill. It was not the cold, but fear that caused me to tremble.

The phone was ringing. How loud it sounded in that empty house! It carried above the sound of the wind. Only Bill and the Colonel knew I was at home; there were no lights shining in the house so the neighbors would not be calling. My two friends were merely checking on me, I thought as I lifted the receiver.

"Hello," I said.

"Mark, it's the Colonel. I have bad news."

My heart fell. At once I knew something dreadful had occurred. All evening I had felt a foreboding sense of tragedy.

"What happened? Tell me quickly," I said.

"I just received a call from Dean's wife. He shot himself."

"He's dead?" I asked.

"Yes. Dean wanted to be sure. He used a shotgun against his head."

"My God," I whispered.

"I thought he was fine when we left him. Didn't you?" asked the Colonel.

Recalling Dean's wild eyes and his agitated state, I said, "No, Colonel, I did <u>not</u> think he was all right–but that hardly matters now."

"Dean seemed confident that the Vets would help him," said the Colonel.

Anxious to end the conversation, I said, "He gave up. For reasons known only to Dean, he thought the struggle was not worth the effort. Do you know Dean's wife?"

"Yes, I've met her several times. She's quiet as a mouse."

As the Colonel recounted the details of each time he had talked to Dean's wife, I was thinking about Mary and her chatter and the long walks Dean and she had together. I pictured Dean's lonely figure, his head bent forward, listening, rarely speaking, always kind, never forward or aggressive. What had happened? Later I learned that Dean had gone to bed shortly after we left him. When his wife returned and everyone was in bed, Dean said something about being unable to sleep. He got up and went to the basement. There he shot himself.

The Colonel's voice cut into my thoughts.

"Mark, what are you going to do?"

"Nothing," I replied.

"Are you going out there?" he asked.

"Colonel, I don't know the family. His wife called you, not me. Did she want to see you?"

"I think I'll go out," said the Colonel, "but my eyes are bad. It would be hard for me to see in this rain at night so I'll get Bill to drive me."

"If he doesn't want to go, call me. One of my cars is here. I'm not going anywhere."

"Fine," said the Colonel. "I'll call you when I get back."

"Do that," I said. "I'll be waiting for the call."

I returned to the living room and lay down on the couch. Lying there I tried to find some meaning in what had happened. Dean had been no different from the rest of us. What was in him to cause him to take his life? Such a senseless act of violence, so final, so irrevocable: to send his spirit into the unknown by his own hands was an act of madness. That was it: he was insane, driven mad by despair. Alcoholism had consumed him, had destroyed all hope.

Again I tried to reconstruct what had happened. I could see Dean turning to his wife in the darkness saying that he could not sleep. Silence: he sat in his bed saying that he felt like ending his misery. His wife listened in sullen, angry silence. Dean left the room.

He was overwhelmed with the conviction that he was no longer a man; his life was futile and worthless. He was an outsider to his own family, isolated, lost: an outsider of whom they were ashamed, whose usefulness was spent. Far better if he were gone. This, I sensed, was how it ended.

I sat up feeling heaviness all about me. Rising to my feet I began pacing the room.

Death, violence, insanity. How senseless to end in this way, jettisoned by the force of one mad act into eternity–and into whose hands? Surely a benevolent Providence would receive the sad Dean: the friendly, helpless soul of this man would not be condemned. Who had he hurt? He was the victim.

Alcoholism is reinforced with human frailty: it is a disease that feasts upon weakness like worms upon a corpse. A hidden force rises up; in time it withers the heart and rules like a tiger. This arrogant power consumes the man. Dean was buried, submerged by this alien force, even as he attempted to reestablish his supremacy over this dark power. He failed. He refused to submit any longer to drunkenness. He saw he could not win. The strength to resist was not there.

Dean, what you have done is so final. You have bolted free into that mysterious world of darkness where I would fear to take the plunge. Are you free now? Have you broken loose from the grips of that monster that dominated your life and mine? Are you free to stand up and say, 'I am a man. I am what I was intended to be.' I believe you are no longer controlled, no longer a clown, like me, who prances about on the stage of life making a mockery of what I was intended to be.

How my mind reaches out to know the truth. How restless I feel in this dark house. I could read. No, that would not do, not after this senseless death. No reason for it, no force could make an old soldier, who had faced death many times, take a shotgun and place it against his head. No lack of self respect, no cries of revulsion from within, no self reproaching could push a man seasoned by the trials of life over the brink. Something else entered in to make the difference. The trials of winter could be endured, and the heat of the summer, and the dry anguish of spirit, and those long dreary endless days that seem to go on and on leading nowhere. All the disappointments of life–the loss of ideals, the romance of life, the good prospects that come to nothing–can be endured, even borne well, but not in the company of alcohol. To be supreme while intoxicated, so sure of success, the master of one's fate and then later cut down with a crash, forced to face reality, is too much for some men. The farce is continued: drinking–day after day leading on into endless tomorrows–this pantomime of a fool builds within a volcano of seething hatred for all of life. No wonder, then, that Dean had erupted.

But suicide. Such a waste. To capitulate and hurl oneself into eternity. Where is the merit? No one can see another's struggle: not

Dean's, not Mark's. Identity is the prize. From my childhood I remembered sitting in the sun, listening to the whispering wind, the sounds of birds, watching insects crawl, the flight of a butterfly, the rich, sweet odor of flowers, the freshly turned black loam in the fields and then the haunting nightmares, when the first darkness crossed my mind, and the struggle first began. So long ago. In those early years, I was so young–yet I remembered them. It is not much to hold to now, but then I was not compelled to be forever moving, striving, seeking, wandering, always searching for the unknown. I never reached a goal. The forest became thicker, the night darker, the heart within me dried up so that now I am lost. I do not know who I am. But I will find my way back!

How cold the house has become. How cold I am. My body is trembling. The house is silent but I feel a presence as if I am being watched.

My heart leaped. The phone. It is ringing again.

CHAPTER 20

Who could be calling? Of course, it would be the Colonel. He would call from Dean's house to see if I was all right and to let me know if he was coming by.

At the end of the hall I reached the phone. Lifting the receiver I said, "Hello." There was silence. This irritated me. Some callers listen carefully for a voice they recognize and if they do not hear it, they abruptly hang up the phone. I had spoken distinctly; I would not play that game by repeating myself. Then before replacing the receiver I remembered the Colonel's difficulty in hearing out of one ear.

I called out loudly, "Colonel, is that you?"

A peal of laughter pierced my ear.

"Do I sound like the Colonel?" the voice asked.

"Lucy! How did you get my number or know I was here?"

"I know! I know everything about you."

"Dean shot himself," I said bluntly.

For a moment there was silence.

"When did it happen?" Lucy asked.

"Tonight, a few hours ago. Coming from Maplewood, Bill, the Colonel, and I stopped by to see Dean."

She cut in, "Why don't you come over and tell me about it?"

"Lucy, at this hour? I'm expecting to hear from the Colonel. He's supposed to be looking after me. He would be alarmed if he called and I didn't answer."

"Oh, just leave a note. Tell him you had to get out of the house. You are a great walker. He'll understand."

Lucy's voice was pleading. There was a change, a stridency—or was it the laughter? She did not seem concerned about Dean.

"Come on, I need to talk with someone. I need help. I'm so confused."

She talked on, and I listened. What could I do to help her? The Colonel would not call—it was too late. I would not sleep tonight. Being alone in this house was too much for me

"What's the matter with you?" she cried out. "Don't you understand? I need help! You have the Colonel to watch after you. I have no one. I left Maplewood because of you. Give me the benefit of your

treatment."

"All right, I'll come," I blurted (even as an inner conviction told me not to go). "Give me your address."

I snapped on the desk lamp by the phone, found a pencil and wrote down the address which was in an older section of the city.

Before hanging up, Lucy said in a warm voice, "I've waited so long. I've hungered to see you. I live in a big Victorian home at the end of the street. The porch light will be on."

"I'll leave in a few minutes," I said. She hung up.

After writing a note to the Colonel in which I explained that Lucy needed help, I hesitated for a moment, then wrote her address at the bottom of the note. In a drawer near the phone I found scotch tape and tore off two strips. I snapped off the light and walked to the front door. In the center of the large glass door I taped the note. I felt that leaving the note was probably unnecessary, because it was unlikely that the Colonel would call or come by at this late hour. At least if he came by, he could not accuse me of going out without notifying him. I was following instructions to keep in contact with him or Bill.

The car responded when I turned the ignition key. As I drove away, happy to be out of the house, I wondered why I had written Lucy's address on the note. I didn't want Bill or the Colonel to follow me. As I drove along in the rain toward the older section of the city, the streets were empty.

My thoughts drifted from Dean to Lucy. She had sounded strange. She hungered to see me, she had said. She was such a simple romantic girl. What was unusual about her? She was pretty, agile and strong. That was it: her strength and quickness had frightened Eva. I remembered something else, something others had said: she was to be feared. How foolish to say that. She was almost like a child around me. Then I recalled how she had looked at Stella at the meeting. Such hatred: her cold eyes had been deadly. She had challenged Stella, even sneered at her. Challenge, that was it. In the cabin she had been coiled to spring upon Eva. I could sense the power in her at that moment. Eva had seen it and had been frightened.

When I reached the neighborhood in which Lucy lived I felt tense, alert, wondering whether to continue or turn back. Then I remembered Dean. I had failed to help him. Lucy was calling for help: I was not going to fail her or turn back, not after having come this far. I saw light in the entrance.

The house was large and old in a setting among trees some considerable distance from the street. From the street lamp, the light from the porch and the faint lighting through the trees from another house I could make out the many windows and the round turret above the third floor. The elaborate display of nooks and crannies, of roof overhangs and porches was typical of Victorian design. This attempt to be startling and innovative had succeeded; the attempt to create a work of art, of distinction and beauty had failed. Yet in its ugliness, its grotesque angles and curves, there was a feeling of strength and endurance. I felt a sense of intimidation as I closed the car door and approached the front of the house. The wind caught me, forcing me to step back quickly to secure my footing. Leaning forward, with deliberate steps, I approached the entrance. Without hesitating I walked up the front steps onto the porch. I stopped at the front door: a heavy carved oak door that stood ajar.

For a moment I stood listening: there was only the wind blowing across the porch and stirring the trees. When I rapped on the door with the brass knocker, the door moved inward. Not hearing anyone approach I stepped closer and rapped again. This time the door swung open even further. I waited a moment then called out, "Lucy, are you in there?"

From the darkness within came a loud peal of laughter. Unmistakably it was Lucy, yet the sound of her laughter was strange and hard; it sent a wave of fear through me. This was no place for me and I turned to leave.

Lucy called out, "Mark, don't go. You must help me. I need you."

Her voice—unlike the laughter—was soft and pleading. I thought of Dean. No one had been present to help him. I turned back and walked slowly through the entrance into the foyer and stood waiting for my eyes to adjust to the almost total darkness in the room. After a moment, I could see that there was an open stairway at the end of the foyer and to the right of the staircase a hallway that ran deeper into the house. To my left was the dining room. Across the entrance to my right was a large living room with a fireplace at the far end. A fire was smoldering.

Except for the faint light from the window and the glow from the fireplace, the room was dark. Near the far end of the room was a piano—a mahogany island in a sea of dark space. Nearer me were heavy pieces of stuffed furniture and tables cluttered with pieces of bric-a-brac.

"Lucy," I called out again, "for heavens sake—don't play games with me."

Then I saw her. She was standing where the living room and the hallway joined. My eyes had come to rest on a chest against the wall laden with bottles and what appeared to be a platter of cheese and meat. The chest had caught my eye when I saw the reflection of the light upon the bottles and the cutlery by the cheese plate. Apparently Lucy had been standing there watching me while I had been looking about in search of her. She moved toward me, appearing to glide effortlessly. As she reached me I caught my breath. She was dressed in almost nothing at all, a thin, transparent slip or nightgown that even in the pale light revealed the outline of her white breasts and thighs. She stopped, stood in front of me so that the light from the window and the hallway revealed her nakedness. Smiling, she turned a complete circle so that I could gaze at her.

She stepped closer, smiling, never taking her eyes away from me.

"Mark," she said, "I've waited a long time for you. Never have I desired anyone as much as you."

With her face close to mine I caught one glimpse of her eyes. They were wild and intense as she put her arms around me and drew her body firmly against me. I could smell the strong liquor; feel the warmth of her body and the strength in her arms.

"Mark," she murmured, "you can take me now. There is no doctor here or that awful Stella or that spy, Eva–just you and me. We are alone, just the two of us. You'll see how good I am. Are you trembling? You are a strange creature. I have waited many long nights for you. A voice within me cried out over and over again: 'You must have Mark.' I have hungered for you. You need not fear me. My ways of making love will carry you beyond anything you have ever experienced before. When you know me you will know love. You will then hunger for me as I hunger now for you." She tilted her head and laughed.

While Lucy had been speaking she had relaxed her arms. Now she again drew her body against me more firmly than before. I felt the fire within her drawing us together. My body felt as if would melt and dissolve and we would no longer be two but one.

"I will ravish you, possess you. You will scream with delight! I'll bring out the devil I know is in you and make him cry out for more. Hereafter, you will always hunger for me. You will never feel that you have enough of me or anyone you find like me. You will go on searching, and wandering, all over the world, for someone to satisfy you again like me. That I promise."

Her laughter again filled the room, followed by a low moaning sound coming from Lucy's lips. Suddenly I realized the sounds in the room were not from Lucy alone. From my lips I heard the mixed sounds of fear and anger and desire, rising and falling like the cry of a wild animal: fading away it ended with a soul wrenching cry of anguish. Searing pain fused with a burning desire, then revulsion and even hatred: my body trembled as conflicting desires shot through me, exploding with ever increasing intensity. In a moment I would explode, go mad, go wild and crawl like a whimpering hound at Lucy's feet.

Glancing wildly about the room I caught a glimpse of a chair beyond the piano that I failed to see before. Someone was in it. Startled, I pushed Lucy away from me and walked to the other side of the piano. Against the wall obscured by the dim light and the piano, was a young man slumped in the chair. From the strong odor of alcohol fumes that filled that corner of the room it was obvious that he'd been drinking.

Lucy laughed. "Let me introduce you. Only I fear Joe won't hear my introduction."

"He's drunk, very drunk, isn't he?"

"Of course he's drunk. You could burn the house or stick a knife in him and he wouldn't mind." She laughed again.

Her voice had a sobering effect upon me: one moment it was warm and compelling, the next filled with contempt and the cold hard ring of hatred. Her laughter was unreal, and it troubled me.

Somewhere before, I had heard laughter that affected me in the same way and I associated it with someone I had met, and not long ago, either. That high pitched ring, not all that strange, yet somehow different, was a haunting, unnatural sound that caused fear within me.

"A pity you can't meet Joe. He's a real tiger, but he wears out so easily." Again the empty laughter.

The man was young, although perhaps older than Lucy. He was muscular, but even in the weak light I could see that he was dissipated. Lucy appeared to accept his presence as nothing unusual; boldly she had indicated why he was here. She was not the young woman I remembered, the frightened woman who was lost, and uncertain of herself. She was charged with energy, in command, a wild, provocative creature–and frightening, too.

What was I doing in this room with this fierce, exotic creature? My eyes were drawn to her firm, white body, her black hair and pale face. She smiled, revealing white teeth, and her black eyes gleamed with pleasure as I stared at her. There was unnatural longing in those eyes.

The battle was raging again within me. I felt pain and longing and knew that I was a pawn in a mighty conflict. Feelings of hatred, lust, fear and pride–even pain–flowed through me.

"Mark," she said, taking my hand, "let's go upstairs. Don't think about Joe. I have much to do, much to show you. You will never be the same again when I have finished with you. I will show you your possibilities beyond anything you have experienced before."

Strange memories clouded my mind: stories of perversion, half forgotten scenes of men and women sent forever wandering throughout the world in vain search for fulfillment; always seeking to satisfy that craving that once ignited could not be extinguished. Could one night do this? Was it possible to be carried beyond the addiction to alcohol into something worse–or better? Beyond alcoholism, beyond lust and pain (as I had experienced both lust and pain) there was something else: a new world of perversion, the fruits of which I had not tasted. This is what I was being offered.

"Come."

She tugged at my arm. Desire flooded through me. I wanted to ravish and to be ravished. The excitement and the need to consume and be consumed was intense. Lucy laughed again. "Come. Must I force you?"

That laugh! The same laughter as Mary's. And Bernice had laughed like that once, out among the trees, when we had seen the druggist. The mad laughter of Bernice and Mary was pitiful and empty and wild, whereas Lucy's laughter rang with malice and an unnatural hunger. She would send me forth in the world, after tonight, like herself: a wounded animal, unsatisfied, filled with a craving to satisfy a hunger she had ignited, cutting loose all the discordant powers within that would never be caged again.

"Mark, I'm going to get us a drink. You are trembling so. You must relax or you'll explode."

She disappeared, gliding softly around the corner of the living room and into the hall where I had seen the bar and the buffet table. In a moment she was back, offering me a large glass.

"Here, take it." By the strong smell I could tell it was Scotch without a mix. She smiled while I watched her. Then she drank deeply from her glass. She smiled again at me.

"Drink it, drink it."

I lifted the glass, choked, and dropped the glass on the carpet.

"I'm sorry," I said. "It's been a long time since I've drunk anything. It was too strong for me."

"Never mind. I'll get you another one."

"No, don't bother." I was irritated with my display of weakness. I picked up the glass and walked toward the chest where the bottles were sitting. I glanced at the empty bottles, the assorted cheeses and meats and the cutlery and decided to leave. I walked to the front door.

"Where are you going?" Lucy cried out.

"I'm leaving. There's no way that I can help you."

"Wait, don't go. Not yet!"

"No, Lucy, this is not good," I replied, pulling open the door.

Lucy ran to the chest that held the bottles as I was opening the door. She was swift as a cat. She seized a carving knife and ran back across the room to where Joe was still slumped in the chair. Her movement had startled me and I stood in the entrance watching her. She held the knife like a dagger raised in the air. Crazy shadows played on the wall, upon Lucy's face and her transparent gown. She stood still, poised, waiting. A sudden draft caused the smoldering log in the fireplace to flare, and I saw Lucy's face in the light for the first time. Her eyes gleamed and her face was contorted with a crazed look of rage. I turned and started through the doorway.

"Stop!"

I turned in the doorway and looked back into the room. Lucy had not moved except to raise the knife she was holding.

"Mark, you are not leaving me. Once before you refused me. You wanted me, but we were interrupted by that spy, Eva. Then in your prissy manner you refused to see me again. If you go through that door, I'll stick Joe with this knife."

My nerves tingled, my skin tightened, as fear crept through me. She was mad. Such talk was utter nonsense. Why attack Joe? Surely she was bluffing. No one was mad enough to stick someone for no reason at all. Nor could she be drunk –not completely anyway– otherwise, she could not move so swiftly. But her voice, cold and harsh, and her wild eyes, made me tremble with fear. What a fool I had been to come here. I wanted to run but my legs felt heavy. If I ran from her sight she would recover her loss of sanity.

"Goodbye," I said, turning to step onto the porch. I heard a wild cry and turned to see the flash of the knife as Lucy drove it into Joe's chest. He grunted once and rolled over onto the floor. For a moment I stood stunned at the horror of her action.

I reentered the room and heard my voice saying, "Lucy, you fool!"

Frightened, almost in a state of panic at what she had done, I wanted to flee at once but I feared that she would stab Joe again if I left the house. Although Lucy was swift and strong, she had been drinking before I arrived, probably with Joe. She had consumed a full glass while I had been there, and the liquor was certain to have affected her movements. As I walked into the center of the living room, Lucy slipped around on the opposite side of the piano and ran toward the foyer. I found Joe lying on his side unconscious, his shirt stained with blood. Finding a switch to a floor lamp, I flooded the corner of the room with light. I opened Joe's shirt to examine his wound. Judging from the point of entry, Joe was not seriously injured. He was safely out of it. My deadly combatant awaited me.

Rising to my feet I saw Lucy standing at the far end of the room with the knife. She held it poised, ready to strike again. I forgot Joe, concerned now only with my own safety, in getting out of this house as quickly as possible. The only exit was through the front entrance, or through the rear of the house, which was blocked by Lucy standing in the foyer.

Seizing an iron from its bracket by the fireplace, I walked toward Lucy. She was just closing the front door. I heard the key turn in the lock. As she turned to face me, she saw the short, heavy poker— and laughed. It was not a pleasant sound.

"Mark! My dear Mark—you are no match for me. You're slow and awkward. You don't stand a chance against me—not even with that silly poker."

"Lucy, remember why I came to see you. We were going to talk about Dean, his death, his family. And what his death meant to his family and to us."

"Beast! You don't want me. You never wanted anyone but yourself. Don't talk to me about Dean. You are a hypocrite. You don't care about Dean. You are only concerned about your image. Isn't that what you worship? Some glowing fancy in your mind that you consider the real Mark? You live on a pedestal, pretty boy, worshipping yourself–and I'm going to cut you down."

"Put down the knife and show me where the phone is. I'll call the Colonel and Bill. They'll come and help Joe. No need to call anyone else."

"No! You are too good for me. You don't want what I can give you. Who are you, anyway?"

What a challenge! My nightmares had become real. How could I answer her? There was more than a shadow of truth in what she was saying. I knew that I was a fool to be here–a frightened, terrified fool, up against a crazy woman. She was not going to allow me to escape, and as she moved a ray of light caught the gleam of the knife blade as she changed her grip so that she could slash from side to side. The same light, for one instant, showed Lucy's face and eyes, wild and unnatural, contorted with rage and hatred. She had been turned into something I could not recognize: a ferocious beast whose sight chilled and terrorized me and made me feel that withstanding her was beyond my strength.

There was no sound in the room as we stood facing each other. The wind rose again and as I heard its moaning wail, the coals in the fireplace ignited again. Lucy appeared, for a fleeting moment, like a naked, white goddess. The illusion vanished as I saw the movement of the knife, the cruel smile, the cat like movement as she thrust the knife toward me.

"Stop, Lucy, this is madness!"

She stepped back and laughed. "Pretty boy. This is real. This is not some dream of yourself you are protecting."

With a feinting movement she stepped toward me, thrusting the knife toward me with the quickness of a serpent's tongue. I swung the poker iron but too late. She stepped back and laughed with a bitter, empty laughter.

"You don't want me. You are too good for me, pretty boy. Such a pretty boy. I'm going to fix that face so you'll remember me. When they see you again at Maplewood they'll say 'There goes Lucy's lover. See, she's left her mark on him.' They'll all laugh at you."

While she was speaking I took one quick step toward her, swinging the heavy poker to disarm the knife. I missed, but in that fleeting second, as she jumped back, I moved onto the lower step of the staircase.

Infuriated by my unexpected attack, she leaped at me, bringing the knife upward, ripping open my shirt. As I swung the poker again in defense I lifted myself to a higher step. I was far too slow for her.

"Mark, you are no match for me. But don't fear me. I knew what I was doing when I stabbed Joe. It's only a scratch. I'm not going to kill you. Oh, no, that would be bad. Don't you know a girl must protect herself from men like you? I'm going to castrate you: one cut, off they go!"

As quick as a jungle cat she leaped at me; the knife moved upward, cutting through my pants near the crotch. The blade grazed my thigh. As she made her thrust I swung down and across with the poker and caught her arm and deflected the blow. Otherwise I would have been mutilated. The impact of the heavy poker caused her to cry out and step backwards as she rubbed her arm. She did not drop the knife. I turned and bolted up the stairs, instinctively I whirled with the poker as I reached the top of the steps. Lucy was upon me. She shrieked as she brought the blade toward my face. I turned my head to avoid the knife, but the blade caught my left cheek and laid open the side of my face. I dropped the poker and gave her a violent shove. She fell backward: with the skill and agility of a gymnast she caught the balustrade to prevent falling down the stairs.

I retrieved the poker and moved back along the hall. If I attempted to disarm her, she was too fast: she would dart under or around my intended blows. I thought the liquor would slow her. I was injured. Blood was running down my face onto my shirt. Seeing the open doorway to my right I stepped toward Lucy, who had regained her balance, and swung the poker from side to side. She leaped back. In that momentary retreat I was able to run into the bedroom, shut the door and place my full weight against it. I almost collapsed from the violent exertion: my chest heaved as my breath came in sudden bursts. With my full weight against the door I closed my eyes and muttered over and over again: "Fool! What a fool. She's mad, but I am a fool." My outrageous vanity prevented me from seeing Lucy's insanity.

All my life I had lived by my instincts, much like the fox. Whether I had retreated along the lower hall or taken the steps to the upper floor did not matter much against this wild tigress. She was more than a match for me. My only hope was to stay away from her long enough until help came, or if she sobered up, she might recover her sanity. But I did not know if she was drunk. She couldn't be, to move so quickly.

Suddenly my heart leaped within me. The creak in the floor, the movement of the air, my mind flashed scenes before my eyes of old houses–the odd arrangement of bedrooms–the floor plans, the bedrooms connected by closets. The evil dreams of my youth: the darkness, the ominous presence, the closet door that slowly opened while I watched in terror unable to cry out or move. But I was not a boy now. This was not an evil dream. This was reality: the darkness, the blood dripping from my face, the terror I felt–all this was no illusion but a nightmare in which I was the intended victim.

My back was pressed against the door. My heart pounded as my eyes strained to see every object in the room. A small dormer emitted enough light so that I could see shadows move across the wall. Grimly I remembered similar scenes so long ago.

The iron bed had been near the window; across from the bed a chest of drawers; on the other side of the bed a stand and a lamp. Then, as now, shadows danced on the wall. My skin began to crawl as shivers shot through my body. The door to the closet along the far wall was ajar. My eyes were riveted upon it. It moved.

A thousand pent up demons of fury were released within me– the fears and hatred of all the nightmares of my youth exploded at once. Then I was paralyzed with terror; fearful of the dark. I always approached the long night in dread of what evil awaited me. Now, in this room, I was face to face with what I hated. I had the sealed room (which once I had longed for) in which to lash out in fury. Was I mad? I was filled with hatred and a blind fury–even though I still trembled, half paralyzed with fear. Was this the encounter that I wanted? To crush and tear and lash out at my tormentor? So often I sought this as a child. But then I was frozen with fear. No longer young, now it was different: I longed with every fiber within me to have this encounter now. As I leaped across the room, the closet door flew open. A wild demon leaped at me with a cry more savage than the cry of any animal. Had I been a boy I would have died of fright. In the light from the window (all in one instant) I saw her eyes, her white teeth, the knife as she struck at my throat, which I warded off with the poker. Before she struck again I dropped the poker and seized her arm. We rolled across the bed and onto the floor. She fought, she cursed, she screamed, like a thousand demons unleashed. All the closets within my mind were opened. All the deep caverns and passageways, the hidden dungeons were propped open and allowed the demons out. I fought them all in one–all in this tigress who was determined to have my life.

With both hands I held the arm with the knife. She kicked me in the stomach with her knee, sank her teeth into my chest, bit my jaw. I fought on against her; I sensed the fury within me was hardly a match for her. Where did she get such strength? She was not human.

With a sudden burst of strength she freed her arm and made a wild thrust with the knife that I barely deflected. As she pulled back her arm again, I reached for the knife. Another arm seized the knife.

"A Southern lady would never cut a gentleman," a voice said.

I rolled free of Lucy and laid upon my back on the floor gasping for breath. The Colonel held Lucy's arms: she was strong, but no match for that man. She screamed and kicked; unable to break free she stopped. She began sobbing.

The Colonel stood over me while he held Lucy. He reached over and snapped on the light by the bed. On my back I blinked and tried to focus my eyes upon the Colonel.

The Colonel's expression was serious. "You have a nasty cut on your face. How do you feel?"

"I never felt better than when I saw your ugly face."

"That's good. For now I'll leave you there. Come, Lucy. You and I must get some help."

She walked along with him like a child.

"Colonel," I called out, "take a look at Joe. He's at the end of the living room. I don't think he's hurt bad."

But Joe, I learned later, had already departed. He knew Lucy. He had come and drunk and had satisfied his needs. Since the point of the knife had not awakened him, it appeared he was either very drunk or on both drugs and alcohol. Whatever it was had worn off. I never learned any more than just his first name or if he ever returned again.

From below I heard another voice. It was Bill's deep baritone. Someone was on the steps, then coming along the hall. "So here you are," Bill said.

"Pull me up, will you?"

Bill swore, which was unusual for him, and his expression showed alarm. I felt the side of my face and discovered a bad cut that would probably require stitches. The blood covering my face may have frightened Bill. I sat on the bed while he examined the cut in my trousers that reached nearly to my crotch.

"Just missed you," he said grimly. "Let me help you to the car."

"No, Bill, I can walk."

"Well, we're going to Seattle General Hospital to get some stitches for that cut on your face. You'll have a bad scar if we don't."

Until now I had felt nothing except fear and anger. As soon as I realized the deep cut on my face I felt the pain. I walked slowly out of the room followed by Bill. As we descended the steps I saw the Colonel talking to Lucy who appeared calm as if nothing out of the ordinary had occurred.

Joe's gone," said the Colonel. "Are you sure he was ever here?"

"He was here. It was no apparition."

"I've seen war casualties that looked better than you, Mark. You sure make seeing a lady friend a painful experience," chided the Colonel.

"Say whatever you like. I'm still grateful for the help."

"We saw the note. I thought you might be in for trouble. I didn't want to explain later to Stella that you got away. You can't say I didn't warn you."

"I was foolish," I said lamely.

"You boys go on. I hope to keep the police out of this. Lucy's ex-husband is coming by for a chat. He's an attorney. I think he understands. He's bringing a head doctor with him. I think you know the doctor." I feared to ask his name, knowing in my bones that it would be Bogleman. It was not an unusual coincidence; after all, he was well known among those with alcoholic addiction.

The front door was open. It was a welcome sight to see the out of doors as I walked across the porch and down the steps. The wind was blowing and the air was cold, but I hardly felt it. Before getting into the car I looked back at the large, old house where I came so close to losing my life. I prayed that all the demons that haunted me remained there.

There was little traffic. Bill explained how he had driven out with the Colonel to see Dean's widow. Bill glanced once at me. He decided not to go into details, I assumed, about Dean's appearance. He was pale and alarmed.

When we arrived at the emergency room, we went to a waiting room where I sat and shielded my face from any curious onlooker while Bill talked to one of the nurses. In a matter of minutes I was in another room with a doctor who examined the wound while Bill answered a few questions. The doctor was quite professional: all this seemed routine to him. He washed the wound.

"I can put you out or deaden the pain locally before sewing you up."

"Just deaden it," I said.

He didn't say anything more. He made no jokes about the other guy nor asked any questions. He worked fast. I appreciated his efficiency. Within an hour we were in and out of the hospital.

Bill drove to his apartment in silence. I dozed off before we arrived. Only vaguely I remembered going up the elevator to his room, where he gave me his bed and took the sofa in the living room for himself. I dropped my clothes on a chair and fell asleep on top of the bed.

CHAPTER 21

Bill was pulling at my arm, and, as I attempted to speak, I felt the stitches on my cheek. Bill saw my pained expression and drew back his hand.

"Hurts, does it?"

"Not much," I said.

"You saw the cut. With all the blood it looked bad, but it wasn't deep. I'm just sore all over from the exertion."

"Deep or not, she almost got you." Smiling he added, "I'm not impressed with your taste in girls."

"Neither am I. Hey! Do I smell coffee?"

"You bet! Let me get you a cup."

I sat up slowly while Bill walked across the hall into the kitchen. I was glad that he couldn't see my efforts to dress. My body felt as if I had been involved in a violent contact sport like ice hockey. I was struggling with my shoes when he returned with orange juice and coffee.

"I see you are able to bend down to reach your shoes. Thought I'd hear you groan."

"I'm too embarrassed to groan."

"Don't put yourself down. Last night was a chilling experience, especially for you–but for the Colonel and me as well. When we arrived at Dean's house, the body had already been removed, but the sight of so much blood nearly made me sick. Later, seeing you wounded and bleeding gave me an added jolt. All in all it was a grim night. If Dean hadn't shot himself you wouldn't have been caught off guard."

"Bill, you always mean well, but what you probably don't know was that I was warned about Lucy, not once but several times— even by the Colonel. Only when it was nearly too late did I appreciate that she was probably crazy—certainly so when she had been drinking."

"So you made a mistake. Your good judgment was overcome by a desire to help her."

"Or I was flattered by her attention, Bill. That's closer to the truth. I saw signs of hatred and violence in her, but in my lofty self esteem, I felt that none of this hatred would be directed toward me. Oh well, I've learned something. My face will show a scar, which will remind me for a long while that I must not overlook the role played by pride when I make decisions."

"You looked bad when I first saw you. All that blood on your face made you look worse; after I saw that bloodstained floor at Dean's house, seeing you was almost too much."

"Lucy was a devil. Was Dr. Bogleman the one called to help her?"

"Yes, he's the one. Specializes in alcoholism. Lucy gave us his name."

"I heard he was coming to Maplewood, shortly?"

"That's right. I understand he comes several times a year when asked to help out. I've heard he's a mysterious character. Do you know him?"

"Yes, I know him." The thought of Bogleman, for some reason, caused me to feel anxious and tense. I feared him. At the moment, I didn't want to talk about Bogleman. I sat on the edge of the bed, sipping coffee, and I was scarcely aware that Bill had slipped out of the room. My mind was miles away dwelling upon half formed thoughts.

Suddenly, I was aware of the sound of music, and I realized that Bill had gone to the organ which I had seen in the living room, and begun to play softly. The sounds filled the small apartment and the melody affected me like wine. I was drained of strength, for the moment, and I was moved almost to tears. I hungered for some nameless something, and longed for the kind of peace and tranquility I had not known since childhood. I didn't understand the cause for this sudden yearning, nor did I know how to satisfy it. It was just there–a powerful entity which I could not deny.

My thoughts turned again to Lucy and the doctor. What would Bogleman make of my relationship with Lucy? How closely was he following my progress? He hardly knew me well enough, even if he cared, to make an accurate diagnosis. The doctor would not know that taking away alcohol brought me face to face with a stranger; that the continuing struggle within often left me confused, weak and unstable; and that fear and anguish mounted as the opposing sides of my nature struggled for supremacy. If the voices within were only clear (and therefore enabled me to understand), I would throw the entire weight of my will and the strong passions of my nature into the battle. But I could not choose sides; I could not clearly determine what was good and what was evil. I could not choose one side of me against the other. I was forged into a creature I could not recognize. As I saw glimpses of what I thought was myself, I was filled with self-loathing and self-hatred. I had no sooner resolved to change my life than, moments later, my resolution cooled as I saw again what I had become–but in another light. The other side–the hard, cold, defiant, cunning nature was what I saw, and this portrait appealed to me. Why let go? I loved that monster, didn't I?

Suppose I opened up, exposing myself? Begin by telling Bogleman of the two dominant forces which raged within my heart, splitting me into two persons. One voice directed me to remain as I was–proud, strong and self-reliant. From the other voice I heard a pathetic cry: 'Stop violating your nature! Stop following the course that has hardened and embittered and disillusioned you. Wrench yourself free. Break the chains that bind you. Survival as an individual means changing now! Your old thoughts and old habits and old attitudes must go. Your craving for wealth, your insatiable ambition, your building of dream castles must end. This will be accomplished by discovering new interests, by pursuing worthwhile goals. The price of peace for you will be found in serving others, in finding ways to use your talents to help those who are weak and subdued by life and unable to help themselves. That is not much to ask from you; just a helping hand is all–wherever you can offer it. In this way you will turn away from your preoccupation with yourself and the building of dream castles; away from seeking wealth that focuses your eyes upon yourself–away from growing sublime in your own eyes until you are unable to free yourself from pride and egotism.'

Suddenly I realized that this voice proclaimed my real self, or at least what I ought to be. But I could not change what I had become. My nature was formed; it was molded over many years and I found that old habits and old thoughts were as much a part of me as my limbs and the blood that flowed through them.

At the very thought of changing, a strident voice cried out within. "Give up alcohol, but nothing more. Alcohol served its purpose. Of course, you went too far, you always did. You were made that way. You were always a man of powerful drives. When you wanted something, you were not easily stopped: that was good as long as your desires were under control. Give up alcohol and continue your life as the person you have become, and you will reach your goal. In time you will see how carefully I led you. Really, to change your thinking and your way of life–except for the drinking–would be madness. You cannot change totally–it is too late for that. Once your demands upon life were made (and you worked unceasingly to see them fulfilled) a change in you was inevitable: your ideas, your mode of life, your feelings came together in perfect harmony forming you into what you have become: the center of your universe–a star forever rising in your own eyes, forever enhancing your own self esteem.

"Your character is now as firmly set as the Northern Star. All that you need now is to live according to the rules set down long ago. After all, there is really no other 'will', no other 'real' course to follow but self-will. Let the idealists and the reformers and those who prate about religion call this selfishness or egotism or pride, we do not care, we know the world—we know, you and I, that the strong devour the weak. Look at history. Look around you. Success is built upon the broken bones of the weak—not upon the acts of do-gooders bent upon helping them."

Enough of that voice. It has led me to a dead end that weakens and confuses me. It is only a small consolation that this side of my nature tells me that I can now do without alcohol, but otherwise, my life should remain unchanged. This is what I am. This is the being I now see through clear eyes, a being undistorted by the confusing mist of alcohol that had heretofore made me see myself only with self-loathing and hatred. Without change I will be only a dry alcoholic who will feel that something of value has been taken away, and will live mired in a selfish life with a long train of accumulated vices without liquor to conceal their presence. Without changing my life I cannot live long without alcohol. I must opt either for change, or for a return to alcohol. One option will be difficult—the other unthinkable.

If I told Bogleman that my nature was split and that I did not know who I was or what I ought to be, he would surely say that I was mad or a fool. If I was to say that I was not certain what voice within me was directing my actions he would say, "Why not? Your voice is the same. You are seeing life for the first time in years through sober eyes. No doubt, this is a strange sight for you. For too long you attempted to live your life according to your terms, following your passions, your will, your desires."

While I drank this was true. Now my life has changed. I felt ripped, torn loose from my moorings; there was nothing left to hold onto, no markings to guide me. I was lost. The old ideas and feelings of certainty that I leaned upon as evidence of reality were gone. So, I feared, was my sanity.

Between two worlds I hovered. Viewed from the outside, my life moved along, at times exciting, at other times, insignificant and dull. On the inside, in those dark and hidden caverns–those mysterious regions of the mind and heart–a battle raged.

As a young man I had followed my desires and that siren voice (then scarcely audible) that urged me to go along a path that each year appeared more fruitful. Success drove me. Self approval, recognition, and the grand display of all that was achieved was my goal. To rise in the world, higher and higher, outstripping all competitors was life. Success carried me aloft. Pride sustained me. I lived in a world of enchantment breathing in the fumes of flattery. Intoxicated by pride, I wanted more. Alcohol was the elixir that promised fulfillment, which created an illusion of happiness, contentment and solid growth as an individual.

Slowly I changed. Years passed before I saw that I was growing hard and bitter and filled with hatred and resentment. No longer did the simple pleasures and joys of life appeal to me. I looked into the mirror and saw an aging face: the sight of the empty eyes and haunting look filled me with dread and self-loathing. Alcohol was no longer creating an illusion unless I was drunk. Wherever I turned I came face to face with my real image, a creature I despised but could not escape. My nature was shredded, torn by self pity, by violent emotions and a torrent of conflicting thoughts that raced through a mind running out of control. My mind reeled with clashing thoughts, with strident voices, saying 'Do this,' then 'No, do that,' leaving me helpless, feeling that I was not a real person. Unnatural fears followed these unnatural thoughts: they followed me into the night and into my dreams.

With alcohol behind me I thought all these conflicts would end, all the nightmares would go away and my feverish mind would grow calm. There were moments of peace, after giving up alcohol, I saw, for brief periods, that there was another course my life could follow which led away from pride and ambition. But time was running out. I feared that a new life with new interests, with kindly thoughts and actions, was beyond me. It was too late. I was frozen into a callous, hard and embittered man.

Each year the pace quickened. Step by step I was being absorbed, more and more coming under the domination of a power I could neither understand nor resist. While I felt that I could not change, in my heart I could still hear the faint cry that perhaps it was not too late. If I could but believe this to be true, I would be given the needed strength. 'By good will, by constant effort,' the voice said, 'your hardness can be pierced, and the warm flow of human feeling will enter your heart.'

"Mark, are you talking to someone?" Bill asked. Bill had quietly entered the room, and was looking down at me as I sat upon the bed. His eyes were concerned. Even though he was smiling, there was worry in his voice.

"Are you thinking about Dean or Lucy?"

"Neither, just poor Mark. I had nothing to offer Dean. What Lucy wanted I could not give. When I see Bogleman I'm afraid he might accuse me of leading her on."

"Why?"

"By now Dr. Bogleman knows all about what happened at Maplewood. He will have heard the story from Stella and, no doubt, from Dr. Neilstrom, too, about my supposed affair with Lucy. They will be convincing because they are sure they know all about me. Heaven knows what Lucy told Bogleman about me coming to her house. What do you think he will believe? I suspect that even you and the Colonel think that I was having an affair with Lucy."

"Come on, Mark, that's not fair. You're not yourself. You're wrought up. I wish you could resolve your conflicts. I believe in you, and the Colonel, I'm sure, believes in you. Must I tell you that again?"

"No, I'm an ass! An egotistical, drunken ass. My eyes are set only in one direction. They bear inward searching for answers—something tangible to grasp. I am afraid I've never admitted this to anyone before."

"What do you fear? You have character. Everyone knows that you are strong."

I stared at Bill. He was genuinely concerned with my welfare, and a most generous soul. Whatever the hidden weakness that condemned Bill to alcoholism, it was not exacerbated by pride, ambition or a divided nature. I could not burden him further with my problems.

"Bill, we'll be going back to Maplewood, and Bogleman will be there. He was the doctor retained by my wife to treat me. Much as I appreciate your offer of help, I don't want to burden you with talk about my schizoid tendencies. The doctor specializes in that sort of thing. Let him find an answer."

"As you wish, Mark. But we'd better give the Colonel a call. I asked him to check in with Stella. After all that's happened I was relieved that he was calling in."

Bill dialed the Colonel. As the phone began ringing I continued dressing. The Colonel answered, and his booming voice carried clearly throughout the small apartment. I caught the gist of the conversation, and from Bill's responses I gathered that the Colonel had talked with Stella, and the talk had not gone well. At one point in the conversation Bill sounded exasperated.

"How in the world, Colonel, could I know what Stella said?" he asked.

The voice of the Colonel grew louder. He was angry and Bill listened patiently with a half smile on his face. Finally he said, "Yes, that's right, Colonel." He cupped the phone into his hand.

"Are you well enough to travel, Mark?" he asked.

"I'm ready."

"Mark is ready. I'm ready. We'll be by within the hour." He hung up before the Colonel could begin another long monologue.

"My," Bill laughed, "we alcoholics have tempers. Apparently Stella berated the Colonel for not watching after you. She reported that all the repairs had been made to the heating system, and that we must return at once because of what happened last night. The Colonel told her we would not be treated like children. Stella then reminded the Colonel that he was a commanding officer in the war who insisted that orders must be obeyed and that he had also told everyone at Maplewood that he was a Southern gentleman. Stella then asked if he believed in accepting orders or in fulfilling his pledges given as a gentleman."

"From what I was able to hear, it sounded as if the Colonel was not happy with this frontal assault on his honor," I said.

"Stella can be harsh. She is almost a fanatic about those under her care. I think you learned that, too, the first day you met her."

"Indeed, I did, Bill. She is a match for any man. Well, what's up?" I asked. "Are we leaving now?"

"As soon as we eat something," Bill said. He poured me another cup of coffee.

In less than thirty minutes we ate a roll, drank our coffee, gathered our few things together and left the apartment. Nothing much was said as we drove across town to meet the Colonel. If Bill was irritated he gave no sign. Whenever he spoke he was cheerful. We did not mention Dean.

As we drove up to the Colonel's house Bill honked the horn, and he obligingly came out to meet us. As the older man climbed into the front seat Bill observed, "I've never seen you move so fast. Stella is sure one tough commanding officer, isn't she? Makes you jump right through the hoops!"

The Colonel grunted. He looked first at me and then at Bill, then asked, "What's Mark doing wearing a Halloween mask?"

"Don't be cruel, Colonel," Bill said.

"Aw, come now, Colonel, you've seen much worse faces after combat."

"So I have, but she was out to get you. You were lucky to save your plumbing. After this maybe you'll listen to me."

"That I will. I've learned a lesson. Thanks again for appearing on the scene when you did."

"Forget it. I promised Stella I'd look after you. If I've guessed right she'll be waiting at the gate for us. She said it was important that you be there to see Dr. Bogleman. He has a busy schedule, she says."

"So I must fit into it at his convenience?"

"I'm guessing that Bogleman wants to measure your progress. After what Lucy told him he'll want to put you away with Bernice. Lucy made you out to be a real Jack the Ripper, saying that you tried to rape her and she defended herself with a knife."

"Be sensible for once, Colonel. I have the marks to show. Lucy doesn't have a scratch or a bruise anywhere to show."

"You inflamed her, Mark. You drove this girl into a state of frenzy until she lost her sanity. When I was with her and her ex-husband, the lawyer, she was sweet and shy and somewhat bewildered."

"A touching scene, no doubt. Were you present when Dr. Bogleman arrived?"

"Yes, I was there. He's a big strange looking man. He gave Lucy some pills to calm her, although she seemed calm enough, and then sat on the couch and stared at the three of us. While I told him what had happened he smoked one cigarette after another. When I mentioned your name his eyes widened and the strangest look came over his face. He looked at Lucy and raised one of his big hands signaling me to stop talking."

"That wasn't easy," I said.

"All right, do you want to know what was said or not?"

"Sorry," I said, "go on. I'm all ears."

"'Lucy,' the doctor asked, 'do you feel up to talking about what happened?'

"She nodded. She began in the softest voice, like that of a young girl.

"'Mark called me,' she said, 'to tell me about the sad fate of Dean.'

"For a long moment she paused. I thought she was going to weep but she maintained her composure," the Colonel said.

"'Mark insisted upon coming to see me,' she continued. "I told him if he wanted to see me so badly he should call in the morning. Then I hung up. Imagine my surprise when I heard him at the front door. Foolishly I had left the door unlocked and he came right into the foyer.'

"The doctor interrupted, 'What about the other man who was there? The man you stabbed.'

"Lucy drew back in her chair clasping her breast. The look on her face was of pained innocence. In all my life," the Colonel said, "I have never seen such a look"

"'What man?' she asked.'There was no man here but Mark. If another man was here he would have defended me, wouldn't he?'"

"She looked as sincere and innocent as any woman I've seen in all my years. She would have, I believe, convinced anyone that she was telling the truth."

"What did her ex-husband have to say?" I asked.

"He said nothing. However, he appeared alarmed when I described what happened to you and what you had said about the stabbing of this fellow, Joe. While Lucy talked he watched her then slowly lowered his head and stared at the floor. The doctor made no comment and continued to smoke his cigarettes. The pills on top of the booze relaxed her; she laughed once when she referred to the statement I'd made about another man being in the room. She was so sweet and innocent, and rather shy, that I almost believed her myself until she laughed. Her laughter sent a chill through me; for the first time I began seeing what you were up against."

Bogleman cut in. "Tell me what Mark did to you."

"Did to me? "

Her eyes flashed. She reached for a cigarette; even with the pills and the alcohol she moved with the swiftness of a cat. I looked at the doctor. Whenever he spoke, he enunciated his words in a tone which was low and even, without emotion. But I noticed he never took his eyes off of her.

"'Mark,' she said, 'was such a strange man. I was attracted to him at Maplewood because he was somehow different–sort of lost and helpless, always dreaming. He was either reading or strangely silent or wandering about in the woods. His sadness caused me to pity him. So I befriended him, never dreaming he would come after me, apparently interpreting my simple offer of friendship as a sexual overture.'"

"True, I offered him something to drink, which he spilled on the carpet. I was ready for bed wearing a sheer nightgown, the one under this robe. That appeared to inflame him, seeing me almost naked. He tried to embrace me. I pushed him toward the door. He was wild. He grabbed me and tried to pull me onto the couch. While I struggled to free myself, he kept saying that I must give in and stop resisting. I broke loose from him. In desperation, to defend my honor, I seized the knife off the chest and ran up the stairs and into the bedroom. I closed the door and locked it, but I forgot the connecting closet to the other bedroom. "

"The room was dark except for a little light from the bedroom window. I saw crazy shadows on the wall; trees moving up and down– and then I saw the closet door slowly opening. I was terrified, but I didn't wait for Mark to attack me again. When I saw a shape emerge from the opening I screamed and leapt at him. I fought for my honor. I fought for my life! The Colonel saw us struggling. He didn't know that I was fighting for survival."

As Lucy finished, she lit a cigarette, inhaled the smoke, and appeared to be pleased with her story. She looked at me and then at the doctor. Her ex-husband slowly shook his head.

"Are you going to call the police?" the doctor asked, turning to her former husband.

"No," he said.

"What do you have to say to all this?" the doctor asked me.

"'I'm an old army man,' I said. 'In my day I've seen many men die. Suffering, death, brutality were part of my life as a combat soldier. For over twenty years I was trained to observe and act under fire. What I saw earlier tonight convinced me that Mark would be mutilated or killed if I had not arrived when I did. You saw her move; she is fast and strong. And deadly.'"

The doctor looked at me for the longest time and then got up slowly and lumbered to the fireplace where Mark said Joe had been sitting. He bent over and rubbed the carpet. I could see him rub his fingers as if they were moist. Then he said to Lucy's ex-husband, 'Do you have a flashlight?'

"When a flashlight was found, the four of us walked up the stairs. Flecks of blood were to be seen in the hallway by the bedroom door, but on the bed and on the floor near the bed there were considerable blood stains. Lucy was composed as she described her struggle. I watched her former husband. He was frightened. The doctor didn't appear frightened, but his dark face was set; his voice was low and hard. I couldn't tell whether he was angry or pondering over the events of the night.

"'Go, Colonel,' the doctor said.' You performed a service that I will long remember. Perhaps I'll see you again at Maplewood when I visit there.'

"Without a word I walked out of that bedroom into the hall, down the steps and out of that house. I didn't even pause to call a cab. When I reached the street I turned and looked back at that big old house. The Colonel is not ashamed to admit that he felt a sense of fear.

There was something evil in that place. I had never felt anything evil in a house before, but I felt the evil there and then. In combat I had often felt a sense of danger; my senses had been alert, and I would be ready for the enemy. This was different. In that house, as Lucy explained what happened–then led us into the bedroom I understood for the first time the terror of what you experienced. When Lucy changes roles, I would not want to face her.

"After pausing for several moments to look back at the house, I walked along the streets toward the nearest business district until I found a phone booth outside a service station. After calling a cab, I waited for at least thirty minutes in the fog and rain. But I didn't mind the discomfort. I was just happy to be out of that house."

We were out of the city and high into the mountains by the time the Colonel finished with his story. Snow was falling. I could hear the sound of the windshield wipers and the engine laboring as we climbed toward the summit. No one spoke for several miles.

"That was a hellish experience," Bill said at last.

"You believed my story, Bill?" I asked.

"Of course. Lucy is crazy. She may even believe what she told the Colonel to be the truth."

"Old soldier," I said, "I owe you much."

"You owe me nothing–and don't call me an old soldier. Next time you go out looking for a woman, I want you to listen to me. She nearly got your manhood on the end of that knife."

"Yes, I know."

"You've got to listen and take better care of yourself. You look like you've been hitting the deck too many times," the Colonel said.

"I'll make it," I told him. The Colonel was determined to lecture me.

"Of course you will make it," the Colonel said, turning to peer at me from the front seat. "Next time pick one of my women, a real Southern girl."

"All your tastes are carnal, Colonel," I said.

"No," Bill interrupted, "it is just that the Colonel is so much in demand, so big, so handsome, and, best of all, so virile."

"A real Casanova," I said.

"A what?"

"Casanova was a great lover of the eighteenth century. Women could not resist him. He was much like you," I said.

"Say, when do we stop for lunch?" the Colonel asked.

"Food or sex," I said. "Are you always hungry? You have a hump on you like a water buffalo. Don't you carry supplies in there?"

The Colonel started to say something about an empty larder when Bill cut in saying, "We'd better stop at the first place we see. A tavern will have coffee and sandwiches."

We drove along in silence, looking for a place to eat, and stared out at the endless expanse of snow. After what seemed like an hour I saw the neon light of a beer sign in the window of a log building near the highway. Bill saw it at about the same instant.

"Colonel, we could stop here," he suggested, "or we are only an hour from Maplewood if you think you can wait."

"No, no, stop here," he said.

Bill applied the brakes. The car skidded as we turned into the parking lot in a flurry of fresh snow that clouded the windshield.

"That's the way to drive," roared the Colonel. "My jeep driver drove just like you."

As the snow settled, the Colonel bounded out of the car as if he were reliving his army days. Bill and I followed him through several inches of soft snow to the entrance of the log house. The inside of the place consisted of one large room. There was a bar at one end, and the shelves on the back bar were lined with bottles of various kinds of whisky. A door off to the side appeared to lead to a small kitchen. An elderly man greeted us.

"What do you have to eat?" asked the Colonel.

The menu was simple: hot chili, cold sandwiches and coffee. We ordered the full menu and seated ourselves at a table in the middle of the room. Outside the snow was falling. The days were short and soon the white trees and the snow drifts would be enveloped in the gathering darkness.

The sandwiches and chili were served. As we ate the tavern keeper brought us coffee. Through a small window with wooden cross bars I watched the falling snow. Then the silence was broken by the sound of a diesel truck pulling up a long grade.

The Colonel looked up from his bowl of chili and said, "Diesels! Noisy, aren't they; but you know, there was money in them for a spell right after the Second World War. I sold several of them to one of the banana republics in South America for a huge profit."

"I thought selling diesels after the war to South America was illegal. Or maybe there was a limit on the amount charged," said Bill.

The Colonel laughed. "I delivered them to the pier and got my money; where they were sent afterwards was no business of mine. I didn't ask."

"But you knew," I said.

"It was a long time ago. I could only guess who the buyers were."

"And all along I thought you were an honest citizen," said Bill.

"I wish that was all that troubled my conscience," I added. "Wasn't it Lamb who said that he knew things about himself that would cause all his friends to avoid him like the plague?"

"He was an alcoholic, too," said Bill.

"Who was this Lamb?" asked the Colonel. "I just sold some diesels–that was all."

"Lamb was a nineteenth century essayist, playwright and critic. He was well liked in his day."

"Oh, one of your literary friends," said the Colonel.

"Most men of Lamb's day are forgotten, whereas he is still read, at least in the classroom."

"People who write don't interest me: I sold some diesel engines as war surplus and made a lot of money. An agent made the contact and paid me off. I never saw the buyers." The Colonel paused, then continued on another tack. "Say, Mark, this Bogleman is really on your case. Why is he waiting to see you at Maplewood? Why not in Seattle?"

My heart leaped. Even the mention of Bogleman's name had an effect on me.

"My guess is that he has other patients at Maplewood or he was scheduled to give a talk as a guest speaker. My wife hired him to counsel me. It appears he has taken a special interest in my case. I find him to be a strange man, but gifted with unusual perception. It's uncanny what he can learn about a patient. In his quiet way he is forceful: he cuts right to the heart of a problem."

"Now you know all about him, Colonel," Bill said.

"Know what?" the Colonel snapped. "Mark says he's low-keyed and perceptive. I already know that. I saw him with Lucy. I wondered if he was at all like the old army doctor I knew when I was a young student at the military academy."

"What was he like?" Bill asked.

"I thought he was one of the boys until I got into trouble. At the military post the girls came around and I took care of my share. Old Doc Steinman would ask me about my love life and I would embellish it a bit to make the tales more colorful. He would laugh until the tears came into his eyes. Then he'd grow serious, and would say,

'Remember, my boy, that everything has a price. The joys of sex are no exception.'

"One day I got a bad dose. Old Doc Steinman actually appeared happy about my fate. He was all business. When they laid me out on the table he turned to Big Bertha, his nurse, and said, 'I warned our boy—but he wouldn't listen. He thought that thing—pointing to my penis—was hung on there just for a good time!' Then he shook his head as if he were really sad about it. If the truth were known, I think he delighted in teaching me a lesson.

"I didn't know what was coming but I was scared. Big Bertha looked grim. I looked to one side and saw two male nurses come into the room. 'Let's get started,' Dr. Steinman said.

"Big Bertha bent my knees down over the table, the two male nurses held my arms, while the doctor ran a long instrument up my penis. I screamed, the sweat ran off me, I was frightened and in pain. 'Doc! You're killing me!' I yelled.

"'No, no,' he said, 'you are just experiencing the pleasures of sex.'"

"Did you give up sex after that?" Bill asked.

"No, once a bear tastes honey he will endure any hardship. The bee stings, however painful, will not defeat his purpose. Unlike the bear, I took precautions after that."

"I think you are ruled by your appetites, Colonel," I said.

"What's wrong with that?"

I didn't answer. Once I was considered to be a respectable, disciplined man, one who never went beyond the bounds of propriety (although in truth I was filled with ambition and pride, and was slowly being possessed by alcoholism). No one saw me in the right light in those years. On the other hand, the Colonel was shrewd, strong and straightforward, gratifying his appetites; he was intensely human with human weaknesses; he was the totally uninhibited man—and courageous, too. His zest for life made it a pleasure to be in his

company. The Colonel accepted his alcoholism as a fact of life–
something distasteful that had to be faced and overcome. What
happened because of drinking was in the past and forgotten. 'Make the
most of the moment' seemed to epitomize his belief. He did not appear
to be concerned with changes that had taken place within him; he saw
what had happened as irreversible. He accepted Dr. Neilstrom's
explanations on his alcoholism; now he would take the necessary steps
to stop drinking.

When the Colonel drew out one of his big cigars I knew it was
time to go; otherwise, he'd forget where he was, as he began one of his
long tales of love, of war, or of some half forgotten experience out of
his life. Bill apparently saw the danger and picked up the check and
walked to the counter. I followed to settle the small account, then
walked to the door. Bill said something to the Colonel and he muttered
to himself and followed us to the car.

After we left the tavern we drove the last hour of our journey
with little conversation. The nearness of Maplewood created a tension
in the car. In the past I had solved many problems. In my present state
of mind I felt weak, tense, confused, and in no condition to face the
doctor about my relationship with Lucy. I was unstable and unsure of
myself, as if I were embodied in a stranger, no longer in control of my
thoughts, my moods, or what I might say or do. My nerves were
shattered. That must be the answer.

If the doctor concluded I was deranged, in danger at any
moment, under certain conditions, of losing my self control (and it
would be easy for him to believe this if he accepted Lucy's story along
with the true account of my wife), then he could recommend a private
or public institution for mental cases. I knew at this moment that I did
not have the strength to resist. In an institution I could not recover.
Despair and the loss of the last vestiges of reason would follow: total
emptiness, the end of my resistance would soon make me a plaything
of all wayward impulses. My days would revolve around doing
nothing, as I became a plaything for all the destructive forces that
reeled about within me. With the victory of this evil force my real
nature, hidden somewhere within me, would be consumed. I would not

recover; I could not because my nature would be changed. Then, there would be no confusion, no great struggles–just an idiot's peace and an idiot's happiness.

Day after day–through endless days and nights and years–until time ended I would wander in and out of rooms, through open corridors engaged in endless chatter, listening to the babblings and ravings of men and women more possessed than myself. Before time ended I would have long forgotten my struggle or even what it was all about. If foolish dreams persisted of the past, of happier times, if I cried out in the night that my true nature was locked deep within me– that I was actually a person–then a doctor would give me a pill to keep my true nature in submission. Such a fate would occur if I conceded defeat, if I lost hope and allowed myself to surrender.

Grimly I set my mouth until I felt the pain from the stitches. I could not succumb, not now, not ever. I must try again and again to match my true nature against my lower nature until I prevailed against those evil forces within me. I would meet this enemy by turning anger against anger, hatred against hatred: then my true nature would become strong, crying out, "How dare you mock me by making me a possession, without will, a plaything to be dissembled, mocked and sifted like wheat? I refuse any longer to be tossed upon a sea of resentments and illusions, being possessed, consumed, and filled with hatred for all things that stand in my way, opposing my will and my desires. Because it was this way in the past does not mean that I cannot change the present and therefore the future. For once I know that I want to be free of ambition, of pride, of hatred and above all free of the hardness that these enemies create–this hardened and callous nature, unable to care or give, or express any feelings of sincere warmth and love toward anyone."

Soon I would meet Bogleman. True I feared him; yet I would match my will against his if he sought to condemn me. I was learning. I felt grateful for the particles of light that were given me.

Bill turned in his seat. "Maplewood ahead. We are home, at least home for us."

CHAPTER 22

The long twisting road from the highway into Maplewood was just wide enough for one car. Snow as piled high on either side of the road, which wove its way in and out, among the snow covered maples. Bill stopped the car in a space near the front entrance. Cars covered with snow were visible in the dark. The air was cold and still, and the snow squeaked and crunched underfoot as I walked away from the car. Bill and the Colonel went inside. Snow hung over the roof and the dark vines which long ago had been stripped of their leaves and were now clinging to the brick walls waiting for spring and the renewal of life. In the stillness, under the stars, I could make out the dark mass of pine trees that enclosed us on all sides. There were three buildings in the cleared area near the river surrounded by the ancient maples that give Maplewood its name. The light of the stars reflected upon the snow, and softened the outline of the trees and the entire landscape about me. In the silence, as often before, I felt the peace and harmony of nature.

At the moment it did not seem to matter that I was one of those in treatment because I had been deeply wounded. Once I had sought to be the master of my fate; now I was among the refuse of society–shunned, scorned, unwanted–a slave to alcohol and a social outcast no longer capable of moving about freely. None of these truths bothered me now; in the snow I felt calm and at ease as I breathed in the cold air and stared at the maple trees–those worn and twisted shapes, so very old yet still so strong. They bore up each year under nature's fiercest onslaughts. They survived: they would outlast us all.

"Someone will be wondering about me," I mused. "I will go in to see if the doctor is here."

As I entered the warm building I thought about alcohol and the effect it once had upon me. While I drank I could not conceive of living a meaningful life without it. Often I had heard someone say that drinking with control was important for everyone. Control was a simple matter for social drinkers. For them no effort was needed. It was the alcoholic who was constantly firming up his will, hating himself while he made fierce resolves never to drink to excess again, resolving never to lose his temper and say (or do) frightful things– never, never to act again without complete mastery of self. Control was the difference! It was the key that opened the door to social drinking and closed that same door in the face of alcoholics. There was the difference–not in the superior virtue, the will power, balance and sense of purpose of the social drinker–but in the very makeup and constitution of the alcoholic. Some tragic malformation (for which there was no answer) had taken place within every alcoholic that singled him out for destruction. All that was necessary was the right set of circumstances: the future alcoholic established in a drinking society, time (say fifteen years), and the eroding forces of life, disappointments, the loss of idealism, the growth of pride, the habit of drink, and the stage was set for true addiction. The social drinker could never understand this inordinate desire for alcohol–the compulsion was totally foreign to him.

My drinking helped to create my world of insanity. When I drank I wanted to soar upon the wings of my illusions, to live above the masses who sweated and toiled, who lived dull, drab lives. I wanted a different life free of boredom and any constraining force upon my ego–an ego that wanted to grow and grow, never satisfied but always crying out for more. I had accumulated a sufficiency of the world's goods–but it never seemed enough. The hunger to accumulate more still remained.

What a price I paid. I subverted all that was kind and creative in my nature. The change at first was imperceptible, but with the erosion of time a new man emerged–hard, calculating, and strangely suited to live a life of illusions. For over twenty years I burned each day with renewed ambition. Nothing else drove me, but only ambition, and ambition's close ally, greed. And fear, too, was always close at hand: in the darkness, in the silence of the night, in the shadows behind every tree and strange shape, and even in my dreams, was fear. Ignored, or unseen at first, it grew slowly until I was always aware of its presence. Fear strutted in locked step with ambition and greed, the two inseparable companions. Now that the fires of ambition had cooled, and also the desire for further gain, I had expected fear to diminish and go away. What a fool I was! Fear was a monster: it invaded my pores, shattered my nerves, pervaded my mind, stirred up wild fantasies that threatened my sanity. With fear consuming my will, my control was gone; my moods, no longer controlled by reason, carried me aloft one moment and the next plunged me into despair.

At the end of the dimly lighted corridor I saw the light in the counselor's office. The building was silent except for the sound of somebody turning in his sleep. Where the hallways joined I saw Audrey working in her office. She looked up as I approached. Her eyes widened as she looked at my scarred face and shook her head sadly.

She smiled, saying, "Experience is a school where most of us learn about life."

"And a fool learns in no other," I added lamely. "I can't say I wasn't warned."

"Why blame yourself, Mark? The Colonel told me enough about what happened so that it was easy to see why you went over to see Lucy." She smiled. "You are learning about women –at least about Lucy."

"I didn't know. Lucy looked so helpless to me while she was here."

"Helpless? She was dangerous! She was ready to explode. All she needed was a few drinks of alcohol to set her off."

I remained silent. Audrey knew Lucy better than I. She had warned me to stay away from her, and I deserved this reprimand for ignoring her advice. At the moment, I felt no desire to excuse, or to explain why I had gone to see Lucy. The kind, thoughtful role bringing comfort to Lucy in the middle of the night, did not suit me. I was a fool to go there and I knew it. Audrey lit a cigarette and studied me while I also lighted a cigarette. She did not appear conscious of my eyes as I boldly stared at her figure compressed in a tight fitting blouse and skirt. I thought she accepted my gaze; she saw the hunger in my eyes, felt flattered by it, or considered such desires as natural in a man—a desire she knew her charms ought to arouse. Her pale skin and grey eyes and appealing figure were in contrast with white walls and glaring lights in her office which cast a pallor over everything. The lights only emphasized our sickness by showing the contrast between our pale skin and the darkness that encircled our eyes in which the flame had disappeared. Some patients retained only the look of despair, while in others there was the wild look of indecision and conflict. More often there was no discernible light in the eyes—only dullness. The flame of life had gone and only signs of death and decay remained.

The sick, the deeply wounded, those whose minds and characters had been diminished by alcohol, were in their rooms at this hour. Was every heart, I wondered, empty, embittered, disillusioned and despaired? Were the lost hopes carried into their dreams, wondering (as they dreamed) what they had done to lose their wives and jobs and friends and everything of any meaning—their health and all hope in the future? We were all alike; we were beaten by life; we were slowly consumed by our enemy, alcoholism. No matter how much talent we possessed, or no matter how high we rose in the world, this disease, this insidious cancer, this enemy of all that was decent and good in us, would, in the end, destroy us. With all semblance of dignity gone, we were the refuse of society, not even sick in a decent, acceptable way. We were sick because we could not drink like men. It did not matter that "drinking like a man" was misunderstood and therefore could not apply to the alcoholic. Society had its collective judgments: we were weak, unstable, perverse and arrogant beyond the reach of understanding—and forgiveness.

Most of us, society felt, would never see the truth because in our strange perversity we refused to hear the truth. As I stood there smoking, someone cried out from somewhere down the long, dark hallway.

Audrey ignored the cry. "Mark," she said, "one moment you were staring at me, the next moment you were gone, as though I weren't here. You just faded away into some far off land. The sound you just heard–well, there are some new faces here, but Gene, the druggist and the Admiral are gone. Whoever cried out was one of the new ones."

"Another week or so and all of our old group will be gone," I added.

"When you leave with them I'll miss you prowling the halls and the woods at night," she added, smiling.

"Oh, come on, Audrey. You know how much more peaceful Maplewood will be when I am out of here."

"You're a strange one, Mark. I don't understand you or what kind of struggle goes on within you; from all outward appearances it must be considerable. At times I hardly know you; your eyes are wild, they appear to light up as if there was a fire within you. When I heard about Lucy and the knife I wondered why you went to see her. I concluded that Dean's tragedy so upset you that you called Lucy and she asked you to come. I can see that you are a changed man. You are not the same person who arrived here in the fall. Dean's death and your encounter with Lucy accounts for some of that change, I would guess."

I ignored her observation. There was no way I could evaluate what was taking place within me. What was seen from the outside was merely the opinion of the observer.

"Where is Lucy now?" I asked.

"She's insane from what I've heard."

"I know that, Audrey, but do you know where she has gone for treatment?"

"Ask Bogleman. He's here now. Earlier, Stella was asking him about Lucy and your name was mentioned. He said something about seeing you. At the moment he's in Dr. Neilstrom's office at the other end of the hall."

"See me? Now, why does he want to see me?"

"Come, Mark, surely you know. After your encounter with Lucy he wants to know what happened. You are his patient."

"Yes, I know–my case is so fascinating."

"Mark, we're all interested in you–certainly all of the staff. You are aloof except for your friendship with Bill and the Colonel. And we all know you've been having a tough time of it–it shows. Sometimes you seem so preoccupied it's rather scary." Audrey laughed nervously. "Not scary in a threatening sense–except maybe for you."

"I must be an awesome spectacle," I said, attempting a smile.

Audrey took a puff from her cigarette and inhaled deeply. As her eyes looked at me casually, her expression changed. Suddenly, her smile was warm, and her eyes were inviting.

"You would have no trouble making friends anywhere if you just opened up more. Even with your face badly cut you're not a bad looking fellow. You just seem to have so many conflicts."

I laughed. "Once this business with alcohol is resolved, I'll open up plenty–but I'm a loner, a dreamer, I guess. That I can't change."

"You'll change. You'll make a lot of changes in your life, if you are like the others."

"Change? I can't account for all the changes now. You're right about conflicts. You might say that giving up alcohol has brought me face to face with my 'daemon,' a friendly spirit whose guidance is hardly clear or easy to follow. Another force (an evil spirit, if you like) haunts me especially at night. The worst part is I don't know what to do to pull out of these conflicts to find peace and normalcy."

"I can't understand everything you're going through, but I see what it is doing to you."

Her voice changed. For the first time there was a note of concern in it.

"Mark, I don't have the training or the experience to help you. You need someone like Bogleman. He's good." She glanced at the clock. "It's late. That meeting with Dr. Neilstrom ought to be over with. Maybe I should call Dr. Bogleman, only it's so late. He didn't say when he would see you. You can't afford to lose this struggle to recover your real self. A fate like Dean's or Lucy's is unthinkable."

"No, nothing like that will happen to me. You needn't call the doctor; I'll just wander down the hall to his office. If he is talking to Dr. Neilstrom, I'll let him know I'm here, then wait outside his office until he can see me."

"He's known, I've heard," said Audrey, "for helping those with unusual problems. There are strange stories about Bogleman. Some say that if you take your eyes off him for a moment, while you are talking with him, when you look back he will be gone."

"Bogleman is clever," I admitted, "but he is so big and moves so slowly I cannot imagine him disappearing. I grant you, though, that there is something mysterious about him."

I rose to leave. Audrey followed my movements, and her eyes met mine.

"Good luck, Mark. I'll miss you when you're discharged."

I stared at Audrey for a moment and wondered at her show of concern.

"I'll miss you, too," I said.

I began walking down the hall with slow steps, my mind racing, wondering with each step what I should say to the doctor and what he would say to me. I gave a dozen answers to imaginary questions I thought he might ask. It gave me pause that he might not ask any of these questions that flooded my mind. I assumed that most of the questions would be about Lucy and about my own internal struggle. I was not at all confident that the doctor could help me, but I was aware that I had come to a dead end. I must find peace. I could not afford to sink more deeply into depression, nor could I continue the struggle much longer. If I saw that the doctor's only solution was further treatment in another institution, among the insane, I would not stay here another hour. I would begin walking into the woods and continue as far as my strength would carry me. I would go tonight, but not yet; first I would see the doctor. If I saw no future I hope I would not end up like Bernice, Mary, or Lucy.

Such thoughts caused the tension and the irritation to rise within me. I could hear the deep breathing of patients asleep in their rooms. Some moaned, long, deep heartrending sighs of anguish. The heart was exposed in sleep: the cries of pain told stories of the failure and emptiness of our lives. The heart and mind converged and wept in the darkness. There were dry tears, unseen tears, but I could not hear them fall: I could hear a heart break as I passed each room. Fools, we are all fools, our lives condemn us. We did not fail like other men after a long struggle: we raced headlong into defeat by our own efforts–by refusing to listen to anyone who could help us. Alcoholics we were, and damned by our own willfulness.

Whoever speaks of alcoholics without contempt? In my heart I know that I am culpable. If my values had not been mistaken, had my life been disciplined, directed toward higher values, to service, this passion for alcohol would not have overtaken me. My nature revolted at my weakness, at such incredible stupidity, at allowing myself to have been pulled down so low, so that I lay prostrate before my own eyes, judged by my own convictions as a fool–one who has prostituted every decent feeling.

Why did I become an alcoholic? Because I was human? Because I was weak? Because I could not see the truth? Life unfolds slowly. It was as if I was always wandering about in a mist where I could see the outlines of shapes and forms without seeing clearly what they were or why they attracted me. When the mist cleared I saw the forms which attracted me were ambition and pride. Was it innocence or some compulsion that caused me to accept their embrace and to follow them wherever they led? Soon alcohol was discovered, too, and embraced with the same innocence and lack of caution; so that while I thought I was pursuing success, and the freedom and good things of life that wealth provided, I was actually being led. Without alcohol I might have seen the folly of being led by ambition and pride. It seemed that I was chosen, picked out from a group for a special prize: I was mounted on the stool, given the fool's wreath, and allowed to prattle long hours all alone.

Yet many of my faults seemed no more than those of other men. There was a mystery here, beyond human comprehension. Why was I chosen? There was no answer. There was only silence when I asked. Faith was what I needed; a conviction that my life was worth something, had meaning, and had an ultimate purpose.

The pressure was building again in the back of my neck. I felt the steel bands around my forehead and the electric shocks through my body. Nerves. I was so close to collapse. Frustration, depression, the curse of this sickness increased my irritation and sense of failure. As my feeling of self-worth diminished, my sensitivity to any criticism increased. Anger rose within me as I neared the end of the hall where I heard voices.

Before my eyes flashed vivid scenes from the past. I saw a friend dying from cancer, lying in a bed, his emaciated form weak and helpless: yet in his shining eyes I saw a mind that was alert, a spirit that was serene and resigned—waiting in patience to be set free. A far cry from the shattered life of an alcoholic, who played out to the end the role of a fool, whose total concentration upon self blinded him to all reality, even to the angel of death who was waiting in the wings. Nothing could jar loose or break into that total concentration upon self. In that world of madness one man was king, who saw the entire world revolving around his desires, his pleasures and his suffering: life did not exist, did not in any way concern him unless he was at center stage. This was my life too; I saw that now—but how could I change it?

Being possessed by alcohol did not come about in a few weeks or months: addiction took many years. My approach to drinking seemed innocent enough. At first I drank for pleasure and to be sociable. Only later, much later, did the first subtle changes take place as I became dependent upon liquor. A gradual deterioration followed: as my mind became dark I became hard and ruthless allowing pride to justify my life. 'Do as you will,' said pride, 'soar with me over the valleys, above the mountains where the air is cold and there is no sound from below–no cries of anguish to be heard.'

Had I paused and listened to those voices I might have heard these words, 'Stop! Stop now! Never drink again. Children who could be useful in society were lost because of you. Their lives were twisted; their values were false because you were false. They have not learned to love because they could not give what they did not receive. They entered a hard world crippled without the tools of survival. With the advantages of the best schools, with leisure and material benefits, none of this mattered without a home in which there was love and stability. There was no substitute for a family life in which children were reared with care and discipline, and nurtured by gay, wholesome laughter that enabled them to develop their individuality. That radiant glow of affection develops strength and confidence and values.'

Alcoholism was a loathsome disease: it possessed the devil's tongue, the devil's pride and the devil's hatreds. At times in my life all these evils were combined in me. I was pulled in all directions. My nature–the essence of what I am–was fractured, with every fragment straining one against the other. My Daemon, if such a ministering angel existed, 'Hear me, help me to bring this shattered nature, split and confused, into harmony. I can no longer smile and hide behind an empty facade exhibiting a calm exterior with a face frozen in a smile like the painting of the young man in my home.'

If I could reach within my mind, or within my heart I would choke that image that alcoholism has created; with intense hatred I would seize that evil creature and tear him limb from limb until the blood ran through my fingers. I would delight in the red glow, in seeing life slip away knowing that I had killed that monster at last. As

I listened to his death rattle I would stand aside and mock him and spit upon the fast decaying flesh. I would gladly give up a leg or an arm or any part of me if that was the price of driving out the monster that tormented me.

My thoughts were interrupted. I heard loud noises from the lighted room. The talk was about me. My name? I heard my name! I stopped at the doorway and stood half concealed in the shadows. Dr. Neilstrom was talking. His voice sounded agitated

"I realize, doctor, that Mark was your patient–but he was my patient, too. Stella was hasty in asking him to return. I felt that she had made a mistake in doing so. Now, I understand she received these instructions from you."

"Now, Walter, you and I are old friends. What do you fear? That Mark will ruin the reputation of this clinic?"

"No, but I am concerned. The story I heard about Lucy was frightening. After the trouble Mark caused here with that girl, why did he go to see her?"

"Did Mark cause the trouble here with Lucy?"

Dr. Neilstrom shook his head. "You know how stories are exaggerated. The girl was trouble. I knew that much. I thought Mark had more sense. I grant you that he was caught off guard in the woods, but why did he go to see her in Seattle after he was warned to stay away from her?"

"Walter, I don't know. Perhaps you should ask him. If I'm not mistaken, I think I saw Mark just now, outside the office. Mark? Is that you? Come on in–we were just talking about you."

At Bogleman's invitation I stepped into the room. Dr. Neilstrom rose to his feet. As he stared at my face his mouth slowly opened. His face expressed pain and his voice was almost apologetic.

"I'm sorry about your injuries," he said softly. "I must not forget that you met Lucy at Maplewood." Turning to Dr. Bogleman he added, "I'll leave now. Mark is in your hands." He glanced once more at me, then walked briskly from the room.

When my eyes adjusted to the white lights I looked about the room. It reminded me of that other office in the city where I had seen Bogleman sitting behind a similar desk in the center of the room, even the position of the two chairs was the same. Everything about this room was equally drab and colorless as the Seattle office except for a window that opened into the night. I could see the maple trees. Dark forms were visible, erect and still, with snow frozen onto every limb. They were waiting (with such patience they waited) to feel again the surge of new life through their ancient limbs. Then, again in full bloom, the leaves in place of the snow would conceal the ancient limbs. How wonderful, beyond all my hopes, to feel this surge of new life within me. Fascinated I sat and stared until I became aware of Bogleman's eyes waiting patiently for my attention.

Now I became acutely aware of every sound and movement in the room. I waited for the doctor to speak. My heart began to pound. There was no other sound and the two of us were here alone, yet I was convinced we were not alone: in the shadows I felt an audience, silent, listening.

The doctor's chair groaned as he moved, with his usual ponderous movements, to light up a cigarette. He then pushed the package toward me as he had done before. His face was unchanged: dark and heavy; his eyes were black and they gleamed when they caught the reflection from the flame of his lighter. His eyes were studying me.

"You have changed. You're thin. Your face is scarred and your eyes are feverish. I hardly recognize you, but I must say that the new man is striking."

"My treatment had its moments," I said drily. "There were challenges." I stopped. My pride would not allow me to admit that I was beaten.

"You are responding to treatment?"

"If you mean do I recognize my alcoholism, the answer is yes." Pausing for emphasis, I added, "Possession–the total control of this drug over its victim–is clear to me now."

Bogleman did not respond at once. "You are an alcoholic," he said finally.

"I am an alcoholic, a full blown alcoholic. I was overpowered and consumed completely by alcohol," I said.

"Fully? Completely?"

"Yes."

Bogleman nodded his head slowly. "Dr. Neilstrom told me that you wandered through the woods alone, sometimes talking with your head bent, as if you were searching within yourself for answers or engaged with someone in conversation. You are an unusual man: you see the two forces within you and you move in and out of two worlds. I wonder if this struggle has taken you beyond your endurance?"

"Are you offering sympathy? If you are, I find your interest very touching," I said.

Bogleman did not respond to my sarcasm. He sat watching me with dark eyes which seemed to grow darker. My heart continued to pound and I felt weak and unable to cope any longer with the confusion and the discord–the conflicting thoughts, the vivid images and wild impulses–that pulled me now in one direction and then another. My condition increased my frustration. Anger was rising within me–anger caused by fear and weakness–by the realization that questions would be asked about Lucy. I felt intensely that I was a fool getting involved with her; now, even worse, it seemed, I did not feel strong enough to defend myself against any of the questions that Neilstrom was raising–let alone any questions the shrewd Bogleman might ask. Couldn't they see that Lucy was mad! That she was a liar, too. Had she fooled Bogleman? How I needed help to survive. This was the end of the line if the light did not break through. That decision, at last, was made.

Bogleman began speaking. The room was strangely silent except for his voice. My senses were unusually alert: this was my final hour and that knowledge seemed to relax me. There were no clashing thoughts or voices now. But there was an audience. In the shadows of the doorway, even in this bright room, I sensed there were many eyes watching the doctor and me. I saw no one but the doctor but I could feel the presence of the "others" crowding into the room.

"You doubtless overheard Dr. Neilstrom in the hallway where I saw you watching us. Like Neilstrom, I wondered about your relationship with Lucy."

"Where is she now?" I asked. "She's mad as a hatter, you know. She ought to be put away before she kills someone."

"Lucy is calm now. She is well cared for."

"Cared for, you say. In a peaceful setting where everyone is dressed in white? I like white, especially all those tube lights over our heads that make us look like the walking dead. As for Lucy,' I know she's at Stiron, or she soon will be there–with Bernice. Mary, too, will join them. She'll spend her days telling everyone how happy they are." I turned and waved a hand to include all those at Maplewood. "Did you know that everyone here is crazy or almost crazy? If your recovery rate means anything, if there are one-half as many recovering as Dr. Neilstrom claims, they are not from the group I've seen here."

"Many do recover and lead useful lives. They come to look back upon this period as the crossroads in their lives."

"You speak of recovery. The losers are soon forgotten, even though many of them fought a good fight."

For a fleeting moment Bogleman's face showed an expression of pain.

"You rode here with Bill and the Colonel?"

I nodded.

"Then the Colonel, no doubt, repeated the story Lucy told us, shortly after you had left the house. The Colonel defended you well.

He believed that Lucy would have maimed you or done much worse if he hadn't arrived at that critical moment. What part of Lucy's story would you change?"

"What part?" My heart was beating rapidly and my voice was rising. I felt the difficulty in holding myself in check. I was desperately trying to end the confusion and conflicts which had shredded my nature and caused my mind to run out of control. Now it seemed to me that first Neilstrom and now Bogleman wanted only to talk about my relationship with Lucy. To hell with Lucy!

"What part?" I repeated, my voice rising. "You ask as if you don't already know." I rose to my feet and stepped toward his desk. "Look at this face! And my pants were cut from the knee to the crotch; a near miss. What other proof do you need? That crazy woman would have killed me and you ask for proof. What is all this nonsense, asking questions about Lucy? I was the one who was struggling for my life."

"I've heard Lucy's story. And only you and Lucy were present. Remember once you almost killed your wife. Her fear of you was justified. You have a scar on your wrist and arm that testifies to your violence when you believed you saw an intruder after you had been drinking. I'm well aware that you are capable of violence. And, Mark, won't you please sit down?"

"Doctor, you know that another man was present. Lucy's former husband ought to be able to find him. The man—Joe was stabbed. Even if his wound was superficial, someone would know of it. Such things are not kept secret. If Lucy lied about Joe being there, and about stabbing him, she would easily lie about everything else."

Bogleman continued as if he had not heard my defense. "You had an affair with Lucy at Maplewood—your wife was in Europe. Then you followed Lucy to her home. When she resisted your advances, you became violent. Is that about the way it happened?"

"I know how unconvincing it sounds to tell you that I was only flattered by her attention. I saw the hatred in her from the first. I saw also the gentle, helpless and innocent side of her nature. We danced and walked together among the maple trees. We did not go into the woods together. She followed me, and that was not prearranged.

"Concerning the night in her house. She has woven fact into fantasy. She has twisted and distorted our conversation beginning with the first telephone call. Lucy called me and insisted I come and see her late at night. Foolishly, I did as she asked. Too late, I realized she'd been drinking, and that alcohol transformed her into a devil—or a madwoman, if you like. She wanted me that night and I wanted her. I saw that she had been drinking. She appeared to be a woman possessed. And I saw Joe in the room. I desired her until I saw Joe. My feelings went beyond lust as I had experienced lust in the past. I actually felt pain. My desire for her seemed unnatural, increasing every moment I looked at her; at first it was lust, a burning, ravaging desire, which even now is not clear in my mind. At that moment her appearance seemed hardly human. She was desirable, and it was plain that she wanted me. She laughed with that strange, chilling laughter, saying that she could show me a form of lovemaking that would change my nature. All this sounds crazy now, but at that moment I was convinced that Lucy could in some way change my nature. At the very least I saw that whatever self respect I had would be lost. But there was also something else, something that the Colonel also felt: a pervading sense of evil in that house."

I finished talking and realized that I was almost shouting. For several moments the doctor looked at me. His face showed signs of strain as if he feared something might happen. His eyes, for the first time, appeared frightened.

"Would you like a cup of coffee?" he asked.

I nodded my head abruptly. Bogleman picked up the phone, spoke briefly, and in a few minutes Audrey walked into the room carrying a pot of coffee and two cups. She placed the pot on the corner of the desk, glanced at me, then withdrew.

After lighting a cigarette and drinking some of his coffee, the doctor began.

"Suppose I believed you. . . "

I interrupted. "That's not enough. There's no reason not to believe me."

"Suppose I accepted all that you said. I wonder if you can control the violence that is in you. Not if you drink again." He shook his head. "Who are you, I wonder?" He appeared to be asking himself that question.

"I am a person," I cried out. "Need anyone tell you that?"

"You are different?"

"I am unique."

He raised his eyebrows as if he were considering whether or not I was unique.

"Yes," I cried out again, "I am unique and a fool, too, if that is what you are waiting to hear."

"Why a fool?"

"Because as a simple man I always sought to know more than I could grasp, retain and understand. When I dreamed of beauty, of achieving perfection, of finding happiness, I struggled to achieve these great prizes, but used the wrong means and looked in the wrong places. In the end beauty, perfection and happiness became an illusion. In developing an insight into business I overlooked the loss of sensitivity, failed to see the growth of ambition, that is inseparable from pride, and my eventual control by that lordly and imperious voice within me—a spirit self-concerned, hard, cold and ruthless. I sought happiness and lived in misery. I acquired wealth and felt naked and abandoned. My fears caused anger to rage within me, followed by the accumulation of resentments: a store of fancied wrongs, and real suffering that hardened into malice and hatred.

"I reached beyond myself in search of a world that did not exist, except in my mind, and fell back upon the sharp and jagged edges of broken dreams and false hopes. Whenever I sought a cherished goal I reaped disillusionment. My pride led to success of a certain kind that always turned to ashes; my ambition drove me like a slave master. I was a slave bound and chained; outwardly I appeared the same; within I burned with resentment and hatred.

"In a world where all of my concentration was focused upon myself, I discovered that I existed in a great void, in a vast emptiness where there were no boundaries, only the sound of a strident voice whose harsh cries urged me on toward success. At night and alone, without anything to distract me, I stared at the strange shapes I saw in the darkness and then I realized with fear and trembling that within me all was dark and empty. I felt lost. Fear flooded my mind and heart. Fear came over me in waves in those early hours before dawn. Slowly, then, I began to realize that my life was not growing and expanding, but rather turning inward upon itself. In this unnatural state of mind I felt intense loneliness; as I sank deeper within myself, into a nightmare state, I felt that I could not escape, nor would I ever see a friend again. I would be alive in a dark world where I could not see and where I would be all alone. This was my reward, my kingdom, that fulfilled the promise of the voice I often heard, 'Now we shall be one, you and I.' Then I understood, with horror, that fulfillment meant that I was totally consumed–that I had already entered this nightmare for the last time and would not return."

The doctor's face appeared darker under the lights. His black eyes appeared to smolder as if they would suddenly burst into flames. His voice changed: for the first time I detected a note of anxiety.

"No other voice? You heard no other voice?"

I hesitated before going on. I felt bitter and contemptuous of myself for exposing this nightmare world in which I lived with all my wild fantasies. The sight of this self-centered world revolted me; like an angered serpent I wanted to lash out at the doctor–and strike back at myself. I felt reckless. This was the end. My senses told me that this was our last meeting. I was finished. Nothing would matter after tonight.

The doctor was waiting for an answer. His eyes gleamed under the light as he sat, rigid and still, waiting.

"Another voice? You asked if I heard some other voice." I lowered my head and stared at the tiled floor. "Yes, there was once, long ago, a gentle voice. For years it was silent; now, I have been hearing it again, hardly a voice at all–just a feeble voice that pleaded with me to change."

"And your answer?"

"Change to what? Why should I struggle against the tide?"

"What did the voice ask of you?" the doctor persisted.

Dark lines began to form on the doctor's face and beads of sweat began to accumulate on his forehead. His eyes were changing, showing anxiety–then fear and anger. His eyes seemed to be searching for something. What was he pursuing with such interest and such intensity?

Excited by his interest, I hurried on. "After I stopped drinking, I became aware of the two sides of my nature. Often at night in the silence of these rooms and when I walked among the trees alone, I could hear two voices contending, as they sought to persuade me which course of action I ought to follow. One voice attempted domination of me by appealing to my pride and ambition. Slowly through the years I accepted this voice as an integral part of my nature–as my true self.

"But on a few occasions I suspected that my nature was divided; a second voice was also contending for the prize: my reason, my will, my heart–all that I am. At first when I stopped drinking I felt a thrill and a new surge of life and a sense of independence, accompanied by moments of peace, a feeling of self worth and, in a vague sense, that my life had meaning–that a power beyond my understanding cared. Then I heard this other voice: a sorrowful, desolate voice, pleading to be recognized as the true side of my nature, as that power that instilled my love of beauty and idealism and desire for kinship with others. While I listened to that voice I experienced utter peace. Over and over again I heard the words repeated that my life had meaning, that someone (who resided within me) cared and would always care for me. As my mind dwelt upon these words I felt unusual warmth toward everyone near me. No longer did I feel bitterness or resentment even when I saw myself as I was meant to be— just a servant. Yet seeing myself as less, I nevertheless saw my individuality in a much clearer light than ever before. The voice was ever so gentle and kind and said, 'Come, how long I have waited for you!'"

"All too soon the vision ended, and with it, the peace and joy that I felt. Then my ears rang with the imperious voice that governed my actions. As I listened, my mind was flooded with a whole series of arguments. Facts were marshaled forth. They were persuasive arguments. With a haughty air, the voice conceded that alcohol had served its purpose in my life. Obviously, if my mental and physical health were endangered, alcohol ought to be set aside at least for the present. No mention was made by this demanding voice that it had long encouraged the use of alcohol to enhance my self-esteem. The voice told me that if I was to continue as a hard businessman in a thankless, selfish world, and remain on top, I could not concern myself with others. Self-awareness, exalted self-esteem, self-concern— following the dictate, <u>my</u> will be done—was the only course to follow.

"As I followed my will and bathed in the light of success and burned with the intense heat of ambition and pride, I felt that I was losing myself. As that dominant voice grew within me, I became weaker: I felt that I was being absorbed, consumed by another power that glorified me on the one hand yet secretly mocked me. I was startled at times by my lack of control; sometimes I experienced feelings of intense hatred that increased slowly and then burned within me with such intensity that I was drawn to the brink of violence.

"At night strange things happened. In my dreams or in a half-conscious state (that was never quite clear to me) I saw myself transported to the scene of a great battle. There was cursing and screaming, the vilest language, and most of all, the savage, unearthly cries of hatred and the ceaseless moaning and wailing of those who had despaired.

"A bloody struggle was taking place. The contest appeared in doubt as white knights struggled against black knights. I heard the ring of steel, the clash of swords, the hoof beat of horses, the impact of bodies as horses and horsemen crashed to the ground. Blood flowed. The earthly sounds and screams of terror and rage never ceased. The frenzied cries of rage were not the worst part of the battle. It was hatred, so deep and penetrating that I felt it everywhere. It pervaded the atmosphere and caused me to tremble with fear–terrible fear–that caused waves of electric shocks to go through my body when I again heard that strident voice (so familiar to me), harsh and clear, commanding the black knights: giving orders to fight, now that victory was near at hand.

"In my latest dream when I heard these words of command, I saw that I was actually standing in the midst of the battle. Then I realized clearly what I always vaguely suspected, that I was the prize. I was frozen and could not move–as in those childish nightmares when I saw the enemy or sensed his presence but could not flee. My terror increased, my heart pounded with such violence I felt any moment it would explode. I felt that I was lost, that all effort was useless, that I had shaped myself into what I was and could not change: that the hatred all about me, which I feared so intensely, was actually a part of me. I would choose to accept myself and live eternally within that completely self-centered remorseless world I had been building throughout my life. I would close my eyes, shut out the battle scenes, shut the door of my heart forever to any outside influences. No one could touch me or even reach out to me again. In that instant when I decided to close my eyes forever and cut out the scene of the battle and abandon myself fully to all the compelling forces within me, I was startled by a brilliant white light rising in the midst of the white knights. There was no sound from that light even though I could hear the screams and shouts from the center of the battle. Strangely, I felt a presence, the same presence that within me brought a feeling of peace and contentment and the realization (faint as it was) that my life had ultimate meaning. There was no strident voice, no words at all, but the thoughts were clear. 'You cannot be defeated, even if you are crushed, and your life was drained from you, as long as you continue to resist,' it said. 'Even if a mother should abandon her child I will not abandon you. Only you can turn away from me. I cannot free you against your will.' The message faded as I became aware that I was lying in the dark with familiar objects around me.

"Drenched in my own sweat, I lay in the dark, considering what I had learned. That my nature was split was clear enough; that I actually could hear the voices of the two sides of my nature convinced me that I must be fast approaching insanity. This sickness–these aberrations of the mind–could be the result of giving up alcohol, or from a shattered nervous system, or an overactive imagination, or any number of natural causes. Then I remembered you and your statement: you said that I was a chosen one, selected to come face to face with My Daemon–that I must make a choice."

Bogleman shifted his massive bulk in his chair. Beads of sweat glistened on his forehead. His eyes showed his concern. The room was still except for the movement of the doctor in his chair. Once more I was aware of the others present: silent listeners crowding in around us, waiting, straining to hear the doctor's words. I could not deny their presence yet I saw no one–but now they could hear with me the verdict from the doctor's lips that I was indeed insane. I had no friend that could defend me on this strange battlefield of the mind; no one who could interpret the voices or show me that my life had any meaning.

"You remembered well," he began, "what I said at our last meeting–that you would come face to face with your daemon. Indeed, you were chosen, you were unique, as everyone is, but there was something different about you. You experienced the division within you and actually saw forces contending for your will and the full possession of you. You heard the two voices clearly within you; this is rare. Indeed you are unique," he said again, slowly shaking his head, "but there was evil you did not see."

"What do you mean?"

"Your involvement with Lucy."

"You do not believe in my innocence? After all you've seen and heard? You saw her! You know she's crazy, and evil, too. If the Colonel felt the evil in that house, a man like you would quickly sense whatever evil was present."

"You asked about evil," Bogleman continued evenly. "I can see that you sensed a presence in this room. Did the thought ever occur to you that what you felt in this room was the presence of evil? Of course, I felt the evil in that house; it was in the air, it was everywhere.

"Do you remember your recurring nightmares as a boy when you saw the wild, frenetic dance of the trees mirrored on the wall? And the door of the closet opening? Something similar to that happened to you while you were drinking, and once again in Lucy's house. Only this time it was not a nightmare–it was real–a hellish reality. Lucy told almost the same story as you about what happened in that bedroom. However, there was a difference. She said you were attacking her! She was strong and cunning and could be dangerous when drinking. She was not as strong or crafty or violent as you."

"So what are you saying?"

Bogleman was so absorbed in studying me he hadn't bothered to mop the beads of sweat which covered his forehead. Clearly he was suffering from intense strain.

"Let me go back over that evening. Not all of it, but enough so that you'll understand what I observed. What happened was this: Lucy called you and begged you to come. When you were determined to leave the house Lucy, who felt rejected, threatened to stab Joe. When you started out the door she carried out her threat inflicting a minor wound. You reentered the room to help Joe, only to be attacked by Lucy. You retreated to the upstairs bedroom. You saw–as you've seen many times in your nightmares–the closet door opening. You once threatened to kill your wife, who was a clear minded woman and who would not imagine such a danger to herself. Yes, I saw and felt evil in that room. I saw evil in Lucy," he said bitterly, and it seemed to me his voice became sad as he measured each word. "I saw the evil in you. What the Colonel witnessed was you struggling against Lucy to protect your life. It was a hellish experience, I don't deny. I do believe, however, that you would have overcome her, and then, convinced that she was some sort of evil person, you might have felt driven to use the knife against her."

I felt bewildered and all alone. Somehow I had expected more from the doctor. It never occurred to me until now that I would use a knife against anyone. Perhaps the doctor believed I was so unbalanced that I was capable of being driven under certain conditions to any act of violence. Well, did it matter?

"What future do I have? And what of Lucy?"

The doctor shook his head slowly. His voice was low and sad with a note of finality in it. "Lucy lost the battle."

"My fate? What is to be my fate?" I asked in a low voice. I no longer cared nor did I even seek an answer. "So you witnessed, Doctor, my evil in that house and here, too, in this room, hatred and violence, and I might add, a warped and twisted nature. You've endured much tonight, coming face to face with evil again. I expected more from you. From what I've told you I thought that you could help." I attempted a smile, but my words sounded hard and cynical even to me. "My apology for whatever you've undergone in my behalf. I was unable to account for whatever evil you felt in my presence. My senses alerted also me to the presence of a hidden audience. But what does it all matter?"

That was the end of our meeting as far as I was concerned. My eyes turned once more to the window. A feeling of peace began to come over me. Was this despair, or the resignation that accompanied death? I saw the dark forest. I wanted to leave the room. I felt my features relax as the desire to leave at once came over me.

I faced the doctor and began rising from my chair. I nodded toward the window and said, "I must walk."

I was startled by a loud cry and the sound of Bogleman's massive fist striking the desk with thunder. His eyes blazed with fire and his voice shook the room.

"Never, never will you go into the forest! As I watched you, each time you looked out that window, it appeared you wanted to leave and begin walking. You can <u>not</u> stop fighting. Not now, not ever can you give in to this enemy. You are winning the battle. Don't despair now. You saw life and death struggling during those long nights. You felt the peace and longing for a renewed life of unselfish purpose–a life of worthwhile activity and growth as an individual. I did say that I saw 'evil in you,' but you are not evil–not yet! More is demanded of you to overcome what you call the 'strident voice,' the arrogance, the ambition and pride that has combined with alcoholism and brought you to the brink of disaster. One more act is required of you. Not even I with all my experience in these matters can help you, unless you take this next step."

"And what is that?" I asked.

"First read this letter, then you might see what act on your part is called for."

"Dear Dr. Bogleman,

"Today I received a progress report from Dr. Neilstrom concerning my husband, Mark. For weeks I have waited, always with a feeling of dread, fearful that he might not respond to treatment. Now my worst fears were realized. The letter was vague. It stated there was some progress, but that Mark was proud and resisted treatment. Then the doctor hinted at some serious trouble. What trouble? I feel I have a right to know. "I remember the early years. Mark was such a dreamer, so filled with idealism, so kind and sensitive. Now his hardness, and the violence I see in him frightens me. Alcohol transformed him. When he drank he was an altogether different man–cynical, cold and ruthless. Now in this silence, not getting any straight answers, I fear the worst. "Until I went away I did not know how much I cared for my husband. If he were lost forever to me I fear my life would end–Mark made up so much of

my life. "My heart is torn. I cannot face Mark as he
was, yet away from him, I remember only the good
years when we meant so much to each other. Then he
was kind and saw beauty everywhere. "He has not
written. He has forgotten me, I fear, but I have not
forgotten him. I love him. I will always love him. My
world is turning black; there is no joy anywhere for me
without him. "I thought that you, with your strange
powers, could save him. If I understand Dr. Neilstrom's
letter, it appears he holds out little hope. You are my
last hope. You must help Mark to win this struggle
against alcoholism!"

Sincerely,

Evelyn Malone

When I finished the letter I lowered my head and covered my
face with my hands.

"This is the end. I am beaten," I said. "Even though someone
cares. I am a fool–a hopeless fool."

"'Beaten and helpless,' you said?"

"Beaten," I said, looking up at Bogleman who was now
standing, watching me, as if he were waiting–waiting for what?

"Yes, you heard me. I am beaten. I am crushed: my heart, my
very nature, whatever I am–everything–is now crying out within me
for help. Alone I cannot heal a divided nature. This battle for life has
finished me. As you guessed, I wanted to go into the forest, alone."

"You are asking for help?"

"That appeal for life within me, which my heart tells me is my
true nature, is calling out loudly for help. Yes, it is I–Mark–that needs
help. Help me or I'm finished."

For a moment there was utter silence in the room. I looked at
the doctor. He appeared to grow larger. His forehead was now dry, his

face relaxed: he was actually smiling. I had never seen him smile before.

"Who are you?" I asked. "Are you my daemon?"

"When you first entered my office," he began, "I saw a great struggle ahead for you. I said that you were among the chosen ones: you were to be allowed to see the struggle, even the two forces of good and evil. Your vision was fascinating. As far as human flesh can conceptualize matters of the spirit world, your vision was realistic. You heard voices–frightening, the power that pride and ambition held over you. You saw that pride was your antagonist; a spirit that desired you greatly and almost consumed you. I was aware of the hatred and violence in you. I saw you that night in your room as you struggled with hatred. As I watched you in a nightmare, or a semiconscious state, I witnessed the great battle being waged within your heart where all the conflicts are won or lost.

"My mission was to save you. Never for a moment have you been out of my mind and my heart. I care. You cannot understand how much I care for you. I wanted to help you much more than this earthly life means to me, but I was helpless to assist you unless you admitted that you were powerless over alcohol and called upon a higher power to save you. Your pride, your hatred, greed or ambition, carried you almost beyond my reach.

"The enemy's power to consume you has been great. You are unable to conceive of that hunger you will now leave unsatisfied. You will succeed. Each day–very slowly at first–you will grow. You will not fail–not now.

"Come, let's you and I go out into the night. I sensed all along that if you succumbed to your pride you would despair and go into the mountains. But now you and I will just walk amongst the maple trees."

Strangely, for the first time in many years my heart began to sing with joy. I felt the kind, warm voice of the doctor who cared for me like another person who was waiting for me now in London. His words flowed through me, lifting me up as we went through the door together, down the hall and out into the cold night.

"See those trees? See what they're enduring? Nothing has caused them to succumb. Look at those twisted limbs! A few of them broke off years ago, yet these battered and ancient trees live on. A certain dignity and grandeur envelopes each one—for they are all different. No one has given any one of us an easy battle. Your battle was complicated with alcohol."

"You are My Daemon! That ministering spirit I learned about when I was a boy."

He laughed, and the laughter seemed to come from the stars. It rang through the cold, clear night: it came through the trees, from out of the woods—from everywhere. The laughter was light and gay and cut through the mist that clouded my mind and weighed upon my heart.

"Who am I? You asked for help. I was sent to help you, to help you in ways you cannot understand, to give you enough help so you can find the road back to a full life without alcohol and with hope for the future. Return to your wife. She is waiting. Listen to that voice that brings peace and joy. Learn to detect the difference in what the true spirit within you demands. As you follow your daemon, the guiding spirit within you, the evil voice that was consuming you will diminish and gradually disappear. I will always be near you. Do not fear."

I looked down at the snow and then I turned to the doctor to ask another question—but he was gone. I heard his laughter fade into the night.

Exactly who the doctor was has always remained a mystery. For reasons unknown to me, he came into my life at a crucial time, when, if his help had not been given, I would have failed. But it was not his help alone that saved me, but also the unfailing love and support of my wife, the accumulated wisdom and spiritual strength of AA, the many AA friends (especially the support of my AA sponsor) and above all the help of my higher power—that spirit which led me out of the darkness–whose inner guidance has brought peace to my heart at last.

After several weeks I left Maplewood for the last time. Then I hurried to London to meet my wife. Our reunion was a joyous one. Our life has grown richer and fuller through the years. I see Bill and the Colonel often. We go to AA meetings together. Others I remember did not fare so well. Gene, my roommate, died from drinking again during his first year away from Maplewood. The Admiral, like Dean, was a suicide. Mary and Bernice and Lucy were at peace, no longer fearful of this world. Their needs were simple and fulfilled by others. A few of our group survived. Many failed.

I never saw Dr. Bogleman again. From time to time I heard stories about this mysterious man. I always felt that he was near–and would come if I called out for him. My life changed when I cried out for help and recognized clearly, at that moment, that I was powerless over alcoholism–that I could not win the battle alone.

Made in the USA
Charleston, SC
07 September 2010